1997 Best Newspaper Writing

WINNERS: THE AMERICAN SOCIETY OF NEWSPAPER EDITORS COMPETITION

D1009033

EDITED BY CHRISTOPHER SCANLAN

The Poynter Institute
and
Bonus Books, Inc.

01   00   99   98   97   5   4   3   2   1

International Standard Book Number: 1–56625–088–9
International Standard Serial Number: 0195–895X

The Poynter Institute for Media Studies
801 Third Street South
St. Petersburg, Florida 33701

Bonus Books, Inc.   .
160 East Illinois Street
Chicago, Illinois 60611

Book design and production by Billie M. Keirstead
Cover illustration by Phillip Gary Design, St. Petersburg, Florida

Photos for cover illustration were provided by Chuck Zoeller
of the Associated Press and are used with permission. Photo
credits: AP photographers J. Scott Applewhite (Bob and
Elizabeth Dole), Lacy Atkins (Jessica Dubroff), Greg Gibson
(Ron Brown delegation), Peter A. Harris (Billy Graham),
Beth A. Keiser (Bernardin funeral), and Mark Lehhihan
(TWA memorial service). AP stringers Mindaugas Kulbis
(Grozny), Fernando Llano (Peru), and Mark Wilson (Hillary
Rodham Clinton). Photos of ASNE award winners and
finalists were provided by their newspapers.

Printed in the United States of America

This book is dedicated to the writer's last line of defense: copy editors.

About this series

APRIL 1997

You're holding a guidebook.

There are no maps, no restaurant lists, no tourist sites. But this book can help you get to where you want to go as a writer.

This volume is, to be sure, a tribute to the talents of the writers whose work it celebrates. It is, yes, a record of some of the events last year that inspired distinctive journalism.

But the reason the American Society of Newspaper Editors and The Poynter Institute have published these collections for 19 years goes beyond those worthy objectives. This book is intended not merely to honor but to inspire. It does so by showing that *Best Newspaper Writing* isn't born, it's made, one paragraph at a time.

The best newspaper writers understand that. One of them, Peter King of the *Los Angeles Times,* said last year in this series:

"We like to pretend that it's easy, that stories write themselves, that you knock them out. It doesn't happen that way. At least the good ones don't happen that way. And I'm reminded of it twice a week, and I should have been reminded of it more when I was a city editor. It is a terrifying process, and it's hard work."

Terrifying. Work. In other words, you can do it. Chances are you're already terrified. That's a start. You may not have realized that just about all writers are angst-ridden. I know I am. That's why I was relieved to learn that Don Murray, the superb writer and gifted writing coach who last year gave his collected papers to Poynter, talks openly in his book, *Write to Learn,* about what happens when he sits at the keyboard:

"Some writers get headaches, others get stomach-aches; I get both."

As Murray's enormously valuable collection of papers shows, writing is work. It's a process. It is a craft. It can be examined, understood, learned.

So, too, *Best Newspaper Writing 1997* illustrates how writers write. Their comments help to demystify the work, to demonstrate that you can do it.

The book's value is increased by the thoughtful work of its editors, each of whom is a writer. Chief among them is Christopher Scanlan, an experienced newspaper writer and coach who directs Poynter's writing programs. He was assisted in the interviewing by Karen Brown, a former reporter and editor and accomplished teacher who is dean of the Institute faculty; by Roy Peter Clark, a founder of the writing coach movement who is Poynter's senior scholar; and by Keith Woods, whose distinctive voice as a newspaper columnist and editor now resonates in his teaching in the Institute's ethics and diversity seminars.

The winners whose work is presented and examined here were chosen by judges of the ASNE Writing Awards Competition and the Jesse Laventhol Prizes for Deadline News Reporting. The writing prizes were initiated in 1978, when ASNE made the improvement of newspaper writing one of its primary goals. The individual and team reporting awards were endowed in 1995 by David A. Laventhol, editor-at-large of the Times Mirror Co., to honor his late father, a veteran Philadelphia newspaperman.

The categories of the awards this year are deadline news reporting by an individual, deadline news reporting by a team, non-deadline writing, commentary, editorial writing, and writing about religion and spirituality. The 1997 ASNE Writing Awards Board was chaired by Mary Jo Meisner, former executive editor of the *Milwaukee Journal Sentinel.* The other judges were:

Peter K. Bhatia, *The Oregonian,* Portland
Kenneth F. Brusic, *The Orange County Register*
John S. Carroll, *The Sun,* Baltimore
Gregory Favre, *The Sacramento Bee*
Robert H. Giles, *The Detroit News*
William Hilliard, retired from *The Oregonian*
William B. Ketter, *The Patriot Ledger,* Quincy, Mass.
Craig Klugman, *The Journal-Gazette,* Fort Wayne, Ind.
David A. Laventhol, Times Mirror Co., Los Angeles
Ron Martin, *Atlanta Journal and Constitution*

Diane H. McFarlin, *Sarasota* (Fla.) *Herald-Tribune*
Tim J. McGuire, *Star-Tribune,* Minneapolis
Rena M. Pederson, *The Dallas Morning News*
Matthew V. Storin, *The Boston Globe*
Gil Thelen, *The State,* Columbia, S.C.
N. Don Wycliff, *Chicago Tribune*

* * *

Congratulations to the finalists and winners of the ASNE Distinguished Writing Awards. Poynter is honored to be associated with them and with ASNE.

The awards complement the role of The Poynter Institute. It was founded in 1975 by Nelson Poynter, chairman of the *St. Petersburg Times* and its Washington affiliate, *Congressional Quarterly.* On Mr. Poynter's death in 1978, he bequeathed controlling stock in the Times Publishing Company to the Institute. The company dividends sustain the Institute's research, publishing, and teaching of excellence and integrity in print and broadcast journalism.

James M. Naughton, President
The Poynter Institute

Acknowledgments

This book reflects the efforts and contributions of many people and organizations, chief among them the American Society of Newspaper Editors, especially Lee Stinnett, executive director, and Mary Jo Meissner, who chaired the writing awards committee. A special thanks to ASNE president Robert Giles for his support. Chuck Zoeller of the Associated Press continued to generously provide the news photos used on the cover.

This volume has been especially enriched by my Poynter colleagues, Karen F. Brown, Roy Peter Clark, and Keith Woods, who each interviewed a winning writer and wrote the study questions accompanying their stories. David Shedden provided his always comprehensive bibliography. Billie Keirstead, publications director, and copy editor Vicki Krueger, ably handled the editing and production responsibilities to produce this book on a journalism deadline. They were aided by Nancy Stewart, Martin Gregor, and Joyce Olson of the Institute staff. Readers benefit most of all from the stories and lessons about reporting and writing shared by the winners and finalists of this year's Distinguished Writing and Jesse Laventhol Awards. *Best Newspaper Writing 1997* is their book.

Contents

Editorial Writing

Religion/Spirituality Writing

Top 10 tools for today's journalists

Annual bibliography

Thinking about stories

It was a great story—a feature about Jed Barton, a 7-year-old boy blinded at birth but attending public school, swimming at the YMCA, even riding a bicycle. I turned it in to the desk and waited for the raves to pour in.

Instead, Joel Rawson, my editor at *The Providence Journal,* wanted to know if I had spent a day with the kid and his family.

You bet, I said. Several, in fact. I had gone to camp with him. Hung out at his school. Watched him bike, dive in the pool. Ate dinner with his family.

No, Rawson said. Have you ever spent an entire day with him from the time he wakes up until he goes to bed?

Well, nooo. But like I said, I went to camp, school, "the whole nine yards," as they like to say in Rhode Island.

Then Rawson leaned in close. "Look, do you know what this story is about?"

"Yeah, it's about a blind kid whose parents are mainstreaming him, who goes to school and camp and rides a bike."

"But what is it really about?" Rawson repeated.

"Well, he's living a normal life and..."

My editor leaned in even closer, eyes aglitter. "I'll tell you what it's really about. It's about not being able to see from the moment you wake up until you fall asleep. For every parent, it's your worst nightmare; the perfect baby you prayed for isn't perfect. So what do you do about it? That's what it's really about!"

So I went back to the Barton house and spent from morning 'til night there. The story I rewrote followed Jed from the moment when a bird's cry woke him from a dream until his mother hugged him goodnight and, without turning around, said for the 10th time that day, "Put your thumb down," part of her campaign to break him of the eye-rubbing that is a blind child's bad habit.

I learned many lessons about reporting and writing over the eight years I worked with Joel Rawson, who is now executive editor at *The Providence Journal.* But that day, when he demanded to know what my story was "really about," I learned the most important one. That day I learned the importance of thinking about stories.

It's a lesson reinforced by the talented writers whose work and reflections on craft fill this book. At a time when readers can get information from a variety of sources, the thinking we do as reporters and editors is the way we transform information into an exceedingly more valuable commodity—knowledge. Journalism, as the contents of this volume demonstrate, remains a challenging and exciting profession because it requires practitioners to think fast and on their feet, to think clearly, logically, soberly, and deeply at moments of intense chaos. To draw connections between disparate events and developments, to fashion a mosaic from an abundance of information, details, and facts. And to do it in a matter of minutes.

Like its predecessors over the past two decades, *Best Newspaper Writing 1997* "focuses on what is at the heart of what we do, the writing that appears in our newspapers," says Mary Jo Meisner, who led the American Society of Newspaper Editors committee that selected this year's winners and finalists from more than 500 entries in six categories.

"Thinking is the great under-appreciated and under-stated part of being a newspaper person." says David Maraniss, whose stories for *The Washington Post* won the Jesse Laventhol Award for deadline reporting. "Think hard. Think long," advises N. Don Wycliff, whose editorials for the *Chicago Tribune* won the ASNE's Distinguished Writing Prize for editorial writing.

You can't have the kind of good writing celebrated by the ASNE's annual writing competition without good reporting. But, as Maraniss points out, "the one ingredient that's often left out of the whole process is not the writing or the reporting, but the thinking."

Consider that process, the series of decisions and steps that effective writers follow.

1. Assign
2. Report
3. Think
4. Plan
5. Write
6. Rewrite

But when I ask reporters to rank how they actually spend most of their time on stories, the line-up changes dramatically:

1. Report (That's why they call us reporters, right?)
2. Write (Hey, we're writers, right?)
3. Re-write (Isn't that what editors are for?)
4. Assign (Does this include the time spent complaining about what a lame assignment it is?)
5. Plan (You don't mean outline, do you? I swore I'd never do another one after fifth-grade English with Miss McGillicudy.)
6. Think (I do that thinking with my fingers: See Step 2.)

The writers represented here do things differently. They have learned the value of thinking about their stories, in a conscious, deliberate, and sustained manner.

For David Waters, the thinking began even before he wrote his first stories on the religion beat for *The Commercial Appeal* in Memphis. He is the first winner of the ASNE award for writing on religion and spirituality.

"I started thinking religion wasn't like any other beat I'd ever had," he recalls. "I'd had government beats and the education beat, the legislative beat, politics. Every other beat I've had had a focal point. There was an agency or a board or a person, someone who seemed to be in charge, where you could go to find the center of that beat. And then I realized God is at the center of this beat. So I decided that my job was to cover God.... And in every story I write, whether or not it's set in a church, I look for God. And it seems to work."

Waters learned that thinking is the way writers, whatever the genre, medium, or deadline, make sense of the material they collect during the reporting. It's the compass that leads the reporter out of the tangled woods of reporting. It's the focusing ring on a camera lens that is turned back and forth until the image is clear.

Critical thinking was essential to the success of *Newsday*'s coverage of the still-unresolved mystery of the crash of TWA Flight 800. Confronted with conflicting theories posed by warring bureaucratic factions, the paper's editors and reporters had to continually separate rumor from fact and decide which elements deserved their readers' attention. In addition to the Laventhol Award for team deadline reporting, the paper's efforts were rewarded with the Pulitzer Prize.

Thinking about stories frightens some reporters and concerns some editors, who fear it sounds too much like a call to inject opinions into news stories. I'd argue that the best stories help readers understand how and why the news has meaning and relevance to their lives, which is a vital part of the journalist's job in a democracy. The way to achieve that is by applying intelligence and critical thinking skills to every story, by reporters using themselves as a resource, as *Boston Globe* columnist Eileen McNamara learned when an editor gave her this piece of advice after she had turned in a story:

"You know more about this topic than anybody and this is a good piece of journalism," she recalls Al Larkin saying. "But run it through the typewriter one more time, and this time, write it like you know it better than anybody else. Write it like you respect the fact that you have spent three weeks living this story. Don't report about it. Write out of the experience of reporting it."

The prospect terrified McNamara, but less than an hour later, her story was "stunningly different." It had, she says, "a voice of authority" missing from the first version. "I thought I couldn't do it. I thought I had handed him the best work I could do. And I'll always be grateful to him because he taught me that there was more in there than I knew."

Tom Hallman's ability to write evocative stories for *The Oregonian* draws from that same inner resource that McNamara's editor helped her tap. Hallman, who won the ASNE non-deadline prize, says, "I view myself as a guide, taking a reader by the hand and saying, 'Come, enter my world for a while and let me show you around.' When I'm reporting, I'm very aware of how I feel and I've learned to trust my voice. As I'm reporting, I think, 'This scene makes me feel that way. Why am I feeling that way?' And then I look for the details I can use to make someone who's not there feel the same way I did."

Thinking about stories helps the writer create the voice—that unmistakable sense of one writer talking to one reader—that takes journalism beyond information into a richer level of communication. "Information also should educate, information also should enlighten and edify and even inspire people," religion writer Waters argues. "That's why people will get up every day and buy that newspaper. They want to be more than informed."

To provide that kind of story, writers need to "think hard, think long," and to trust themselves more. Editors need to encourage reporters to apply critical thinking skills to their stories, to force them to dig deeper, to keep asking, as Joel Rawson once did, "What's this story really about?" Thinking about stories will enable journalists to help readers make sense of the news and their own lives.

A NOTE ABOUT THIS EDITION

The discussions with the ASNE winners in this book are based on tape-recorded telephone interviews by myself and my Poynter Institute colleagues Karen F. Brown, Roy Peter Clark, and Keith Woods. For reasons of clarity and pacing, we reorganized some questions and answers, and in some cases inserted additional questions. The edited transcripts were reviewed for accuracy and, in some instances, revised slightly by the subjects.

This edition also includes an update of Roy Peter Clark's 1984 description of the hourglass story structure, widely used by newswriters as an alternative to the inverted pyramid structure; Karen F. Brown's reflections on the connections between karate and good writing; and an essay by the editor about the top 10 writing tools for journalists.

Christopher Scanlan
May 1997

1997 Best Newspaper Writing

Tom Hallman Jr.
Non-Deadline Writing

Tom Hallman Jr., now in his 17th year at *The Oregonian,* is a senior writer, working on special projects and features. He is a Portland native and a graduate of Drake University. His career began inauspiciously enough: He was a copy editor at a magazine that specialized in stemware. Then he arrived in Portland and was assigned to the police beat, an assignment he says prepared him as much as anything else for the level of reporting he does now. Hallman was an ASNE contest finalist for non-deadline reporting in 1996. He won the Livingston Award for Young Journalists in 1985, was a member of the team that won the National Sigma Delta Chi award for non-deadline reporting in 1989, and was a Pulitzer finalist in beat reporting in 1994.

His work, from the story about being 12 years old to the wrenching tale of a mother about to surrender her baby to a home for incurable children, resonates with deep reporting, rich detail, and a personal voice that Hallman delivers with unapologetic clarity. He brings to his stories the ear of a musician, the eye of a detective, and the fiction writer's sense of complexity and character development. Those combined talents are his gift to readers: a talent for revealing the things that make ordinary people remarkable.

—Keith Woods

Children of a lesser hope

APRIL 28, 1996

Donalda Purrell adds with her fingers and can't make change for $20.

Lennetta Bell can't give directions to her home or read the children's book *Green Eggs and Ham.*

Amber Hancock can't read a thermometer and doesn't understand what it means when the grocery store sells something at 3 pounds for a dollar.

The three are mentally retarded—adults whose minds are trapped in childhood. Yet they have children of their own, youngsters who will be smarter than their mothers by the time they turn 9.

These women and their children are what happens when theories and good intentions collide with reality. They are what people failed to anticipate in the 1970s when mentally retarded men and women were moved out of institutions and into mainstream society.

Forty years ago these women would have been forcibly sterilized. Twenty years ago their children would have been put up for adoption.

But today, they and hundreds of thousands of other mentally retarded men and women across the United States are free to have children and raise them.

Some of the children are born retarded.

But most are not.

And those children are at risk of "cultural retardation," meaning they can't realize their inherent potential because their parents are unable to intellectually and emotionally stimulate and guide them.

Aside from those who get help from extended family, these parents and children go it alone. Beyond welfare and food stamps, there's no government aid or state programs to help them.

These families don't slip through the cracks, they plunge through them.

* * *

Lennetta Bell and her three girls—ages 9 months, 3 and 5, all of normal intelligence—live in a North Portland duplex with standing water in the basement and exposed wires. Mice dart about the kitchen.

Bell is a soft-spoken, 20-year-old who responds to questions with one or two words. If she ever smiled, it was long ago, in another life. She hasn't worked in years. Her last job was handing out hot dogs, soft drinks and snacks at Memorial Coliseum.

When she speaks, it's a monotone. She prefers the company of the television.

Her rent is $600 a month, which seems outrageous for a house that does not meet city standards. She needs to move but can't read the newspaper rental ads well enough to find another home.

Her 5-year-old, in preschool now, can't expect help from her mother with the simplest math problems, the easiest books. Her teacher may assume she's slow.

The child's younger sister hungers for stimulation. She runs through the house, then stacks and restacks video games before sitting on a couch and watching a television talk show with her mother.

Nearby, the baby cries unconsoled. Bell merely kisses her.

Bell doesn't know where to turn. She loves her children and does the best she can.

But it's going to get harder. She is pregnant again.

"It just happened," she said.

* * *

The most egregious examples leap from case files:

A woman released from the Fairview Training Center, a Salem institution for people with mental retardation, moved to Portland and became involved with another former Fairview resident. They had a child each year for seven years. Three children were retarded. All the children eventually were taken away because of abuse and neglect.

In another case, the state took custody of five children being raised by a mentally retarded Portland couple. Officials alleged abuse and neglect.

And seven other Portland women who are mentally retarded have had 38 children in the past 15 years. Some were born retarded; all suffered emotional problems and were placed in foster care or adopted.

No national study has been done to determine how many mentally retarded people have become parents.

But a 6-year-old study by Arc of Multnomah, an advocacy agency for people who are mentally retarded, estimated that 1,000 families in the county include one or two mentally retarded parents.

"This issue did not exist 15 years ago," said Barbara Whitman, director of family services and studies at St. Louis University School of Medicine in St. Louis, Mo. Whitman is an expert on mental retardation and parenthood, a field that has few researchers.

In the 1970s, advocacy groups pushed for people who are mentally retarded to experience what's called the "dignity of risk," which Whitman describes as the opportunity to take the same risks we all take.

Including being a parent.

But who's really taking the risk?

A California study of mentally retarded women found that they didn't know how to respond to a series of common household accidents: a child who drank poison, whose clothes were on fire or who was choking on food. Because reading is difficult, these parents may not understand directions for using prescriptions and over-the-counter drugs.

* * *

Donalda Purrell of Eugene knows about prescriptions and emergencies but only because she is one of the very few mentally retarded parents who is getting some help—even if it is short-lived.

Purrell, 39, has enrolled her 3-year-old daughter, Katie, in a private, nonprofit preschool in Lane County, one of only five programs in the country that helps children with normal intelligence whose parents are retarded.

Purrell, who last worked as a dishwasher, lives on welfare and food stamps. Katie's father, who is not retarded, pays child support but never married Purrell.

Purrell's greatest fear is that she will be labeled an unfit mother and lose custody of Katie. Her apartment is spotless, as if she were always expecting visitors. Her daughter is unfailingly polite and even-tempered, at times acting like a little adult.

Each morning Purrell braids Katie's hair and makes sure the girl's clothes are pressed and color-coordinated. She sends concerned notes to school: *"Would you see that Katie has her coat zip up and her hat put on before she comes home from school ever day thank you."*

"I know I am a good mother," Purrell adamantly said. "We always have food on the table. The house is clean. My daughter has not been abused."

Even with the help they're getting now, an uncertain future hurtles toward mother and daughter.

It's a future of geometry problems, book reports and spelling tests. A life of boys and dates and broken hearts, of important decisions and lasting consequences.

Purrell frowned as she considered the scenario.

"I will be happy if she knows more than me," she finally said. "I don't know math too good."

Then a smile burst across her face.

"But we sing 'Itsy Bitsy Spider' and 'Two Little Monkeys Jumping on the Bed' together."

* * *

In the 1920s, the U.S. Supreme Court upheld laws that prevented retarded people from having children. "Two generations of imbeciles are enough," Justice Oliver Wendell Holmes wrote.

During the 1930s and '40s, a state board in Oregon authorized doctors to sterilize retarded adults. After the Supreme Court reversed itself in 1942, the board disbanded. But parents continued to have retarded children sterilized. And retarded adults were institutionalized or kept on the fringes of society. If a woman did give birth, the child was quickly given up for adoption.

Then, in the 1970s, mainstreaming began. At that time, 200,000 mentally retarded people were living in public institutions across the United States. By 1994, that figure dropped to 65,000.

Mentally retarded children entered public schools in 1975, when it became illegal for schools to turn them away. At the same time, advocates successfully pushed for a broad range of rights, including sexual relationships and parenthood.

"Sexual drives and the desire to be loved are as strong in people who are mentally retarded as it is in all of us," said Sharon Davis, national director of research and programs for the Arc, formerly known as the Association for Retarded Citizens. Davis has a 29-year-old mentally retarded daughter.

"It is clear, however, that persons with mental retardation can be vulnerable to many sorts of things when you are talking about sexuality," she said. "They can be taken advantage of."

Bell, for example, had her first child when she was 14. She was in special-education classes and dropped out of school. The 18-year-old father said he loved her; he fathered a second child.

The man is now in jail.

Bell never sees the father of her third child, and she receives no child support. The father of her unborn child doesn't know she's pregnant.

Davis said she's talked with her daughter about using contraceptives.

And if her daughter did get pregnant?

"I would be very, very concerned," she said. "She loves children and is a good caretaker. And yet, she would also need quite a bit of supervision. That would fall to me because there are no programs to help her."

* * *

That's what happened to Melissa Isom. The McMinnville woman's 25-year-old daughter, Amber Hancock, is mentally retarded, as is her son-in-law. When Hancock became pregnant, Isom considered telling her daughter to give the child up for adoption.

But her daughter wanted this baby. Isom felt she must honor that wish.

The baby, a boy, is now 7 months old and of normal intelligence.

The burden of his upbringing has fallen to Isom and other family members.

"We've assumed tremendous roles," said Isom, an administrative assistant for the special-education department with the Yamhill County Educational Service District. "My daughter isn't comfortable giving the baby a bath, so I help her and show how to do it. She's feeling more at ease. If the baby's fussy, she gets nervous that he's sick. I'm teaching her that it's OK for a baby to be fussy."

Although Isom's daughter and son-in-law are capable of leading independent lives, a baby has raised the stakes.

"They love the baby and are good parents, but they need extra help," she said. "They wanted to buy third-

and fourth-stage toddler food because it was cheaper. I had a hard time getting them to understand why they couldn't feed a baby toddler food."

Isom realizes she will always have to be involved in her grandson's life.

"I will always be within driving distance of my daughter's home," Isom said. "I'll volunteer at my grandson's school, enroll him in baseball. She needs me. He needs me.

"Some days it scares me."

* * *

Severely retarded adults—people who can hardly function in society—usually don't have the opportunity to have children. When they do, adoption is still typical.

That's not the case with adults with IQs between 65 and 80. Someone with an IQ of 100 is considered average; someone below 80 is considered retarded. People in the 65 to 80 IQ range can live alone but have difficulty holding even a menial job. These people, often described as mildly mentally retarded, have trouble with abstract concepts.

Bell, for example, knows her address but not the name of streets just a few blocks away. If she was dropped off downtown, she would be unable to find her way home. She knows what a $20 bill looks like, but she isn't sure what it will buy.

"They do just well enough to stay out of trouble," said Bill West, a case coordinator for Arc of Multnomah. "Their kids come to school every day, Mom and Dad may seem slow, but they can talk with the teacher."

Over the years West has worked with about 100 families headed by retarded parents.

"The vast majority were struggling," he said. "Maybe 12 were doing OK. And those 12 had extra family help. About 30 families had kids taken from them, and I was in favor of many of those because of abuse and neglect."

In a perfect world—one with proper support for the parents—West thinks people who are mentally retarded would be able to raise children.

"This is troubling to me, but I try and dissuade them from having children because it's not in their best interest," West said. "I try and be realistic."

But not everyone listens.

"This is an issue that is literally growing bigger every day," said Davis, the researcher at the Arc's national headquarters in Arlington, Texas.

* * *

Sometimes the extended family helps raise the child. In other cases, relatives persuade the parents to give up the child. Sometimes, the parent makes that ultimate choice.

In Eugene, a woman—after much soul-searching and anguish—allowed her 6-year-old son to be adopted. He was gifted—far above average intelligence—and she believed she would hold him back.

Often no one realizes a child's parents are retarded until the child is in school.

And by then, it's often too late for the children, said Whitman of St. Louis University. Cultural retardation has set in.

Whitman began studying children born to retarded parents in 1981 after a woman brought her 18-month-old daughter into the university's clinic to find out why the girl wasn't talking.

"The woman had been in the state hospital all her life," Whitman said. "When we tested her, she had an IQ of 35. The girl didn't talk because her mother could barely speak."

Whitman knew she had to do something. She set up a parenting class to teach the mother how to be a parent.

She then set out to find other mothers in similar situations. The parenting class ran for seven years—helping nearly 400 families—until funding ran out.

There's never been enough money to conduct a follow-up study of the children.

"I often wonder about that first little baby," Whitman said. "Her name was Annie."

Even after years in the field, Whitman doesn't know if mentally retarded adults should be parents.

"Do we have a criteria for who can be parents?" she asked. "It's a moral question for which we have no answer. What can be said, however, is that if these folks have the right to the dignity of risk, we as a society better be there with supports when the risks backfire. It's the kids who pay for their parents' risks."

* * *

It's a risk that David and Rachel Beem, who live in Salem, wanted to take. Now, though, they wonder what became of their two children, Matthew and Sara, both of whom are of normal intelligence.

Four years ago, Oregon authorities took the kids from the Beems' home after saying they were unfit parents.

David Beem, 44, spent 10 years living in the Fairview Training Center, the Salem institution for people with mental retardation. He met his wife, Rachel, 26, at a workshop for the mentally retarded.

Because state officials are not allowed to discuss child-protection cases, accounts of what happened to the Beems are based on their recollections.

"I never knew what the problem was," Rachel Beem said. "They said I shook the kids up or something to keep them from crying. That's not true. I don't do that to kids. I've been around kids since I was 9 years old. I've been a baby sitter. I'm still a baby sitter."

Her husband said state officials never gave the family a chance. He said the couple initially wanted to adopt a child but were turned down even though they passed a test to determine their mental capabilities. The couple then decided to have their own children.

"We tried to do it on our own," he said. "There was nowhere to go for help. Like diapers and what we needed at the store. We did the best we could. Like a family."

Rachel Beem is now sterile.

"I got my tubes tied," she said. "I don't want any more kids after that kind of trouble."

David Beem, his voice plaintive, said he had fun with his children.

"We had them here one day, and then they said we couldn't have them," he said. "We don't know where they are. They don't write to us or nothing. We don't even get pictures. We think about them every day. It hurts us when we see kids."

Beem thinks the state would allow them to adopt children if he and his wife had enough money.

So he plays the lottery.

"I won $300 and paid off bills," he said. "But if I won the big prize, I bet they'd let me have a child. I'm not a bad person."

Writers' Workshop

Talking Points

1) In the story's lead, Hallman uses details that serve as the evidence for the case he's about to make. Where else in the story do details underscore the central theme? Imagine other details you might pursue to make similar points. Remove some of the details and determine which ones are crucial to the story.

2) In describing Lennetta Bell, Hallman says she lives amid mice and chaos, cannot help her children with school work, and clearly is not meeting their emotional needs. "If she ever smiled," Hallman writes, "it was long ago, in another life." Later, he says, "She loves her children and does the best she can." How important is it to the story that Hallman offers up those contradictions? Where else in the piece do you find such contrasts? What effect does it have on what a reader might get out of the story?

3) Note the number of times Hallman uses the word "normal" to describe those who are not mentally retarded. Mentally retarded people, he says in one passage, are allowed to take "the same risks we all take." What point of view comes across in this piece? How do you think it helps or hinders the writer's message?

Assignment Desk

1) In interviewing people with limited mental abilities, Hallman manages to demonstrate both critical analysis and sensitivity. Find an interview subject you might regard as difficult. Alone or with an editor, think through the potential problems and pitfalls of such an interview. Conduct a tough interview and write about your experience.

2) Construct a list of sources Hallman might have used. Do some research on mental retardation and suggest other resources a writer might employ.

Mount Hood's deadly deceit

MAY 12, 1996

No mountain in America is more climbed than Oregon's beloved Hood. But our easy trust was shattered during a spring storm in 1986, when Mount Hood claimed a sacrifice of nine lives. As the search dragged on through four chilling days, The Oregonian's Tom Hallman bore witness. Ten years later, he returns to seek lessons from those we lost.

In the decade since the mountain's betrayal, I have traveled back many times. Never once have I thought of anything but the children.

Now the anniversary approaches, and the mountain calls again. I share the front seat with memories that have not faded, with names as familiar as the faces of my own children: *Patrick McGinness, Richard Haeder, Brinton Clark, Giles Thompson...*

They were among the 13—three adults and 10 students from Oregon Episcopal School, an elite private school in Southwest Portland—who failed to return from a one-day spring hike to the top of Mount Hood.

They set out in the wee hours of Monday, May 12, 1986.

By nightfall they were several hours overdue.

By the second day, two from the party stumbled down in a desperate gamble to get help. The other 11 were trapped above, huddled in a snow cave. Searchers cursed the blizzard winds that kept them grounded.

By the third day, spotters found three dead on the slope. One wore no parka, another no gloves. Two had peeled off their boots. The madness of hypothermia— the severe loss of body heat—made them think they were hot. Parents prayed aloud to the dark face of the mountain, where eight still were lost in the snow cave.

At the end of the fourth day, a searcher's probe found the cave. The eight climbers huddled inside were so cold that intravenous lines could not pierce their frozen skin. By midnight, only two survived.

Mount Hood stands a majestic 11,240 feet.

It is Oregon's tallest peak, its post card and land-
mark and playground. After Japan's Mount Fuji, Hood
is the most-climbed mountain in the world.

The climb to its summit is so pedestrian that 10,000
trekkers make it each year. So routine that OES made
it a rite of passage for sophomores. So casual that one
of the kids on this trip lugged along a six-pack of pop.

The days after the OES disaster—the second-worst
climbing accident in U.S. history—were filled with
funerals and memorials. Then came weeks of investi-
gations and, later still, legal inquiries.

All but one of the families settled with the school's
insurance company; only one, the Haeders, sued, winning $500,000 from jurors who found the school had
negligently caused the death of their son, Richie. A report outlined mistakes made on the mountain and rec-
ommended changes in the school's Basecamp program.

Climbers continue to trek up Hood each spring, but
few take it for granted now. They wear proper gear
and carry cell phones. They watch the weather. They
honor the mountain's dark power.

Later that summer, I encountered the parents of one
of the lost climbers. Their presence embarrassed me. I
felt awkward as I cradled my baby daughter, a cooing,
living reminder. I made small talk and tried to ease
away. But the father clutched my shoulder.

"Cherish her," he said quietly.

I thought it was over then—until this anniversary,
when I again travel this highway, a journalist in search
of a sequel. Now that I'm at the base of the mountain,
I'm a father who wonders whether he understood what
happened on that mountain, to those who survived, to
those who died, to those left behind.

* * *

Firefighter Rick Harder hunkers on a bench outside
the station house in Southeast Portland. Harder, also a
master sergeant in the U.S. Air Force Reserve's Portland-
based Aerospace Rescue and Recovery Squadron, was
summoned to the mountain 10 years ago.

He doesn't want to remember. He leans away from
the questions as if they were a swarm of hornets. At
times his emotions threaten to breach some internal
dam he has constructed.

"We thought we'd find them that first day," he says softly. "We gave it our best shot."

His descriptions come shrouded in the safety of clichés—packed like sardines, stacked like cords of wood. But that's what rescuers found in that cave.

Those on the bottom had to be cut from their clothes, which had frozen into the snow. A girl's core body temperature was 39 degrees. A boy's teeth were clenched so tightly that medics couldn't maneuver breathing tubes into his mouth. They were raced by helicopter to Portland hospitals, where the formal declarations of death began.

By midnight only two—Giles Thompson and Brinton Clark—were left.

"I see death all the time on my job," Harder says. "But these were kids and...

"I've got kids of my own."

He mutters.

"You know, we searched that area four or five times," he says. "Everyone in the world tried as hard as they could. But they were buried under snow as hard as this."

He stamped his foot on the driveway.

"Buried alive."

He slumps in the seat.

"To die on the side of a mountain."

He bows his head.

* * *

Brinton Clark has kept her silence these 10 years. The last time anyone heard from Giles Thompson, he was in college in Colorado.

Ralph Summers and Molly Schula—the two who stumbled off the mountain the second day in search of help—let it be known they don't want to talk. Summers, who was hired by the school to help guide the trek, no longer leads climbs. Schula, an older student who had the strength to make it down the mountain with him, later married one of the attorneys who represented OES in the lawsuit.

Eighteen people began the climb. Five turned back before they even eclipsed the Palmer chairlift. Among them were Sharon Spray and her daughter, Hilary. Spray, who now lives in Laguna Beach, Calif., is stunned by the telephone call.

"Mount Hood," she says. "Oh, my God. I moved away from that mountain. I couldn't bear to look at it any more."

She cries.

"I'm sorry. For years I had nightmares. Those kids calling for help and I couldn't do anything. I knew every one of them. One was my daughter's best friend."

From the moment they set out, Spray sensed it was a mistake. Most of the kids had been in a school play and had attended a cast party Saturday night. On a short night's sleep, they set out about 2 a.m. Monday, the standard time to depart. The ritual of Hood is to reach the summit in time for sunrise, then cruise back down in time for dinner.

But newfallen snow had sculpted deep drifts. The climbers were weary; an adult and several students were so slow they fell behind schedule within the first hour.

Spray had climbed Mount Hood before. She complained loudly that this march was ridiculous.

"You don't climb like that," she says. "We were all carrying 50-pound packs. And it was cold, the kind of cold where you feel it in the marrow of your bones. Your stomach is cold."

For some reason, the Rev. Thomas Goman, a teacher at OES and the climb's leader, didn't listen. They pushed on.

"Then a storm hit, and there was a whiteout," Spray recalls. "We had no sense of direction or balance. I said this was stupid, we needed to turn around."

When her daughter, a diabetic, grew nauseated, Spray told Goman they were turning back.

"My lasting image is those kids walking past us, disappearing into the falling snow," she says. "They were exhausted. None of them said a word.

"We never said goodbye."

They buried her daughter's friend, Erin O'Leary. At the funeral, the girl's grandmother asked Spray why she didn't grab Erin and make her come down the mountain, too.

"That will haunt me until the day I die," she says.

Eventually, the questions drove Spray into therapy.

"What if I hadn't been there? Why did Hilary get sick? What if Hilary had refused to turn back? I finally learned that for some questions there are no answers. I just, I just..."

The telephone falls silent.

Then comes a resigned, exhausted whisper.

"We came back. We just came back."

She clears her throat.

"Hilary and I turned back. And two people came out of the snow cave. And that's the way it was."

* * *

The telephone rings.

"Yes, this is Brinton."

She listens to the question.

"Yes. Next week."

* * *

The cold is a gentle killer.

When they found Patrick McGinness, he didn't have a mark on his body. He was 15 and sang in the school choir. He was different from other OES kids because he didn't come from money. His family lived in Northeast Portland, and he attended school on a full scholarship.

"At the hospital, they pulled down the sheet, and I looked at him," his father, Frank McGinness, says. "He looked like he needed to be kicked out of bed and told to get ready for school."

McGinness, sipping tea in a Northwest Portland coffee shop, apologizes because his thoughts tumble at random. In the month before the climb, he and his wife separated, and she moved to Philadelphia. Patrick and his younger brother were to join her when school ended.

"In early April I had a wife, two kids and a business," he says. "By late August, I was divorced and had filed for bankruptcy. I had no job, no money. One son was dead, the other was 3,000 miles away.

"I was drinking pretty heavily to kill the pain," he says. "I was doing a little consulting work to make ends meet, but not much more than drinking."

In the brutal days after the climb, McGinness was more approachable than most.

"You know, it was such a public thing," he says. "Not knowing for days, the media. Always the media."

Patrick was buried in Philadelphia, near his mother. The funeral was front-page news. Seven TV crews, two from New York, showed up at the church. When McGinness returned home, he says, he went through the floor.

"I had nothing to distract me from the grief," he says. "I cried, but I was in denial. One night I heard some music that Patrick liked and I realized never again would I hear him sing. I pulled the blinds and started drinking at night to go to sleep."

He failed to tend to his wood-finishing business; orders dropped off, and he was forced to let employees go.

"I crapped out," he says.

And so it went until 1990, when he met the woman who would become his wife.

"She stopped my freefall," he says. "I won't say I got better right away; it took time. But with her I felt safe."

What would Patrick think?

McGinness smiles. His eyes glisten.

"I'd like to think he's seen it all," he says. "He'd be proud because I've taken care of myself. I have flaws, but I deal with them. I'd like to think my son would be proud that his father had the courage to change."

* * *

The woman at the front desk would be about his daughter's age. Another one of those reminders. He strides into the reception area, dispenses a handshake and leads the way to his office.

"*The Oregonian* made this dreadfully difficult 10 years ago," Don McClave says. "Pursuing information about the insurance settlement; harassing families about the investigation. Ghoulish behavior."

He shifts in his chair. He moves as if his shirt is too tight or the chair too small. He braids his hands behind his head, tucks them between his knees. Anger and disgust seep out of him. He hasn't been asked about the climb for eight years. But if there is to be a story, he wants his say.

He waits for the questions.

He gives terse answers.

Yes.

No.

He bristles against a long silence.

Then he fills the gap.

"Losing a child is the worst thing that can happen to a parent," he says. "All of us were beset by the media, by movie companies, by television producers, by insensitive and self-serving groups trying to capitalize on the incident."

He is proud that none of the families sold its story.

"We didn't hurt each other," he says.

He and his wife didn't know most of the other families. The climb was for sophomores. His daughter, Susan, was a senior. She had made the climb as a sophomore and went along to help.

Her father softens.

"It never goes away," he says. "You learn to live with it with the help of the church, professional help, friends. But we deal with it every day of our lives. We always will."

We face each other across a gulf miles wide, each in our roles. Me the inquisitor. He the guardian of the past.

He snaps to attention.

"My son is grown and married," he announces. "My wife and I are here. Other than that, I'm not going to talk about our lives. Anyone interested in reliving the accident can read the papers from 10 years ago. It was awful then. It is awful now."

* * *

She is wary.

"I had lots of requests for interviews," Brinton Clark says. "I never gave one. I never wanted to be a public person."

She talks now, she says, because it seems right. But she is as evasive as a boxer. She ducks and bobs. A certain intensity radiates from her. Talking with her is like playing chess with a grandmaster. You think four moves ahead and find she is there, waiting.

When she was pulled from the cave, she was in critical condition. She spent six weeks in the hospital and nearly nine months undergoing rehabilitation to repair nerve damage in her arms and legs. She sustained no permanent damage. Doctors said she survived because she was dressed more warmly than the others and because Giles Thompson lay on top of her, his life stoking hers. At the time, doctors said she might never remember what happened.

"I remember a lot of things," she says. "I don't want to talk about them. They should stay private, with me."

She admits to mood swings and depression the first year. She does not know why she lived.

"I don't want to guess," she says. "I don't want to rehash it 10 years later."

She leans forward.

"Look, I was only 15." She says, "I needed to work on getting better. It's not productive to look back. I don't do a lot of second-guessing. I survived, and many wonderful things happened to me."

She graduated from Stanford University with a degree in human biology and joined the Peace Corps; she taught health education in a West African village. She plans to get a master's degree in public health-care, then a medical degree.

And she has been kissed by death. She has stared over the abyss. You can see it in her eyes.

She knows.

But she will not discuss it.

"It is an element of who I am," she says. "But only an element. It does not define who I am."

She knows.

We stare at each other.

She does not fill the silent gap.

"I lived," she says. "Why is not a question that has plagued me."

* * *

She answers the telephone, but hands it to her husband, who does all the talking.

"She's crying," Richard Haeder says. "This is still too hard for Judy. The real tragedy of this is that it never ends."

From the beginning, the Haeders were different. On the mountain they wore city clothes. She carried a handbag; he wore walking shoes. The rage they felt about their son's death was apparent even then and finally boiled over when they broke ranks with the other parents and sued OES. They won a wrongful-death suit, but no comfort. They fled Portland and settled in Rapid City, S.D., near his parents and brothers.

He practices law, much of it pro bono. Only a few people there know about their past.

When the Haeders filed suit, some people thought them vindictive, unable to let go.

"The suit was not easy," he says. "It kept open an already raw wound. But the school would not take any responsibility for their actions. Their blunders put young lives on the chopping blocks for no more than pride in a program."

Long before it was fashionable for fathers, Haeder put his family ahead of his career.

And he feels cheated.

"I could have made more money, but I never missed it," he says. "Everything was for the family, not living through Richie and my two girls, but looking forward to being with them as we grew older....

"You cannot raise a person and lose them without heartache and regret. You see their potential. Not that they were going to be kings and presidents. But they had a future."

Richie's baby sisters are now older than he will ever be. They don't want to talk about their brother.

When the Haeders were flying out of Portland for the last time, the pilot announced he had a treat for the passengers. He instructed them to look out their windows for a breathtaking view of Mount Hood.

* * *

Giles Thompson is friendly on the telephone, but firm. No interview. We talk awhile. I ask again. He waits and waits. He goes to ask his wife and returns with directions to his home near Seattle.

I ask one more question: Do you remember?

"Yes."

* * *

In the need to blame, a school is too vague to satisfy. A villain requires a face. This time it belonged to Father Thomas Goman.

He taught physics, ethics and math at OES and led the yearly climbs up Mount Hood for the school's Basecamp program.

An investigation noted that his decision not to turn around early in the climb was inconsistent with his long record of safe climbs. This, his last, was his 18th. His reasoning, the report noted, will never be known.

His widow, an artist, lives a quiet life in North Portland.

"Big anniversaries are important," Mar Goman says. "A decade is a way of measuring changes in a life."

Others can speak to the climb itself, the decisions made, the mistakes. But I turn to the priest's widow for questions about God and where he was that week. We sit near a window. From time to time she says nothing, but stares out at a rainstorm. Her eyes twitch, and most of the time she looks away.

"God could have changed the weather," she says. "But that is not how God works. Tom would say that we only see a small piece of the picture. That what looks unjust to us is part of a larger puzzle. God doesn't make things well in life."

She remains a religious person. God did not let her down.

"What happened ripped my life open," she says. "I had to redefine myself as an unmarried person in a married culture. As painful as it was, there was new growth for me. My spiritual depth is there in hard times as well as in joyous times."

Yes, she says, her husband was at fault. But so were the school, the administrators and all those who oversaw the program. Tom was dead and unable to explain his actions.

"He was an easy scapegoat," she says. "People who knew him have memories of him. Those who don't know him can make up their own minds. He is out of this world. What is said does not affect him."

She does not think that she must defend her husband. But she says it is better that he died on the mountain.

"It would have destroyed his life if he had lived and those kids had died," she says. "He could not have lived with himself. They trusted him to bring them down safely. And he didn't do that."

She grapples with her own questions, not theological, but practical. Months after the climb, she visited a local sporting goods store and stared at the climbing gear. Goman didn't own any Gore-Tex, any special underwear. His gloves were U.S. Army surplus. What if he had spent $500 for better equipment?

"Would it have made a difference?" she asks.

She looks out the window. She answers her own question.

"Maybe.

"How I wish.

"How I wish."

She sighs.

"As a Christian I believe in the resurrection," she says. "I waited and waited for a vision of Tom. I dream about him from time to time. He still plays a powerful role in my life.

"He was the first person who loved me unconditionally," she says. "I never felt I fell short in his eyes. I miss his sense of humor."

She stares at her hands.

"I miss the smell of him."

* * *

He moves so gracefully. It is hard to believe he wears prosthetics, that both his legs were amputated after they pulled him from the cave. Each year since the climb, OES has a memorial to mark the event. Giles Thompson does not attend.

"I learned not to count the years," he says. "For a long time, I wanted it to go away. I wanted to be like everyone else. And I wasn't going to be."

He cannot straighten his fingers. Thick, wide scars from skin grafts map his forearms.

"I will die this way because of something that happened 10 years ago," he says. "Something horrible."

There are no tears. No long pauses. He remembers everything. His wife, Marie, has heard the story, but he speaks with such passion that she stares at him, captivated.

"We should have turned around," he says simply. "We were only at the halfway point at the time we should have been at the top. And we kept going. Father Tom was focusing on one of the teachers, who was having a difficult time. He kept telling her that this was good for her, that she should push on."

The climb began to unravel when Patrick McGinness, suffering from hypothermia, fell over and knocked others off their feet. "He got up and pushed himself to continue," Thompson says.

They were all so tired. On a steep incline, they took one step up only to slide down two.

"Then all hell broke loose," Thompson says. "The weather got even worse. We turned around, but Patrick was in bad shape."

The group stopped to try to warm McGinness. They zipped him in a sleeping bag with another student and fed him hot water flavored with lemon. About an hour later, when they should have been approaching Timberline Lodge, they remained nearly 9,000 feet up the mountain. They continued their trudge.

"Ralph Summers was holding onto Patrick, who was like a sack of potatoes," Thompson says. "They were falling. Down a ravine, wandering off course. We'd lose sight of them. It was snowing like hell. I was carrying Ralph's pack and mine. The wind was blowing so hard that the snow was horizontal."

Goman was at the rear, tending to signs of hypothermia in the teacher, 40-year-old Marion Horwell. He and Summers devised a plan: Follow a 160-degree compass reading, which would veer them away from treacherous Zig Zag Canyon, where climbers often end up in whiteouts. The adults were busy helping the sick, so they passed the compass to a student.

Thompson, in his bright yellow gear, stepped out in front a few paces to serve as a compass beacon for Susan McClave, the next student in line. Step, read and follow. Step, read and follow. In that way, they would curve the group into the Palmer chairlift and follow it to the lodge.

"But we didn't start reading the compass at the right place," Thompson says. "We cut too early, missed the chair and started back up the mountain. Then I fell in a hole. We were lost and thought we'd fall into a crevasse. But there were no crevasses. Turns out we were just on the side of a hill."

By now it was nearing dusk. They should have been sipping hot chocolate at the lodge and congratulating themselves.

Instead they were high above, trapped in the whiteout. No one could see. Summers took over the lead.

He instructed those with enough strength to dig a snow cave where they could ride out the storm. McGinness was tucked back into a sleeping bag; the others huddled under a tarp.

"I have no idea how the cave was dug," Thompson says. "It just was. It was so small."

They stowed their gear under a tarp. Summers led the climbers—all weary, some sick—into the cave two at a time.

"I went in first," Thompson says. "Brinton was on my shoulder. Someone else butted up against my crotch. Half of someone else on my legs."

And they began a wait that would last three full days, long enough for death to visit.

"Scoot over."

"My arm is cramped."

"My legs hurt."

"Let me out."

The cave was about 4 feet high and 6 feet long. To get inside, the climbers had to lie down and slide through a tunnel made tight to keep out the wind. They had no insulation beyond the clothes they wore, and much of that was inadequate.

Body heat caused the snow ceiling to soften and fall in on them, the floor to melt and leave them in a shallow lake of slush. Ice formed around the entrance, tightening the hole, which had started out horizontal, but turned upward because of the snow and ice. Climbers took turns crawling out to make space, to get air. Those inside used an ice ax to keep the entrance chipped open.

"But it wasn't working," Thompson says. "Our shovel was lost, buried outside in the snow. And the hole got smaller and smaller."

It was only the first night. But already, Goman was severely hypothermic.

"One time he was outside the cave, shivering so loudly that it scared us. He was just screaming," he says. "I remember that sound."

Thompson struggled outside to search for the group's packs.

"The tarp was under a foot of snow," he says. "I couldn't lift it. It was insane—the wind, the snow, the cold. I couldn't get back in the cave. I panicked and just wrenched myself in."

By morning, most of the 13 were in bad shape. The students were listless. The teacher was no longer talking. Summers asked Goman to count to 10. He couldn't. His mind was gone.

Summers tapped Schula as his partner in the attempt to march out. He told those left behind that he and Schula would "keep walking until we found help or until we died."

Thompson pauses before speaking again.

"We were scared," he says. "That sound of people shivering."

Only the kids were awake. At first, they nursed their hopes. Summers would bring help. The weather would blow over. Rescue would come.

But the hours passed, and kept passing. Someone asked whether they were going to die. There was no answer. They lost track of time. At one point—most likely Tuesday night—three students went outside.

"Maybe to pee, maybe they were claustrophobic, I don't know," Thompson says. "But they couldn't get back in. We tried. All that could fit through that tunnel was a leg. I saw this boot. That's all. I chipped away with the ice ax, trying to make the hole bigger. But the boot disappeared.

"I looked through that hole," he says. "It was like looking through a telescope, just an image of gray. I wasn't at peace or terrified. They were out there and we were in here."

Thompson had no way of knowing that searchers were on the slopes, desperately probing the snow. He didn't know that they had come within 15 feet of the buried snow cave the day before. All he knows is that only he, Brinton and Richie Haeder were awake at the end. Their friends and teachers, cradled with them in that icy hollow, were dead, or near death.

"We hadn't eaten," he says, "We had no water. The weather wasn't getting better. We were cold. So cold. I never thought I would die, but I was pretty scared. It was so bizarre. This howling wind outside, the silence inside. And then a lot of hallucinations, pain."

The doctors never lied to him.

"They told me that I lost my legs and that six others in the cave died," he says. "I just cried. I cried. And I cried some more."

He returned to OES the next school year in a wheelchair and his physical recovery progressed rapidly. It wasn't until he went to Colorado College that the depression seeped in.

"I had to let my old self go," he says. "I just wanted to be like everyone else, and I wasn't."

He went to a counselor. He dropped out of school and began skiing in competitions for disabled people.

"I needed some success," he says. "I found it."

He returned to school, where he earned a degree in drama and met his wife. Their son Lewis, 2½, looks like his father.

"I'm not rooted in the past," he says. "Nothing is going to change. I am rooted in reality. Every morning I put on my legs."

He stands up and walks down the hallway of his home. He returns with a piece of graph paper. He has drawn a pencil rendering of the cave. He does not want it to be reproduced, but he needs me to see it, to understand.

It is a simple sketch, and small. But the terror cries out.

The cave is shaped like an old-fashioned water bottle, the kind tucked at the end of a bed to warm your feet. A side view shows there was no room to sit up. Thirteen bodies are jammed together. There is no free space. They are curled and draped, in balls and angles, clinging to one another.

The drawings have few features, but neither are they stick figures. Here is a boy, there a girl. There are shadowy eyes, almost personalities. One girl holds a head in her lap. Another, her head buried in someone's shoulder, seems so sad.

Thompson points to a figure shoved against one wall, hugging the girl next in line.

"This was me," Thompson says.

He doesn't know why he lived.

"I was slightly bigger, I had skied more and was wearing some ski gear," he says. "I don't know. I gave up second-guessing long ago."

There was a time he felt guilty, like giving up.

"But eventually I realized I could not give up or waste an opportunity that none of them would have."

He sighs.

"Erin and Susan and Eric and Patrick and Richard and Tasha..."

His wife rubs his arm.

"They all had such special qualities," he says. "They all paid such a terrible price. In my heart, they are all with me. Not daily, I don't live for them. But they are there. The reality is that they are with me, and I with them."

Thompson's son toddles over to him.

"When I held my child for the first time, I realized that I am part of the cycle of life," he says. "And for the first time, I understood what those parents went through. Those hours, those days of waiting."

He bends down. He kisses his boy.

Writers' Workshop

Talking Points

1) Tom Hallman weaves his own memories into the lead of the story, telling the reader about encountering one of the parents of the children who died on Mount Hood: "I felt awkward as I cradled my baby daughter, a cooing, living reminder," he wrote. Hallman says that his perspective, as one who knows the stories of all those involved in the tragedy on Mount Hood, required that he be a part of the story. What do you think about his use of first-person in this piece? Where else do you hear the writer's voice beyond first-person passages?

2) Some of the strongest moments in this story are carried in quotations. Hallman quotes Mar Goman, wife of the priest who led the expedition: "I miss the smell of him." Where are quotations used most effectively? Discuss the way Hallman uses the fact that Brinton Clark and Don McClave were reluctant, difficult interviews. Does Hallman reveal anything about interviewing technique in his stories?

3) Hallman tells this story in snapshots, each segment ending with what verges on a cliffhanger. The author says he wanted to leave the reader wanting more than what he provides. Does this strategy seem to work? Would you do things differently?

4) Hallman offers graphic, gripping details about how the climbers died and the conditions of their bodies when rescuers arrived. Discuss his handling of those descriptions. Were they handled sensitively? Were there words or phrases that increased or lessened the impact of such description?

Assignment Desk

1) Brinton Clark did not want to speak to a reporter. Don McClave is still angry at the newspaper 10 years after the accident. Prepare a strategy for pursuing an interview with each of them. How would you get their stories into this piece if they refuse to be interviewed?

2) Reconstruct a story using only physical sources: civil and criminal court documents, coroner's reports, police reports, press clippings. Note how much information you can put together without conducting an interview.

Diana's choice

Diana Sullivan chose to join the Navy, to marry, to have a child. Then, putting family ahead of career, she chose to have a second child. That's when her real choices began.

After all this, she still flinches at each cough. One... two...three...He hacks and wheezes and gasps, like an old man in the grip of emphysema.

Five...six...

She shoves her cereal aside and stands guard outside his bedroom door.

Ten.

Silence.

She eases in, peers into his crib.

"Are you ready, honey? Are you ready to go on a long trip?"

Nothing.

"Oh, my son," she whispers. "I..."

She kisses her fingertips and slides them across his cheek. She lingers, memorizing the curve of his face. She lays hands on his chest and feels the life beating there.

Then she turns to confront the suitcases that taunt her from the living room. The choice, her husband said, was hers to make.

Never has she felt so alone. She gave up on God long ago. If only someone could tell her what to do.

No.

Yes.

No.

Yes.

She packs his few, small things. A shirt. A sleeper. A pair of shoes whose soles will never be scuffed. Her husband appears, wordless, and takes over, leaving her to dress her boy one last time.

Now it's just the two of them.

"Shh, it's OK. Mommy's here. Your mommy's here."

She rubs his back, but her touch carries no comfort. She struggles to wrestle pants and shirt over limbs that flop and sag. She hears her husband, outside now, loading the suitcases into the car. She has but moments left.

She scans the room.

His favorite animal?

Yes.

His blanket?

Without question.

A musical toy?

She kicks it away. "Rock a Bye Baby" fills the room, mocking her.

* * *

"I used to think the worst thing that could happen to a parent would be to have their child die. Was I wrong. When someone dies, it ends. But my boy...Well, my boy is just...He's just there.

"Most people don't know how I really feel. It's funny how good I got at hiding what's there. I guess I keep everything inside to make it easier on everyone else.

"I'm the one who wonders what's really going on in his brain. Is he scared? Does he miss me? Does he wonder where I am?

"This is right, I know this is right.

"But there are moments when I'll glance in the mirror, and I'll ask myself: What kind of mother does this to her son?"

* * *

Pressed to name a hometown, Diana Sullivan picks Albany, an industrial hamlet 60 miles south of Portland.

Truth is, she took root in people, not places. Her family followed the farm harvests across the Pacific Northwest until Diana's senior year in high school, when her father found steady work in Albany.

Even now, at 26, she honors small-town ways. Strangers get a howdy. Waitresses get respect. She knows how many children the grocery clerk has and likes it when a man holds the door.

She grew up wearing the musty scent of Goodwill clothing as her perfume. If she was allowed to pick a new winter coat, she knew she had to make it last. During the worst times, relatives offered to take the kids. But her father, abandoned himself as a child, preached that family is everything, as important as life itself.

After high school, Diana toyed with notions of college. But she never considered herself book smart. She joined the U.S. Navy in 1988 and was stationed in San Diego, where she trained to be a firefighter. There she met Mike Sullivan, a slender Navy welder, 2 years older.

Mike knows a lot about things—carburetors and buckshot and tools. But when it comes to feelings, he speaks as if he pays by the word.

They were married a little more than a year when Brandon was born. Books and classes taught Diana how to care for a baby, but nothing had prepared her for the enormity of the love. Brandon was just 5 months old when Diana was shipped to sea for two weeks; she thought her heart would break.

And so it was that Diana Sullivan made a choice: She would find a way out of her standard six-month duty tour at sea. She would be home when Brandon dared his first steps and cooed his first words.

She scoured the Navy's rule book and found an exemption from sea duty: pregnancy. Mike said he wasn't ready for a second child. So Diana just decided: She stopped taking her birth-control pills.

* * *

The pregnancy is unremarkable until one night in the seventh month. Her stomach hurts. Diana thinks it must be the hamburger she ate. She lies down, tries to relax. When she can't stand the pain any longer, she asks Mike to take her to the hospital.

The doctors find nothing. Her cervix isn't dilated. No contractions. Blood tests and amniocentesis are normal. The baby's heartbeat is strong and steady.

But this pain...she's never known anything like it. The soft touch of the hospital bedsheet on her stomach makes her writhe.

And suddenly the baby's heart is racing, 200 beats a minute. Contractions rip through Diana. The doctor says she has little time to decide: Bear the pain and risk of a vaginal delivery, or have an emergency Caesarean section.

Mike can't help.

She doesn't know what to do.

The doctor is waiting.

It hurts too much.

End it, she begs.

After it is over, after the tiny creature is lifted from her womb, she lets Mike name his second son.

Christopher.

Christopher Sullivan.

He tells his wife the name sounds so innocent.

* * *

Christopher weighs barely 5 pounds. The top portion of his right lung is hyperinflated, trapping oxygen like a balloon; blood flowing through receives no oxygen. And he has bronchiopulmonary dysplasia, an asthma-like condition in the main branches of the windpipe.

These are minor problems, the doctors say, all to be expected. A ventilator will help him breathe. He will outgrow the dysplasia. And, when he is older and stronger, surgery can fix his lung.

Diana sits beside Christopher's plastic-walled crib in the pediatric intensive care unit, watching him doze beneath the heat lamp. How does she mother this child? She can't cradle him lest she disturb all the tubes and wires that attach him to the terrifying machines. She can only touch his fingers and wonder what he feels like, smells like.

For the first five days of his life, he lies motionless in the incubator. On the sixth day, he opens his eyes. They are brown.

It is another two months before Christopher meets the criteria for release from the hospital: Maintain a normal body temperature, feed by bottle and sleep in a proper crib.

When Diana gets him home, she does not want to be apart from him. She holds him constantly, showering him with kisses and gentle hugs. His stomach is so small that he must be fed every three hours. But he's a good suckler and easily drains his bottles. Mike takes the first night feeding and alternates with Diana until morning.

Friends drop by. They pack the boys in strollers and wander the mall. They stroll through the park. Brandon, 19 months, wants to hold his brother and give him his bottle. He shares his toys.

They are a family.

* * *

The coughing begins on a Friday, on Christopher's ninth day home. Nothing alarming. Just little baby coughs that signal a baby cold. Maybe four an hour.

Just to be safe, Diana takes Christopher to the pediatrician, who sends her home with medicine.

On Saturday, he is still coughing, 10 times an hour now.

On Sunday, it's up to 20. He sounds like a barking seal.

The pediatrician's office is closed. Mike is at work. Diana bundles the boys into the car and drives to the emergency room. All kids have coughs, she tells herself.

By the time they reach the hospital, Christopher's cough is almost constant. He is whisked to a room jammed with doctors and nurses and machines. They cover his face with a breathing mask, draw blood from his arm, scrape cultures from inside his mouth.

The tests show that Christopher has respiratory syncytial virus, which clogs the airways of the lungs, blocking his breathing.

It is a common enough ill. Perhaps Brandon, who has a cold, spread it to a toy that spread it to Christopher. But given the baby's medical history, the doctor wants him in the hospital, on a ventilator, until the virus runs its course. About five days, he says.

Diana isn't sure. Maybe she should just take him home. She wants to talk to her husband.

No time, the doctor says. You must decide.

She signs the admission papers.

Two days later, Diana receives an urgent message at work: Call the hospital.

She dials the number.

Christopher had a series of bronchial spasms. They were so severe that his heart stopped.

Twice.

* * *

"You know what haunts me? Maybe I shouldn't have taken him to the hospital. If I had taken him home, maybe this wouldn't have happened.

"So was this a consequence of my choice? There was no answer. No one to say if it was fate. Or if it was me."

* * *

The young mother stumbles off the elevator in a stupor. She asks questions. The answers make no sense, incomprehensible terms rushing by.

"...*Gastroesophageal reflux*..."

"...*Atypical hyaline membrane*..."

"...*Hyperbilirubinemia*..."

She does not consider herself book smart. But certain words leap out, and they stick.

Mental retardation.

Cerebral palsy.

Blind.

Failure to thrive.

She stares at this...this...thing in front of her. A tube runs from his stomach. Machines click and rumble and whirl. He cannot breathe on his own. His arms move a bit. Twitches, really. Mostly, he just lies there.

He had a cough.

Just a cough.

"You may hold him," a nurse tells her. His gaze up at her is blank, empty.

"He can't see?"

"You'll have to discuss this with the doctor."

This can't be her son.

No.

"All he had was a cough."

She gathers him up. He feels the same in her arms. He smells the same.

"He wasn't that sick."

"You'll have to talk with your doctor."

The nurses watch.

"He didn't even have a fever."

She asks for a bottle.

They hesitate.

She asks again.

She places the nipple in his mouth.

He will not suck.

The formula dribbles down his lips and chin.

Now come her tears.

"He's OK."

She tries again.

The nipple slips from the slack rosebud of his mouth.

She tries again.

Again.
Again.
"Mrs. Sullivan, he's not going to eat. You're going to wear him out."
She pulls away.
Again.
"He needs his rest."
Again.
"Mrs. Sullivan."
"Mrs. Sullivan, please."

* * *

"When Christopher was born, I pumped my breasts so I'd produce milk until he came home. I wanted to breastfeed him. I figured he'd be home in a week. Well, you know what happened. He stayed in the hospital a long time, and I quit, and my milk dried up.

"Now what I'm going to tell you makes no sense, but the day I saw him all hooked up to those machines, I went home and looked for that breast pump. I dug in the closet and looked in the drawers. I yelled at Mike to help me find it, but he couldn't, and he got frustrated and said I was crazy and to give up. I finally found it and started pumping. Of course, my breasts were dry.

"Like I said, this makes no sense.

"But I tried and tried.

"You see, I never got a chance to bond with my son. I never got to nurture him. Eleven days is all I had.

"Tell me, what can you do in 11 days?"

* * *

The doctors hedge. He is young, and, please understand, it is impossible to accurately predict the future with someone so small because, of course, there are many variables and...

She demands the truth.

The central portion of his brain has been severely damaged, if not destroyed. He will never sit up. He will never eat on his own. He will never walk. He will never talk. He will never use his limbs. He will never see.

Why?

They don't know.

The tiny lungs.

The hyperinflation.

The virus.

Fate.

Please understand, they say. His heart stopped for a total of 45 minutes during the seizures. His brain received no oxygen. If doctors had not performed heroics, if machines and drugs could not work miracles, he would have died.

Christopher, they tell her, is lucky to be alive.

* * *

A mother's first priority is her child. That is the only truth Diana knows. She will quit work to care for Christopher. That is what a good mother would do.

But people can't just quit the Navy. The doctors write letters describing her situation, but her commander denies her request for a release.

"I know it's hard to take care of two kids," he says. "I have two kids. My wife works. What we do is use day care."

Diana is in full uniform for the meeting and chooses her words carefully.

"Sir, your wife is not in the service. My job requires more time than a civilian job. My son has many problems. I cannot drop my son off at day care. I don't have that option."

Her commander reconsiders the file.

"The Navy has a program for outstanding children," he says finally. "Kids who are special and need help."

Diana controls her rage.

"Sir, I don't need your counseling."

"What do you need?"

"To be with my son."

* * *

Diana blames herself. She should have been a better person. She should have accepted sea duty. She should have stayed on birth control.

She tries explaining it to Mike, how guilty she feels, and confused. But he won't talk to her. When tears threaten to betray him, he turns away.

Maybe he thinks that silence will protect her, that words will only reopen the wounds. She doesn't know how to tell him that she never healed.

With the help of a chaplain, she is released from the Navy. But the staggering medical bills add to their tension. Insurance covers 80 percent. But without her salary, they fall further and further behind, trying to make it on Mike's monthly take-home pay of $1,500.

Diana hates the solution: She will take the boys to Albany to live with her parents. Mike will move into base housing until he can get a discharge.

The U.S. Coast Guard flies Christopher to Portland, a courtesy to a military family. A special ambulance charges $1,500 to take him to Doernbecher Children's Hospital for lung surgery. It costs $15,000.

The day before the baby is released, the doctors suggest that Diana spend the night in his room. Christopher hardly sleeps. He cries. Diana asks whether something is wrong.

"No," the nurse says. "This is how he is all the time."

Diana's parents share their modest Albany home with an aging parent and a son. To make room for Diana and Christopher, they give up their own bedroom, sleeping in a 15-foot trailer parked in the driveway.

Christopher's crib goes up near Diana's bed. She monitors his feeding tube and administers his medicine. He screams and chokes and vomits. He sleeps no more than an hour at a time, and then only when she rocks him.

She doesn't watch television. She doesn't read or go to the movies. Friends don't visit. The bedroom becomes her prison, the rocking chair her bed, Christopher her tiny cellmate.

Sometimes, when she is alone and too tired to stop herself, Diana takes stock of her life. If Christopher were deformed, if his face were hideous, she could detach, look at him as though he were a piece of broken machinery.

But his cheeks are plump and kissable. His eyes deep brown. His brown hair has grown in thick and silky. And when he sleeps, she can adjust him so he nuzzles her neck, the way Brandon used to. She likes to feel his soft breath on her cheek.

To complain would be to betray him. What happened to him happened because of her. She chose to give him life. She is responsible.

Brandon wants her to hold him.

Not now. Christopher needs her.

Brandon cries.

She ignores him. Christopher is fussing.

Brandon wants her to play.

She can't. It's time for Christopher's medicine.

Brandon can wait. Mike can wait. She can wait.

Christopher needs her.

When he screams and screams, she tells herself it's not his fault. He is innocent, a doll with a beating heart. Be patient with him.

And so it goes for three months. Until one morning, when Christopher screams, Diana screams back.

"I can't handle this," she shrieks at her mother. "I'm taking Brandon. He's my baby. You want to take care of Christopher? You take him."

She runs to another room and locks herself in. She slumps to the floor, sobbing. She dreams of driving somewhere no one knows her. Her mother knocks, asking whether she can help.

"Leave me alone," Diana screams.

She hears Christopher choking.

She doesn't care. Let him die.

She hears Brandon crying.

She doesn't care.

She hears her mother pleading.

"Don't give up. Christopher needs you."

My God. She doesn't want Christopher to need her.

"Diana, open the door."

She sobs.

"Diana."

"Go away."

She slumps in the room, her mind blank. She can't think. She hears voices—her mother, her sister, her aunt. They cry and call to her, begging her to come out, to let them help.

Beaten, she opens the door. They hand her a Diet Coke, hug her and promise that everything will work out, that she isn't alone.

They lie. They will leave. They will go back to their lives.

Only Diana will be left.

* * *

"Loneliness is heavy."

* * *

The Navy arranges a temporary assignment for
Mike in the Salem recruiting office. He moves in with
Diana and her parents and commutes from Albany.

Being together feels awkward. Mike seems distant.
Diana is self-conscious about the weight she has
gained. She has little time to fuss with makeup. She
longs for him to hold her, to tell her that everything
will be fine.

Nothing. He goes to work. He comes home.

Two days before his return flight to San Diego, she
confronts him.

What's bothering you?

Nothing.

Tell me.

He hems.

Mike?

It's just that he can't handle this. Life used to be so
good.

No kidding.

And...

What?

He's not sure he wants to, well, stick around.

Diana thought she had spent her tears. She is
wrong. Frantic, she wonders what she can change,
what she can do to make him happy, to make him stay.

Then she knows.

Nothing. There is nothing she can or should do.

This time, the choice is his to make.

She rehearses her speech all day the next day. She
steels herself not to cry. When Mike gets home from
work, she asks him to sit down.

"If you leave, don't come back."

He blinks at her, stunned.

"No one will ever love you like I will. But the good
comes with the bad. This is our life. You have one day
to decide if you want to be a part of my life or not."

The next morning Mike tells her he loves her. But
he is scared.

So, she says, am I.

When Mike's discharge comes through, they rent an
apartment on the north edge of Albany. Mike sells
used cars for a while, but the lot goes under. He builds
mobile homes and takes roofing jobs when he can,

bringing home about $400 a week. They no longer
have Navy insurance coverage, and Christopher's Social Security benefits are minimal.

The baby's intravenous feeding bags cost $600 a
month. And they still owe $10,000 for various surgeries.

Diana feels as though she has been sentenced to
eternity with a colicky baby. Sometimes she drifts,
thinking she could let him cry until he suffocates.
Who would blame her? Who would ever know?

One morning, Diana settles Christopher on a blanket on the living room floor. She sits down to watch
television, perhaps nap a few minutes.

He begins to cry.

"Oh, Christopher," she snaps.

He stops.

She glances at him.

He is smiling.

"Christopher?"

He smiles.

She shakes his leg.

"Christopher?"

He grins.

* * *

She calls Mike, laughing the news. She calls her
mother. Her younger sister. The pediatrician.

For the first time since Christopher fell sick, Diana
remembers how good it feels to be a mother. Maybe
God is telling her that if she just tries harder, He will
cure her son.

"Christopher."

He smiles.

She can't remember such happiness.

She plays games with herself. If she could choose
to change just one thing for Christopher, what would it
be?

To see?

To walk?

To talk?

She cannot choose.

She will accept any blessing.

The pediatrician examines Christopher, now 19
months old, and notes that he is moving his hands.

Diana is ecstatic.

But the doctor gives a warning: Mentally, your son has the capacity of a 2-month-old. The doctor repeats himself, making sure she understands.

He doesn't know everything, she tells herself. Give me time. She works with Christopher every day. She talks to him, sings to him, tickles him. She sees progress where others cannot.

Smile, Christopher.

For the first time, she has hope. He doesn't cry as often or need as much medicine. He can lie on the floor and play with a toy. Well, not play, really, but the toy doesn't irritate him.

She hangs a mobile over his crib and watches him wave his hands at it. Maybe he can see.

He has a future.

She has a future.

She ventures back into the world.

Her mother baby-sits so Diana can attend a birthday party for a girl born a month before Christopher. The girl babbles and runs to play with her toys. And somewhere after the gifts, but before the cake, it hits Diana so hard that she fights to stop the tears.

That should be Christopher.

He should be learning to talk.

He should be learning to walk.

And what does she get?

A smile.

A lousy smile.

* * *

"Anger grows. Not so much anger that it happened, but anger about why. I wanted an answer. Even if I found out it was my fault, at least I would have an answer."

* * *

On their fourth wedding anniversary, Mike takes Diana on a date. Her brother volunteers to watch the boys.

Over dinner, Mike presents a small box. He has been saving each week, he says, for a surprise. The diamond earrings are tiny, but they match her wedding ring. Mike nods at the pianist, who plays their wedding song, and Mike sweeps Diana into his arms.

She feels like Cinderella.

She feels like a wife.

She feels normal.

A waiter interrupts them. There is an emergency phone call from Diana's brother. Christopher won't stop crying.

Diana storms home, the evening ruined, and retreats back into her world, a world with room only for Christopher.

She leaves dinner to Mike and Brandon while she attends to Christopher's feeding tubes. She sleeps when Christopher sleeps so she can wake with him, at least five times each night.

Her only outside contact is with social workers, who come to the apartment to check on Christopher. Diana relishes their visits with a sort of madness, cleaning the house as if she were throwing a party.

During a routine checkup, Christopher's pediatrician asks Diana how she's doing.

"Fine," she mumbles.

He waits.

"How are you holding up?"

She shakes her head. She won't betray Christopher.

"Diana?"

It leaks out. Her fears. Her doubts. Her loneliness. The doctor just listens. For the first time since her son was born, someone just listens to Diana Sullivan.

And when she is finished, the doctor tells her this: There is life, and there is quality of life.

Christopher has life.

You, he says, have a life.

He pens a number on a piece of paper.

This is the Providence Child Center in Portland, he says. A nursing home for children. There are only about 10 places like it in the United States. And it's not what you think. This is a good place.

She takes the paper.

She would never consider putting Christopher in an institution. But she tells Mike she must see it, so she can tell the doctor she followed through.

It's up to her, he says.

* * *

She signs in at the visitors desk. The literature says that parents pay nothing to keep their children here. Medicaid contributes about $150 a day for each child, about 70 percent of the true cost. Fund-raising covers the rest.

A woman escorts Diana down the hallway, through the double doors, to the children.

She gasps.

She is back in grade school, in the lunch room, where the special education kids had their own table. She hated being near them, watching them eat, watching some of them be fed. It nauseated her.

A cry snaps Diana back. She is surrounded by babies and toddlers and teenagers, none with mental capacity beyond that of a 3-month-old. None can walk or talk or feed themselves. Five sit in wheelchairs, gaping at a Chevy Chase movie on TV. Diana knows this movie, saw it in her life before Christopher. Numb, Diana moves out of the way of the volunteers and nurses, who dispense medicine and adjust feeding tubes and chatter in cheerful, one-way conversations.

No.

Not this.

Not for her boy.

But Diana finds herself staring.

Why? She asks.

Why are they like this?

These are not the products of drug addiction or abuse. These children were simply unlucky. In earlier times, their viruses and defects and accidents would have killed them. Now technology keeps them alive. And hopelessness brings them here.

She peeks into a large dorm room. Four children sleep here, photographs of their families tacked above their beds, sharing space with a Michael Jordan poster.

They will live like this until they are 18 and move to an adult nursing home. Or until they die, which happens to about six children a year. Each death opens a spot on the waiting list for one of the 58 beds.

A girl, perhaps 13, follows Diana's path down the hall with her eyes. Two years ago, on a Monday, the girl told her mother she felt sick. On the following Friday, she suffered 30 seizures an hour and lapsed into a coma. Doctors have not identified the virus that destroyed much of her brain.

Diana smiles at the girl, uncertain.

The girl's eyes follow her, haunting Diana with their silent hint of humanity.

Diana has seen enough.

She wants to go home.

Yes, Christopher is sick.

Yes, Christopher can be hard to take.

But he is different.

Different from the girl who fell into the family swimming pool and now sits in an eternal trance.

Different from the boy who was trapped in a house fire and now is imprisoned in a bed.

No.

Christopher will not live in their world.

* * *

Sometimes Diana wonders whether she is going insane. And if she is, who will care for Christopher?

She calls the center one day. In frustration, she adds his name to the waiting list. Not that she would ever let him go, of course. But the center becomes her safety valve. Knowing it is there makes her job bearable.

And then the center calls her.

An 8-year-old boy died in the night. There is an immediate opening for Christopher.

She has two days to decide.

The choice, Mike says, is hers to make.

* * *

She is his mother and must do what is best for him. Being with her is best for him.

But at the center he will be cared for, constantly. She will not be so tired and angry. When she visits, she will be happy.

If only someone could tell her what to do.

* * *

The first few days that Christopher is gone, Diana sleeps in because she is so tired. Then it is because she can't face the day.

She made a mistake.

She will leave him in the center just a little longer. Long enough to get some rest. Then she will bring him home. She leaves his room untouched. To box up his things, to tear down his crib, would be wrong.

Her family doesn't ask about him.

Only Brandon wonders.

"Where's Christopher?"

"He's sick and in the hospital."

"When is he coming home?"

"I don't know."

"I've been sick."

"This is a different kind of sick. Christopher can't walk or talk or do a lot of things that a big boy like you can do."

"Oh."

One day, Brandon snuggles up and asks her to read to him. She thumbs through the pages but can't concentrate on the simple words. She hasn't read to Brandon in more than a year. She hasn't done a lot of things.

"Just be good, Brandon."

"I don't have time."

"Christopher needs me."

That night, she makes dinner for Mike. They make forced small talk, as though they are on a first date. She has been with this man for more than four years. She hardly knows him.

"Later."

"Can't you understand?"

"Christopher needs me."

She can't do this. She most choose.

Christopher's life?

Or hers?

* * *

A volunteer tucks the sleeping child in a baby seat near the nurse's station.

His mother is coming.

They dress him in clothes from home. They spray a medicine mist near his face to help him breathe.

Diana hangs back when she arrives. She wears a tag that labels her a visitor. The volunteer motions her forward, but she does not move.

"Oh, Christopher," the volunteer croons. "Your mama's here. This is what you've been waiting for."

The volunteer slips away. Diana perches in front of her son.

"Christopher," says Diana.

She wishes she could be a better mother.

"Hey, buddy."

She wishes he had never gotten sick.

She touches his cheek.

He stirs.

She pulls him from the seat and cradles him in her arms. She holds her little boy and rocks him.

She says nothing.

She feels his soft breath on her check.

She listens to his heartbeat.

And she knows.

He has life.

She has a life.

* * *

"Don't call me courageous. And don't tell me what you'd do, because you don't know.

"Every day I tell myself that he doesn't know any different. That he doesn't feel the same emotions we all do. That he's getting wonderful care. That he's happy.

"I do this so I can turn around and walk away."

* * *

She stands by his bed.

Now it's just the two of them.

"My sweetie."

He smiles.

She adjusts his pillow.

"There you go, buddy."

She can't move.

"My precious son."

She reaches onto a shelf above his bed and pulls down his teddy bear. She tucks it under his arm and pulls his blanket over him.

"Christopher..."

Her voice breaks.

"Christopher, I will always be your mother."

He smiles.

"Christopher, I will always love you."

She wipes a tear from her cheek.

"Christopher, Mommy's going bye-bye."

AN EPILOGUE

Christopher Sullivan will turn 3 years old on Dec. 7. He has lived at Providence Child Center for almost a year. His condition is static, and he is not expected to improve.

Brandon Sullivan is 4 and attends preschool, where he is learning to tie his shoes and name colors, shapes and numbers. He says he misses his baby brother.

Mike Sullivan is looking for work after his construction job ended two weeks ago.

Diana Sullivan works as a salesclerk in Albany. She would like to attend school to gain certification as a paramedic but can't afford to quit her job.

The Sullivans are living in Albany with Diana's parents until they can afford their own apartment. They still owe more than $5,000 in medical bills.

They visit Christopher several times a month.

Writers' Workshop

Talking Points

1) Much of this story is told in present tense with Hallman recreating scenes and dialogue. It opens with a scene the reporter did not witness and, throughout, contains conversations he did not hear. How does this writing form serve the reader? What are the advantages or disadvantages of this technique?

2) Mike Sullivan is an off-stage voice in this story, heard from rarely. "But when it comes to feelings," Hallman writes, "he speaks as if he pays by the word." The reporter chose to keep his focus on Diana and all but left Mike out of the narrative. How does this choice affect the way the reader might view Diana? Mike?

3) Throughout this story there are short, declarative sentences and fragments that move the narrative along, sometimes in staccato bursts: "She asks for a bottle. They hesitate. She asks again. She places the nipple in his mouth. He will not suck...Now come her tears." How does this method affect pacing? What tone does it create? What other observations can you make about sentence and paragraph structure in this story?

Assignment Desk

1) Tom Hallman got the idea for this story after a visit to the home Diana found for Christopher. Choose an institution that is rarely in the public eye. Visit and produce a list of stories inspired by your observations.

2) From your list, report and write a story that mixes in first-person with third-person narrative. What feelings and details most influenced your point of view? What are the challenges to weaving those writing styles into one story?

1-2-3-blush

DECEMBER 8, 1996

Life gets confusing when a boy turns 12. Perhaps not all of life, but certainly the part involving girls. When he's younger, girls are no big deal. Then he hits seventh grade and...BAM!

They change. Or he does.

At 12, a boy can find that just thinking about girls makes his hands sweat.

A grown man forgets what it's like to be a seventh-grader.

And so you spend a little time with Scott Dougherty.

He talks. You listen.

You talk. He listens.

The years slip away.

You remember Melanie and Laddie and Becky. And even though you are 41 years old and married and the father of two daughters, the past returns so surely that your palms grow damp.

The process by which boys become men and girls transform into women is as subtle as the fade of daylight to dusk. It is possible to sense, but not see. Unless you wander into the Scottish Rite Center on the southwest edge of downtown Portland and stumble over your past.

There, on the second floor, you find Friday Evening Dancing Class, known to generations of Portland seventh-graders as, simply, dancing school. Since the school's founding in 1922, invitations have been issued to every westside middle school.

Classes run 10 weeks. By the end of that time, most kids truly can manage a fair fox trot.

But, truth is, dancing school is not really about dancing.

It is about boys and girls discovering the mystery of difference.

It is about children standing at the threshold of change.

It is about being 12.

* * *

The guide leading the children through this passage of life is Richard Walker, dance instructor. He is past 70, looks 60 and moves with the grace and confidence of a wide receiver in his prime.

Walker is Central Casting's perfect small-town postmaster. Serious, but not a fogy. Humorous, but not a comic. Mannered, but no fussbudget. His most distinguishing feature is a deep baritone, an instrument as rich and thick as maple syrup on a cold morning.

He uses it now to welcome a visitor to his home and introduce his wife, Dorothy. They have been married 47 years. For 35 of them, she has played his Ginger Rogers as he waltzes through the metropolitan area, teaching formal dance at social clubs and fraternal organizations.

Walker is only the third teacher in the long history of dancing school.

The first was Victor Christensen, a dandy with a Packard convertible and an uncanny talent for wooing women. When he died in 1937, at age 40, his cousin, Richard Billings, carried on.

Billings conducted himself like an English butler. He wore a tuxedo and made his students wear white gloves. Further sophistication was provided by a pianist, an older woman who never smiled.

Walker stepped in some 15 years ago, when Billings retired. He changed a few things—boys no longer wear gloves, and the pianist gave way to a record player. But the basic tenets of dancing school, like good manners, have endured.

On this Friday afternoon, Walker ventures into his basement to find music for that evening's class. He rummages through a record collection that numbers more than 3,000.

"I use contemporary things," he says proudly. "Even Michael Jackson records."

Walker, who insists there is science in learning to dance, warms to the subject.

"First, you have to have a good beat," he says. "I try and find things that don't have lyrics because lyrics distract the kids. And, well, actually some of those lyrics are a little bit naughty."

He shakes his head.

"That Macarena, boy, you don't want them to listen to that."

Satisfied with his choices, he glides back upstairs as he explains why some records made the cut.

"New York, New York"—"Kids like that for some strange reason."

"Hanging Out"—"That's Henry Mancini. There's some whistling in it that the kids seem to like."

"Walk Between the Raindrops"—"A modern swing beat."

He sets the records by a 41-year-old player, a "Califone Promenade," that accompanies him to dancing school. He escorts his wife to the sofa before he commences his demonstration.

"The first dance the children learn is the rhythm dance," he says.

His feet slide back and forth.

"Actually it's the samba, but I don't dare say that," he says. "It sounds too adult. What seventh-grader says he's going to do the samba?"

He sits down.

"Now we don't do the rumba or the tango," he says. "It's just too adultish. To do it right, you have to get close to each other. And I have the children dance quite far apart."

His wife nods her approval.

"Now on the fox trot they have to be a little closer together," he says. "The boy's right hand is on the girl's left shoulder blade. But clothes are not touching. We don't want seventh-graders close dancing. You know what kind of..."

His wife interrupts.

"Honey, tell about the problem with the cha-cha."

Walker hears music in his head and springs from his seat.

"This is the right way to do the cha-cha," he says. "You see that 1-2-3 rhythm? Smooth. It's supposed to be smooth. Well, when the kids do it they think it's fun to stamp their feet."

His wife looks pained.

"That's not dancing," she says.

Walker, still dancing, smiles.

"No, honey," he says. "That's adolescence."

* * *

The transformation begins about 5:30 p.m. when Scott Dougherty sheds baggy pants, his University of North Carolina basketball jersey and tennis shoes and heads to the shower.

He emerges wearing a blue blazer, gray slacks, a white shirt, a tie and black dress shoes. His mother selected the shoes. He didn't care what she bought as long as it wasn't anything fancy, which he describes as shoes with "dots on them."

His mother looks up from the stove and says her son looks wonderful. His father nods. His 17-year-old brother smirks. Dougherty returns to the bathroom to examine himself.

"I feel more mature," he says.

He squares his shoulders.

"Like 18."

He does not wear cologne.

"I don't have any," he says. "My brother does, but I don't think he'd like it if I wore it."

He stares into the mirror.

"My hair won't stay down."

He adds water to a comb.

He examines his hands and rubs them on his pants.

"They sweat. My friend's sister, who's older, went to dancing school, and she told me and my friend that she remembers having a guy's sweaty hand on her waist. So I'm always wiping them off."

He carpools to dancing school with best friend, Tommy Petroff, and Abbey Bowman, a girl he has known since fourth grade.

"You know, Abbey sure looks different in a dress," Scott says. "I've never seen her look like that."

He peers around the corner to make sure his brother isn't eavesdropping.

"You know, Tommy and I don't goof off as much around her when she's dressed up like that."

He checks his hair once more, then walks to the kitchen to wait for his ride.

The kid in him polishes off a handful of Oreo cookies, a glass of milk and a ribbon of spicy beef jerky.

The man in him pats his coat pocket to make sure he has his Certs.

* * *

The boys trade punches and see who can jump the highest, shirttails askew. Shove a 12-year-old boy in a sport coat and slacks and he still acts like a boy.

The girls are something else.

Slip a 12-year-old girl into a fine dress and hose and a pump with a low heel and she is a creature who bears no resemblance to that skinny irritant who sits two seats away in social studies.

The girls exit from cars with grace and beauty, testing a power they don't yet comprehend. Only when they hurry to the ballroom do they give themselves away, running like little girls on the playground.

The boys scramble to the south side of the old-fashioned ballroom, beneath wall sconces and ceiling fans, while the girls hunker down on the north. They glance slyly across the room at each other, taking great care to look as if they are doing nothing of the sort. An anxious electricity ripples through the air.

Max Podemski appears shellshocked. He does not hear the question. Asked again, he repeats it.

"What's most embarrassing?"

He rubs his head.

"Dancing with a girl you don't like or one you really hate."

He looks across the room and grins.

"Or dancing with one you like."

Across the room, the girls register a change in the boys.

"They are so polite," Ally Estey says. "But their hands shake when they hold mine."

Abbey Bowman fiddles with her white gloves.

"Boys are nervous," she says. "They don't look at you. And their hands sweat."

* * *

Out in the empty foyer, at the foot of the steps, Roger Madden patiently sits through another class, attired in a proper business suit and tie.

Madden's family has run dancing school since 1940, when his mother took it over for a friend. In 1976, his wife took over for his mother. One day, Madden's daughter will be in charge.

Dancing school tuition is $65. That covers the invitations, the hall rental, insurance, Walker's tutelage and, on occasion, a minimal profit.

"I'm not into this for the money," says Madden, who has several business ventures. "If a child wants to dance, but the family can't afford it, I cover it. Every child should be able to come here."

Madden is 71. There are other places he could be on a Friday night. But he chooses to be here, to listen to the music float to him from the ballroom, to wait in the foyer and greet the children.

"Keeps me young to be around these kids," he says. "It's funny, though. When I told one boy that I knew his father he told me that was his grandfather."

He shakes his head.

"Where does time go?"

* * *

Ghosts are everywhere. In the ballroom, past, present and future collide and create something so timeless and life affirming that it overwhelms.

The dancers, though, are mercifully unaware.

"My mom made me come."

"I like to dance."

"My brother went so I'm going."

"My friends are here."

They don't know. They can't know. They shouldn't know.

They are children.

They are 12.

* * *

Time to touch.

Walker bounds across the room to the boys and leads them, single file, to the girls, who also are standing in line. They pair up one by one, like gears meshing. A boy offers his arm, a girl slips her hand through the crook. It is strictly random. A girl who is 5-foot-7 links with a boy 4-foot-5.

Smiles are few, and strained. Some girls talk with their partner. Others ignore the boy to chat with a nearby girlfriend. A few couples stare straight ahead, as if trapped in a bad marriage. Beads of sweat glisten on a few foreheads, twinkling in the dim light.

Walker leads the dancers around the ballroom, breaking them off in groups until three circles are formed, one inside of each other. Walker takes the middle.

"Boys turn to your right. If you've met the young lady before, say hi. If not, introduce yourself."

The dancers stand two feet apart.

"Dance positions," Walker calls.

The dancers hold up one arm, as if dancing with an imaginary partner.

"Back to neutral."

"Boys check your shoes. Make sure they're where they should be."

"Dance position."

Walker wanders through the circles.

"That's great."

"Now the formal touch. Dance positions."

Each boy places one hand on the girl's waist, the other supporting her opposite hand.

"Back to neutral."

Hands drop.

"Touch."

"Neutral."

"Very good. Boys, check your right shoe. Now we're going to do the rhythm dance with music. You remember the steps from last week. This song has a good beat."

"Love Talks" blares from the speakers.

Some dancers are out of control. Many stare at their feet or off into the distance. When the music stops, Walker tells the boys to move to the next girl. And remember to introduce yourselves.

Max Podemski sighs.

Abbey Bowman looks up at a boy.

Scott Dougherty wipes his hands on his pants.

The music starts.

One boy can't see fit to make contact; through an entire song, he maintains a six-inch gap between his hand and her waist. Elsewhere, kids relax. They exchange glances. A smile. A gesture. A faint wistfulness when they next change partners.

Walker calls out the next dance, the "Lady Under." Back and forth, back and forth, and then the girl turns and spins under the boy's outstretched arm. Walker and his wife demonstrate.

"Boys, you do the side basic. And boys, please don't grab on to her fingers when she goes under."

"Shug-a-dee-bop" fills the room.

Walker beams.

"This is quite a modern record. The beat is a little faster."

He counts out the rhythm.

"One-two, one-two, one-two. Ready. Lady under."

Some girls get stuck in their partners' baseball-bat grip. A tall girl ducks to clear a short boy's arm. A boy steps on a girl's much-larger feet.

With great fanfare, Walker announces they will try the calypso. He shows them the steps. Instead of gliding, the kids stamp their feet.

"Adults don't make noise," he warns. "Four-year-olds do. If you are next to someone making noise, you know how old they are. Let's try again."

The stomping shakes the room.

"Hmm," he mutters. "I guess we'll have to forget the calypso."

They zip through the fox trot before the hour ends.

"Boys, before we go, I have a question. How many of you helped some lady with their chair at the dinner table?"

About half the hands go up.

"That's much better than last week. Let's see if we can be perfect next week."

Class is dismissed with a parting ritual. Each dance couple must greet one of several patrons—parents who act as hosts to give the dancers the chance to practice saying thank you. The boy's task is to introduce himself and his partner.

A boy approaches.

"My name is...

He freezes. He plays with his tie.

"Thank you," he blurts before fleeing, leaving his partner stranded.

Another couple steps up.

"Um, good morning, I mean, good evening. Let me introduce Jenny."

Formalities complete, they spill out of the ballroom, down the steps and outside, where they wait for their rides.

A boy takes tentative hold of a girl's hand for a moment, before he yanks off his tie and uses it as a whip to chase his buddies.

Another girl whispers to her friends that, during "Walk Between the Raindrops" a boy said he liked her. When her father arrives, she runs to him, offers a hug and slips her hand in his as they walk to the car.

* * *

They hover at a magical moment in life. A time of knowing it all, and of knowing nothing. A time of big talk, and a thick-tongued stammer. A time before bills and jobs, before heartaches and reality.

In the coming years, it is unlikely they will ever formal dance.

Decades later, you barely remember the box step. But you hold the door for your wife, teach your children please and thank you, and are somehow mindful of the value of good manners.

And what you carry with you still is the seventh grade.

You remember the soft scent of a girl, her hand in yours and how, for the first time, your heart fluttered.

Writers' Workshop

Talking Points

1) This story, the reporter tells the reader, is about being 12. Hallman uses several techniques to convey not just the fact of adolescence, but the feel of it as well. "Shove a 12-year-old boy in a sport coat and slacks and he still acts like a boy," he writes. What words, phrases, and quotations achieve the feeling that the story is about prepubescent boys and girls?

2) Hallman says he uses verbs with thoughtful purpose in all of his writing. In his description of Scott Dougherty's preparation for dancing class, he says the boy "*sheds* baggy pants...*emerges* wearing a blue blazer...*examines* his hands ...*peers* around the corner...*checks* his hair...*polishes* off a handful of Oreo cookies." What do you learn about Scott from Hallman's verb choices? Where else in the story are strong, telling verbs in use?

3) Who in this story would you regard as a fully developed character? Scott? Richard Walker? Dorothy Walker? Roger Madden? Tom Hallman? What is it about the story that makes them more or less developed?

Assignment Desk

1) Hallman talked about excruciating moments of awkward silence during his time with Scott Dougherty—moments familiar to any reporter who has tried to interview a child. It helped, he said, to connect personally to that time in his own life. Write an essay about a pivotal time in your childhood. Then interview a child at that stage in life. How did the essay affect the way you conducted the interview? What questions were influenced by the essay?

2) Hallman inserts himself at the beginning and end of the story. In the lead, he tells his story of adolescence. In the kicker, he looks back as an adult. Rewrite both to take the reporter out of the story. Does it hurt the story? Does it make it better?

A conversation with
Tom Hallman Jr.

KEITH WOODS: Characterize for me the kind of story that you're drawn to.

TOM HALLMAN: I'm drawn to what I would call a pure story. It's a story with a beginning, a middle, and an end. And I hope that my words draw readers through this story, that they learn something about the character, the life this character leads. And when they get to the end, I hope that I've changed the way they look at the world or the way they look at people or the way they look at this person I've introduced them to. And I hope that these stories resonate in them and live on in them.

I think journalists have a hard time with, and I quote, "real life stories," because they don't have a true beginning, middle, and end, and the more you dig and the more you report, the more confusing it gets. We look, especially in crime stories, for simple answers. I think readers sense that that's not true.

What guides your writing?

One overarching thing is I'm a guitar player. I've been taking lessons for the last few years, and I find that music and writing are very similar. As a musician, you try to use notes and phrasing and rhythms and tempos to create a feeling in a listener. As a writer, I try to do the same things. And a lot of times, I can almost hear music when I'm writing. I can feel when the score would increase in tempo or when we would have a lull or when we would have a back beat. I really think good writing is rhythmical and has a life of its own.

Do you find the rhythm both as you're conceiving the story and as you're writing it?

I guess I become three different people. When I'm reporting the story, I go a lot on how I feel. I feel the story and if there's sadness or happiness, I want to feel it, and I really try to absorb all that. Then, when I sit down to write, I become more analytical and I think, "OK, how can I get someone who was not there to feel those same kinds of feelings that I felt?" And that's when I use words as tools to recreate those feelings. Then I begin to build the story in a really non-emotional way.

As I rewrite, I start looking at ways to cut. Every time I do a story, I make a printout of it and edit it line by line, strictly with the intention of cutting. I really believe in being spare, and I believe in each word having to carry its weight.

On every story I've ever done, I've hard-edited and cut no less than 10 or 15 percent of the story. So if it's a 100-inch story, I always cut out 10 or 15 inches. And that's before I give it to the editor.

What do you mean when you say you work on the story in a "non-emotional way"?

I don't get caught up as much in the emotion of the story as I do when I'm reporting it. I look at it more like, "What can I do to make the reader feel these things?" So that's when I play around with the tempo. Do I want to start the story like a ballad, or is it going to be like a 3-minute rock song, or is it going to be like a symphony with many different parts? And I play around with that a lot as I'm writing and as I'm rewriting.

How did those techniques play out in some of these stories?

Well, let's take "Mount Hood's Deadly Deceit." Going into it, I knew that I had to be one of the characters. This was a story that almost only I could tell. And I felt as I started approaching this story that I was dealing with history. I felt a responsibility on this story for all the people involved and for myself and for everyone.

It had been 10 years since I had really looked at this story, so I did a basic reading of the clips, trying to get back into the feeling I had on the story. I could always get the facts about what day it was and where these kids were climbing and the elevations and all those kinds of things. But I knew that the story would run on the feelings and the emotions of these people. So somehow I had to recreate in my mind what it was like 10 years ago.

I drove up to Mount Hood, I drove the route and stood in that parking lot where all this stuff transpired, where the helicopters landed. And I drove back up into the Portland hills where one of these families lived, and I remembered how I felt when I had to go talk to these people in their living room. I went out to the school. I revisited the places that became landmarks in this story and in doing so, I was able to remember how I felt.

And then I started on the story, dealing with the people who were the least emotional—the rescuers.

I got all the details from them and then I moved to the next step: the families. And as I moved closer, I tuned in to how I felt at each step along the way. I would do an interview and then I would not come back to the newsroom. I would go get a cup of coffee somewhere and I would transcribe my notes and write down the emotions I was feeling, what the room felt like, because I knew those were all going to be the critical details in this story.

What was the mandate for you to be in the Mount Hood story?

Because I was the only thing that linked all these people together. The survivors knew nothing about what was happening with the rescuers. The rescuers knew nothing about what was happening on the climb. The families knew nothing about what was happening on the mountain.

It could have been written like a traditional feature, probably leading off with Giles Thompson, you know, we're up at his house and he's walking out on the lawn with his little son and his legs aren't there, and you have a little break and then you say, "Ten years ago ...blah, blah, blah." That's a kind of traditional story.

But the power of what happened here on that climb was that it unfolded over a period of days, and the emotions went up and down, and there was tension and sadness and hope, and I wanted to recreate that for the readers. My story kind of paralleled the search; the search for the answers or the search for what happened on that mountain paralleled the search for these kids.

I guess in a way I represented the city in this story. It's a fine line. I didn't want to make this a first-person story because it wouldn't work. It only worked to get the story moving and then I backed out, and by the end of the story, I'm not in it at all.

For the traditional newspaper story, it's awkward being in and out of the story, isn't it?

I'm not exactly sure what all the talk was in the newsroom, but I know there were some reporters who were opposed to this and some who thought it was great. I don't think this would work with every kind of story, but I think it worked with this story.

You dangle yourself in the story in "1-2-3-Blush" in the same way.

This is one of my most favorite stories. I loved doing this story, and I wish I could have gone back and been in seventh grade again and gone to this dancing school.

I went up there several times to watch the dancing school and to talk to the teacher. What struck me was how powerful and how beautiful and, at the same time, how almost sad what was happening up there was. As a 41-year-old man looking back, there's a sadness that these kids don't realize, won't realize until they're 41. What I wanted to do with this story was to make everyone relate to it, even if they hadn't been to dancing school. Everybody's been 12.

And again, I think that the only way I could do that was to state the theme, that life gets confusing when a boy turns 12. You couldn't get any of these 12-year-olds to say that because they don't know that. Maybe with a lot of interviewing, you could get somebody else to say that, but it would be kind of force-feeding them.

You create a certain amount of tension as you talk about the dancing school director and his wife. I see people sitting very straight with very good posture. Tell me how you've created that sense for the reader.

They're almost parodies of themselves, and I wanted to capture that without making fun of them. And so I became observant of everything I could use that would create in the reader what it was like to sit there with them. I guess I'm working as a reporter on two different levels. One, getting strict information from them and, two, trying to work like a fiction writer, creating who these characters are: his wife nodding and sitting across the room, the poodle, the old record player.

What I wanted to create for readers is that these are people from a different era who would probably use the word "hip" and have no idea how unhip they are, but still have a great heart and who really care about these kids. And I wanted readers to see this and laugh with them.

And how did you accomplish that?

This is where I get back to the reporting. I asked him all those song titles. You have to be a real reporter and say, "Well, tell me about 'Hanging Out.'"

"Well, that's Henry Mancini."

I think sometimes there's a misconception about this style of writing, that you turn on a tape recorder and you sit down and all this information gushes out of these people, and then you go back and you play around with words.

And it's really the exact opposite because in every one of these stories, these people have never talked to a reporter and they give you one-word answers. They have no idea why you're doing the story. Some of the questions seem ridiculous to them. And so it requires as much reporting as an investigative reporter or somebody doing an in-depth story on the planning commission. If you skirt on the reporting end of it, you'll get back to your desk and try writing it and realize you're just pumping up a tire with air.

You used quotations strategically in this story and others, particularly when you talk to Scott Dougherty. Talk about that.

I spent probably four hours with this kid. There are a lot of long silences where he can't figure out why I'm there. And you know, after you get done talking about Michael Jordan and basketball, what do you talk about? You really realize the generation gap.

But as we got closer to getting ready for dancing school, that gap narrowed and we found this common area, and he really opened up and I talked about what it was like for me. I wanted to condense all that and give readers a real insight into a 12-year-old boy getting ready to go to dancing school.

So all those quotes came because I spent four hours with this kid and he felt comfortable talking with me.

You pay attention in these stories to some very minute details about people's lives. What's behind that level of observation?

I guess it gets back to being a police reporter and working for this editor. His name was Dick Thomas, and he was an assistant city editor. You would send in a story and he would call back and say, "Are you sure that was Southwest Portland?" "Are you sure it was a one-way street?" "Are you sure the cop had a revolver and not a pistol?" It was beaten into you. You didn't want him to call, and when he called, you'd better have the answer.

Working under that system for so many years, I learned to ask all the questions and to really look at the details. At first, it was just a matter of having the details for my story. As I got more into feature writing, I realized that the details were like little bombs going off. They could do so many things in a story and say so much in a way that I, as a writer, could not.

I want the readers to do a lot of the work for themselves and I want to tap into what's inside their memories, in their histories, and find things that will help them tell the story for themselves.

In "Diana's Choice," more than any of the others, you use a staccato style: single-word sentences, two-word sentences, fragments. Tell me about your preference for that declarative form.

I like using that because it's like the way a boxer uses a jab. It helps set up the roundhouse. For people who aren't boxers, they work on the big roundhouse right, but they forget the jab. So I look at these sentences, these short ones, as working like a jab and also as working, for a musician, like eighth notes: just little blips to move the story along.

And in this story, I wanted the reader to feel the enormity of the situation and the weariness of this woman. And so they might get through a section of reading 30 short sentences and without knowing it, maybe they feel a little weary. They're getting the information, but they're also stepping into this woman's shoes.

Tom, as I look through some of the words you've used in this story, I'm thinking about your music analogy. In the part where Diana is facing the first problem that Christopher has, I hear a soft, even nursery kind of melody that changes into something more sudden.

You're exactly right. I've got two kids and I don't think I could have written this story if I wasn't a father, because I realize as a father the power of a simple phrase like, "It's just a cough." How many meanings that really has. When the doctor said Christopher had a cough, just a cough, I was aware of what this means to this woman and how other readers will feel those same feelings.

The story does shift, and I guess it would be like a lullaby or a ballad, and then you have the foreshadowing with the music, or in this case with the words. And I wanted to really be aware of the use of foreshadowing in the story here, number one, with the idea of choice, foreshadowing that through the whole story, but using things that are common, everyday kinds of things that all of a sudden can become horrible in another setting.

So that builds in some drama by itself.

Exactly. I use the incomprehensible terms from the doctors when they're telling her about what this kid has. I think what I tried to do there and in some of these sections is tap into our own fear about doctors and stuff happening to our own bodies. And so again,

I'm letting the reader do a lot of the work for me by using these terms that I can't even pronounce, followed up by "mental retardation," "cerebral palsy," "blind." Readers go through that, too, and it hits them. I try to be aware of the rhythms of those various words and how they'll play in the reader's mind.

You put a great deal of work into these stories ahead of time; you conduct volumes of interviews. The average reporter out there might salivate at the idea that they could get that kind of time.

When I was covering the police beat, I did these types of stories and I also went out on car crashes, shootings, fires, did the daily beat. I carved out the time to do these kinds of stories.

But did you sleep?

Oh, yeah. But I guess I was efficient in doing those stories. I do have more time than a lot of reporters to spend on these stories, but the techniques that I'm using also work on 20-inch stories that you do in two or three days.

I'm always juggling three or four stories at a time. I'm not just cleared off the decks to write something like "Diana's Choice" for four months. And I like that. I like juggling other stories.

Talk about your relationship with your editor, Jacqui Banaszynski.

She is the perfect editor for reporters who do this kind of stuff because I think all reporters, but particularly reporters who do these kinds of narrative feature stories, at heart are insecure. You launch these big things and at a certain point, you think, "Why in the hell did I get involved with this?"

And an editor plays three or four different roles. One role is enthusiasm. On the Mount Hood story, I would just drop into Jacqui's office from time to time and say, "Gosh, I had this great interview," and she'd be all pumped up and excited and say, "That's great. Things are going really well." Always enthusiastic.

We would have informal talks, and she might say something that would get me thinking about ways to approach an interview or ways to approach the structure of the story.

You said Jacqui gave you some unique advice as you worked on "Diana's Choice." What was it?

Christopher was so normal looking that he kind of frightened me, and for a long time I didn't even pick him up. Jacqui said, "You've got to get to know this child." There was something about coming so close to this world that these people were in that it was frightening. I think that kind of flowed through this story.

One of the issues was if it was going to be a pure narrative story, how we would get Diana's voice in the story. We were talking about that and we thought, what about just having her speak directly to the reader? That was Jacqui's idea. Her exact words, I think, were, "I want this woman to talk to the reader and say, 'Don't you dare look away. I'm going to tell you what this is really like. Don't you tell me how you would feel, because you don't know.'" And then Jacqui started to help build the story.

She's not the kind of editor who rewrites a lot of things, but she knows how to go in with the scalpel and make things better. She'll say, "Maybe we need a little bit more here," so I'll go back to my notebooks and flesh something out. And she asks really perceptive questions that get you as a writer to take that one extra step. So she pushes you in a way that's not pushing you.

Now that might not sound like a big deal, but I'll bet you every writer has dealt with editors who read a 100-inch story and the first thing they tell you is you've got a name misspelled in the last paragraph. Or they watch an editor start editing one of their stories, and they start editing the first paragraph before they read any further. Or they send you a question, "What about this?" when it's answered eight paragraphs down. And that really messes with a writer's mind.

Jacqui's approach is to read the whole story, to get a feel for the story, where it's going, what the story's about, and tell you, "This is a good story," or, "I think something's really working here." She'll start with the positive. So as a writer she's got your confidence. You know that she knows the story, that she's going to make it better now. And then she goes to work on it.

Tom, is there anything I didn't ask you?

If I could pass on any advice, it would be this: Every one of these stories that I've done here can be done at practically any paper in the country. I didn't fly overseas anywhere and not any of these were what you would call big news stories. There's probably a woman like Diana in every city in the country. There certainly are kids who are 12 years old in every city.

I mean, you look around the newsroom and say, how often are we sitting at our desks, waiting for the phone to ring. All these people I dealt with are not newsmakers, but they're out there. It's just a matter of going out and using our skills as reporters and being just as in-depth as if we're covering the city budget or some scandal of the housing bureau. You just apply those skills to talk about their lives.

They're out there. I'm convinced of it.

The Washington Post

Henry Allen

Finalist, Non-Deadline Writing

Henry Allen is a staff writer for the Style section of *The Washington Post*. He joined the *Post* staff as a copy editor in 1970, became a feature writer in 1971, and later served as assistant editor for the Style section and the *Post*'s Sunday Outlook section. Before coming to the *Post*, Allen edited at the *New Haven* (Conn.) *Register*, and covered Congress and the White House for the *New York News*. He has won the Academy of American Poets prize and the ASNE award for commentary. In 1995, he was a finalist for the Pulitzer Prize in criticism. He also has written for *Forbes*, the *New York Review of Books*, the *Paris Review*, *Smithsonian*, *Vogue*, and the *Wilson Quarterly*. Born in Summit, N.J., he received his bachelor's degree from Hamilton College in Clinton, N.Y., and served in the Marines in Vietnam.

After weeks of immersion in the culture of criminal lawyers in Washington, Allen produced a devastating and definitive portrait of justice at the bottom rung of the system. (A portion of his story appears here.) Allen's editor calls him the "Karl Wallenda of risk-taking writers," a journalist who uses meticulously reported detail and scene to take readers on a literary tightrope walk.

A heaping serving of justice

DECEMBER 5, 1996

The Superior Court cafeteria, where a lot of criminal law gets practiced in the District of Columbia, has a warm, used smell like a pay phone that somebody just hung up, somebody with a cough—a smell like a wet bathing suit you left in the car, a compost smell, a smell like the inside of an old Halloween pumpkin with sanitary overtones provided by the wall-mounted deodorizers pumping out a smell like a space station where they replaced the air with something that's supposed to be just as good as air, except it isn't. Another planet is what this smells like, like Mars in the old *Flash Gordon* serials, and the cafeteria, two floors underground, is where the Clay People live, invisible till they step out of the walls to fight against Ming the Merciless.

Red-plastic chairs. Paintings like the ones you see bolted to the walls of motels. Loudspeakers paging the court-appointed lawyers at a pitch so acutely tuned that the noise could shatter...not a wineglass...bigger ...maybe a picnic cooler.

Loud. But mostly the cafeteria smells. It smells like a lost-planet landfill for worn-out civilizations. It smells...do court-appointed lawyers have their own smell, like dentists with their rubber-glove fingers? Or is it the endless prisoners being endlessly processed down the hall in the cellblock known as the bullpen?

The smell is one of the things that led an otherwise gladsome lawyer named Rozan Cater to give up court-appointed Criminal Justice Act work.

"The smell is a cloud of depression and stress and fear," she says, gathering momentum like a radio preacher. "As the day goes on it rises from the cellblock, the cafeteria, and permeates the very crevices of the building until everything reeks with it, nothing is left untouched."

Colin Dunham, a British CJA lawyer with the shabby edginess of a lifer in the class wars, wears Vetiver cologne to ward off the smell when he goes back in the cellblock with its sour-clothes badness, the smell of the effusions of whatever liquids and solids can be released by or on a human body and left there for days at a time, a smell akin to the old dump fires that used to erupt with so much smoke they'd stop traffic on the New Jersey Turnpike, and it was like breathing Jimmy Hoffa.

Dunham says: "The U.S. marshals wear rubber gloves when they touch these guys—we shake hands with them. Most of us get regular TB tests and shots for hepatitis B—that's the one that's going around now."

He is talking about the Criminal Justice Act lawyers known as Fifth Streeters, a name that hangs on from the old days when the lawyers and bail bondsmen had offices on Fifth Street. That was before new federal office buildings arrived with their Nixonian brute-paranoia style. One of them was the new Superior Court building at 500 Indiana Ave. NW, a monument not to justice but to the judicial system, to bureaucracy and process. Nevertheless, you can feel a heart beating in the leatherette infarction of the cafeteria—here dwell court-appointed defenders of the defenseless and indefensible, Clay People battling Ming the Merciless in the form of the all-devouring dynamo of The Law in all its mercy and its arrogant quirks and bad-cop abuses.

Some of these lawyers are like guys who will never be contenders but hang around the boxing gym because they like to hit, no matter how many punches they have to take to do it. Some talk to themselves and comb their hair with their fingers. Some are too mouthy and egotistical to work anywhere else. They are loners, mavericks, freelance gladiators, anarchists, spitball artists, true believers, class warriors.

Some are very good criminal lawyers, a few are very bad criminal lawyers. You see them sitting in the cafeteria with eyes half-closed or half-open and skin the color of mythical New York sewer alligators; with their derelict night-school dreams of enthralled juries and fame, of Darrow and the Revolution, of starting at the bottom and building a paid and retained practice while they fight for the rights of the always poor and almost-always guilty who look so much the same after awhile that the lawyers write down what they're wearing when they meet them in the cellblock down the hall so they can identify them an hour later at their arraignment.

You may have an office at home or someplace like the Bob Hope Building on D Street, but you can run your whole practice down here. Pay phone, a pocketful of documents and a beeper. You meet with your clients in the hallways, the cellblock. You face them across the fake butcher block tables of the cafeteria—the same meeting over and over, the lawyer saying, "I want you to understand..." and the defendant doing the sly calculations of a young man for whom doom and honor are as indistinguishable as they might be for, say, something between a Confederate cavalry lieutenant and a three-legged dog at the city dump.

Day after day, you're talking to another young man with no shoelaces and no belt, which could mean either the police took them away after his arrest or he's just dressing in a prison style that's fashionable on the street where he lives, or hangs, or deals, a young man with a face that looks like he built it himself in his high school metal shop, built it with a big hammer out of a hunk of lead. He is talking to you in a collection of phrases that become a generic conversation after you spend enough time hanging around down here. Like:

"What it is, is, how come you don't ask for a continuance so I can run out my parole before I come up on this one?" "Don't worry about parole, you got a lot of repeat paper, is what it is," you say. "Judge is going to be looking at priors for distribution, possession with intent to distribute, a firearm misdemeanor, unauthorized use of a vehicle, mayhem..."

"Prosecutor just wants me to plead out, is what it is," the defendant says. He has eyes that look like they've just come to a slow but very final decision, and a mouth that looks like it's got a toothpick in it whether it does or not. "Want me to plead out because there ain't no case, is what it is."

"That's not what it is," you say. You're not sure what he's driving at, you know he doesn't know what you're driving at, and you're not sure yet either. You've got your professional face on, a face that doesn't listen as much as it simply waits. You see him checking out your rumpled collar that still smells scorched from where you ironed it this morning. He doesn't understand how somebody can look and live like you, so gray and broken-down.

"Make no sense," the defendant says. "I'm looking at 10 years anyway you look at it."

"You take it to trial, they've got four witnesses— you must've made somebody mad."

"They lie. They say they saw me with those Ziplocs, I didn't have no Ziplocs, I don't do nothing with cocaine. Man dump them by my feet and bucked on me, he's gone."

"Man dumped them," you say. "You find Man, I'll put him on the stand. One of these days we're going to catch Man and the crime rate in this city is going to drop like a stone."

"I should get me a paid lawyer. Get me a Jew. Jew get me out of this."

"You got a paid lawyer last time. He sent his runner out to your mother's house and talked her into taking the case away from the CJA attorney. She paid all that money and you still went down. You can't find any better lawyers than you find right here."

"Can't find any worse ones neither," the young man says.

"You make up your mind which one I am and call me."

It's a hard dollar, being nobody for $50 an hour—a fee that's a quarter, a fifth, a tenth of what you might get in the uptown firms. Uptown, the lawyers are somebody. They can tell from the Martha's Vineyard tans on their faces when they look in the mirror every morning, from the $125 Neiman Marcus suspenders, from the Sidwell Friends and Princeton stickers on their car windows.

When uptown lawyers go to lunch at the Palm, Tommy the manager knows their names. Tommy is the uptown lawyers' pet tough guy. He makes them feel real. Here in the Superior Court cafeteria you feel very real but you're nobody.

"It's just you and Tyrone," the CJA lawyers will say with the racism of people working too hard for the poor and black of this city to worry about political correctness. You, him and fearful grandmothers with their

Bibles and Avon-lady perfume. And the cops stretched out in banquettes with flak jackets, dirty holsters and an unsettling too-relaxed look that reminds you of Bosnian soldiers you see on the news, this being the new breed since the cops had their salary and training cut...The cops don't look at you in that cop way that's worse than a stare.

Sometimes you get a prime candidate for the Palm like Mark Bradley, who describes his affection for CJA work as "a character flaw." He's a cop's son from Roanoke with a cop's way of watching your face while he's talking to you: Washington & Lee, Rhodes scholar, MA from Oxford in history, Fulbright scholar, University of Virginia law school, black belt in karate, former CIA intelligence officer, Criminal Justice Act lawyer, a Fifth Streeter.

He says: "There are people who never touch this world, they never see it, it's like going into a foreign country. I do this job because I like it. I try to take a tragic situation and make a more humane situation out of it—we have a legal system people have to believe in or everything falls apart. But the legal system presumes people will act rationally, that's the problem. And the world these defendants come from is a world where 1 plus 1 doesn't always equal 2. I've got a client that robbed a guy of $5 worth of marijuana, then the guy runs away and my client shoots him. He shoots him because he sees it as disrespect. He says, 'He bucked on me, so I shot him.' This makes sense in his world. Or from my point of view, I've got another guy I'm trying to get off, but I know he's got a prior arrest for soaking his girlfriend down with lighter fluid. When his lighter doesn't light, he cuts her up with a wirecutter. That didn't get prosecuted because she left town. But here I am trying to get him out."

Lessons Learned

BY HENRY ALLEN

I'm 56. I've been at this a long time.

I didn't learn a lot from writing this story because I've never learned a lot from writing any story. The way you learn a lot from writing stories is by writing a lot of them.

What you learn is that you can't beat research, you can't beat people sitting in a cafeteria telling you their terrible life secrets whether they mean to or not, and you can't beat hearing the music of the English language—you have to listen to where it wants to go and remember that it's smarter than you are. It's the greatest computer on earth. It taught me to write.

With this particular story, I was surprised to see how far I could run with the cafeteria smell thing—the image, the metaphor, the trope of smell. Maybe that's learning something.

An editor said: "You took a lot of risks with that story."

I said no, pros don't take risks. They make mistakes, but they don't take risks.

I once asked a Marine fighter pilot if flying close air support over ground troops wasn't dangerous. He said: "Unforgiving, but not dangerous."

I suppose I try to learn a little more about that difference with every story I write.

AP Associated Press

Julia Prodis

Finalist, Non-Deadline Writing

Since 1994, Julia Prodis has worked as part of a six-person team of reporters formed in 1985 to cover topics of strong regional and national interest. Prodis joined the AP in Cheyenne, Wyo., in 1988, and became a business writer in Detroit in 1992. She was the lead reporter covering Dr. Jack Kevorkian's assisted suicide crusade. Two years later, she became Southwest regional reporter based in Dallas and covered the Oklahoma City bombing. A native of Berkeley, Calif., Prodis graduated from Cal Poly-San Luis Obispo and worked as a reporter for the *Tahoe Daily Tribune* in South Lake Tahoe, Calif., and the *Stockton* (Calif.) *Record* before joining AP.

The editor's note that precedes "Dying for Love" says it's a story about three teenagers who "set out for the end of the world, and found it." Prodis makes good on that promise with a riveting narrative about trust, betrayal, and the promise of redemption. The story also won the feature writing award from the Associated Press Managing Editors.

"Dying for Love"

JUNE 2, 1996

ROBBINSVILLE, N.C. (AP)—The trooper's blue lights flashed in the rear view mirror. Peck floored it, Josh grabbed the revolver and Jenny, curled up beside him in the back seat, looked frantically out the back window.

They were far from home on this desolate Arkansas highway. It was the middle of the night and the time had come for the best friends to fulfill their pact: If caught by police, the boys, just 15, and Jenny, 12, would commit suicide.

They had it all planned—or so they thought—days ago. Josh would shoot Jenny first. (She didn't have the guts to do it herself and, if she was going to die, she wanted Josh to do it.) He would shoot Peck next, then kill himself.

They were rocketing faster than 100 mph in their stolen Grand Prix and the trooper was closing in. Just ahead, Peck saw a big rig blocking the only open lane in a construction zone.

They were trapped. It was time.

Peck slowed to a stop 20 feet behind the truck.

Josh cocked the gun, turned to Jenny and looked deep into her green eyes.

"I love you," he said and kissed her.

"Close your eyes."

LOVE TRIANGLE

Just five days earlier, on April 1, they were safely home in Robbinsville, N.C., a town of 775 nestled deep in the Great Smoky Mountains. Joshua Rogers and Kevin "Peck" Hyde cut school for the day—the first time ever—to break into the abandoned science building at the old high school. Jenny would meet them there. She had promised to choose between them.

Both boys, best friends and drummers in the high school band, were in love with the sweet and lively blond girl, well-developed for her age.

Jenny skipped her seventh-period gym class, hurried down Moose Branch Road and slipped through the building's back door.

Peck and Josh were waiting anxiously in one of the classrooms, littered with old textbooks, broken chairs and lab tables.

Josh spoke first, his voice trembling.

"If you want to go to Peck, he's my best friend, I'll understand."

For three months, Jenny had been going with Josh, a shy and studious, rail-thin, dark-haired boy she met on the swim team. They had just had their first real date— a trip to church on Sunday. Josh was a straight-A student, except for a physical science class. He was failing and confided in Jenny that he was deathly afraid of disappointing his father and grandmother.

And then there was Peck. He seemed so boisterous and outgoing, but Jenny knew he was deeply troubled. His mother, a heavy drinker, had died less than a year ago and he was living with his father and stepmother. Peck, nicknamed for his nervous habit of "pecking" on his desk with his pencil, had tried to shoot himself twice before. But each time, his hand shook so hard the bullet whizzed past him.

The three of them were here in this ramshackle classroom because Peck had made her an ultimatum: Take him as her boyfriend or he would hurt himself.

The boys waited. And then Jenny slowly responded.

"I'll be your friend for life, Peck," she said, "but Josh is my boyfriend."

Josh broke down and cried.

As they walked out, an adult passing by eyed them suspiciously and notified the principal.

It seemed so out of character for Josh and Peck to cut class, school administrators thought. They were both smart, popular, well-mannered boys who had never been in trouble before. The boys were punished with in-school suspensions, and word of their truancy was sent home.

Life seemed so unfair to the young trio, so traumatic.

That night, Josh, Peck and Jenny made plans to run away. They didn't want to live in this tiny town anymore, where there was nothing for kids to do but hang out at the video arcade or the Black Knight Drive-In, where the closest big cities, Knoxville, Tenn., and Atlanta, were hours away on narrow, winding roads.

Jenny was scared to go. But she feared that if she stayed behind, Josh and Peck would kill each other or themselves without her.

In life or in death, they all agreed, they would be together.

Thoughts of suicide were not new to Jenny. She had considered taking an overdose of pills once and even tried slitting her wrists. Death would take her away from the torments of her older brother and from her father, a Vietnam veteran who prowled the house in the middle of the night, believing he was still fighting the war. But she would miss her mom.

Jenny, Josh and Peck would leave the next night. The only way they would come back to Robbinsville, they agreed, was in a box.

RUNNING AWAY

Jenny packed a small bag with a small spiral notebook and all the money she had—$9. She grabbed her teddy bear and "dream catcher," an Indian weaving meant to catch bad dreams and let good ones pass through. She threw her brother's black-and-white letterman's jacket over her shoulders and slipped out the sliding glass door.

It was 12:45 a.m. when she met Peck at the foot of Poison Branch Trail, just as they planned. Peck, wearing his marching band jacket and baseball cap, had packed some crackers, peanut butter and a couple of oranges.

He had left a note behind: "Dad, I'm sorry, I got into some trouble and I had to leave. I've gone South."

On their way to Josh's house, they traveled by moonlight along the narrow gravel road that cut through the forest of sugar maples and sycamores, curved around a weathered tobacco barn and passed an old truck rusting in a field of wildflowers.

The dense canopy of trees blocked the moonlight at times and Jenny stumbled into barbed wire. Her legs were scratched and bloody when a snarling pit bull jumped in front of them. In an instant, Peck had drawn a gun—his daddy's .22 revolver.

The dog scampered off, but Jenny was terrified: Peck had a gun, and Jenny had always hated guns.

They picked up Josh and by 2 a.m. had found a car with keys and a purse in it. The gas tank was empty and so was the billfold inside.

Josh got behind the wheel. They bought five dollars' worth of gas before leaving town, then headed down the mountain. They had no destination and no maps, but they were out of Robbinsville and that's all that mattered.

Jenny was asleep in the back seat when they pulled into a gas station across the Georgia state line. It was dawn, they were lost and they were running on empty. Peck pumped five dollars' worth, while Josh shook Jenny awake.

"You're going to have to take the money in there," they whispered.

But Jenny had only $4 left.

"Four dollars in gas," she told the attendant, trying to seem nonchalant.

The woman wasn't buying it and asked to see Peck's driver's license. But he had only a learner's permit. They panicked and ran, leaving the money on the counter. They sped off, Peck behind the wheel.

They were halfway to Knoxville when four sets of police lights charged up behind them. Jenny slept serenely in the back, but up front there was panic: Had the time come to fulfill their pact? But the police flew by.

It was early afternoon when Peck pulled off the highway and into a field. He was bored and started doing doughnuts. Jenny tolerated his antics as she slammed from side to side, crushing the rest of the crackers sitting on the back seat.

By late afternoon, they had arrived in Knoxville tired and hungry. The peanut butter was gone and the last orange had gone bad. They shared the cracker crumbs. For four hours in the hot sun, they slept in a shopping mall parking lot. Some people peered in the windows, startling them awake. They had to move on, but they were dehydrated by now and scrounged around for change. They managed to find 50 cents— enough for a Mountain Dew. They shared it and wandered around to the back of the shopping mall.

A verdant field lay before them, a babbling stream meandering through it. A beautiful, peaceful place, Jenny thought, a place to rest.

But the conversation soon turned again to suicide. If caught by police, they decided, Josh would shoot Jenny first, then Peck, then himself.

Just in case, though, the boys also taught Jenny how to fire the gun: All you have to do is pull back the hammer and squeeze the trigger, they said. That's all you have to do.

As dusk fell, so did the rain. The boys built a crude shelter. As the chilly night wore on, they hugged Jenny and huddled close to her to keep her warm.

At some point, Jenny pulled out her spiral notebook. If anything should happen, they would each leave a note.

In printed capital letters, Peck wrote: "Josh's love for Jenny grows every second, and with every second it hurts me more. Love gives you strength and integrity, but also a weakness at heart."

In a page and a half, Josh recounted their trip and his love for Jenny.

"I'll probably be in a better place by the time you read this," he wrote, part in printing and part cursive. "Tell my dad that I'm sorry and that I love him."

Jenny wrote to her mother.

"I love you mom so please forgive me on this last chance to get away. Josh was my hero. I love him. Peck was and will always be my bestest friend. Just know I will not let you down again. I love you mom."

She signed it with a little curlicue after her name.

DESPERATION

It was dark when they got to Memphis. They had been away from home for almost 48 hours and had nothing—no gas, no money, no food. Jenny felt sick to her stomach and cried.

They had to rob a gas station, that's all there was to it, the boys said. They looked to Jenny.

You have no charges on you and you're a minor, they said, handing Jenny the gun.

She took it reluctantly, stuffing it into the roomy pocket of her big brother's jacket. While Josh filled the tank, Peck and Jenny wandered through the store, picking up a Twix candy bar for Josh and an Almond Joy double-pack for Jenny and Peck to share. Jenny grabbed a Mountain Dew, Peck took a big Coke and Josh came in and got a grape juice drink.

They walked toward the door. Jenny's hands were shaking as she pulled out the gun and waved it around.

"I'm sorry, we gotta go now," she said, her voice quivering.

Peck floored it, turned a corner and hid for five minutes, while Jenny sobbed in the back seat.

In less than two days, the threesome—seemingly model kids at home—had stolen a car, stolen gas, subsisted on crumbs and held up a store at gunpoint. There was no turning back now.

Ten minutes later, they were crossing the Mississippi River bridge. Peck and Josh let out hoots and cheers. Arkansas! They had made it to Arkansas!

END OF THE ROAD

An hour down the road, a trucker noticed the car weaving erratically along the highway and radioed police. Within minutes, the trooper was behind them and Josh had the revolver in hand.

"Close your eyes," Josh demanded.

Jenny closed her eyes tightly and tensed her body.

A shot rang out and Jenny felt Josh's body slump onto her. He had shot himself under his chin and blood was pouring out the back of his head. Jenny screamed loud and hard and didn't stop.

Peck, who had come to a stop behind the truck, reached back for Josh's gun.

"Lean up here!" he shouted at Jenny, ready to do what Josh could not. But Jenny felt paralyzed.

Peck turned forward, jammed the gun barrel in his mouth and fired. His foot hit the gas pedal and he died. The car lurched ahead, crashing into the back of the truck.

Jenny flipped over the seat and slammed her head into the dashboard. Crouching down, she lifted Peck's foot off the pedal and groped around the floorboards for the gun. This isn't how they planned it! They were all supposed to die together!

Smoke was filling the car now and she could hardly see a thing except Josh's eyes, still barely open. She leaned her head back and felt faint.

RAP, RAP, RAP! The trooper's flashlight beat against the window, trying to break into the locked car. Jenny opened the door, and the trooper dragged Josh out and laid him on the pavement, then pulled out Jenny. She sobbed uncontrollably as she watched Josh slowly die, right there on the Arkansas highway.

"Kill me," she begged the trooper, "kill me now!"

LIFE LIMPS ON

Four hours later, Jenny was in the Brinkley Police Department, lying on a bench in an unlocked cell. Every time she closed them, all she could see were Josh and Peck, dying.

"Are you OK?" the investigator asked.

"No, there's blood all over me," she whispered back, looking down at the stains on her brother's jacket and the leg of her pants. "It's his blood, I know it. I was right beside Josh when he shot himself."

She sat down with the investigator and, in a 45-minute taped interview, recounted her story of love and death.

When she went to their funerals, she told him, she would put her friendship ring in Peck's casket and bury her dream catcher with Josh. She would give each of them a red rose and visit their graves every day with fresh flowers.

"I feel so guilty 'cause I feel it's my fault," she told the investigator, tears streaming down her face. "I was supposed to be with them when they died. I was in the middle of both of them. I watched them kill themselves and I couldn't do nothing about it.

"I hate myself. I hate everything," she murmured, her normally sweet Southern accent turning coarse. "I even hate the Lord for doing this."

Her parents picked her up and drove her more than 400 miles home. All the way, she kept Peck's band jacket wrapped around her and Josh's gold chain hanging securely around her neck—two things from the car not soiled by blood. Josh had given the chain to Jenny on the trip, telling her, "I want you to have something of mine."

Jenny spent a month and four days in a North Carolina mental health facility. But she is back at home in Robbinsville now, and receives counseling every day.

On Sundays, she sings in the church choir.

Lessons Learned

BY JULIA PRODIS

THE ELEMENT OF SUSPENSE

An editor of a Texas paper called the Dallas bureau the day "Dying for Love" ran and sheepishly asked the clerk to resend it. The paper had cut off the end of the story to fit the space, he confessed, and readers were calling all morning asking, "What happened? What happened?"

I knew the element of suspense would be key to the story the moment I read the police report. In a page and a half, police summarized their interview with Jenny, including Josh's last words, "Close your eyes."

Reading those three powerful words flashed me back to my own childhood, when my older brothers would say the same thing—right before smashing my face into a bowl of clam dip. In "Dying for Love," I wanted to capture that anxiety-filled moment between trust and betrayal. I wanted readers to cringe along with Jenny—anticipating, but uncertain of, the outcome.

I learned while writing this feature story not to give everything away at the beginning, like most spot news stories do. By not revealing who died and who survived up front, I figured natural curiosity would compel readers to stick with the story to the end.

With that in mind, the structure of my story was simple: Use "close your eyes" as a cliffhanger near the top of the story, then flash back to their hometown scene and follow their journey chronologically until the climax in the back seat of the car.

The police report outlined the trio's journey, but didn't provide enough details to bring the story to life.

Then I noticed what would become the basis of my story—a notation on the police report indicating Jenny's interview had been tape-recorded. Boy, if I could get my hands on that! I figured the police would never release it. But I asked anyway. To my great surprise, they agreed. Lesson learned: Never assume information is secret.

The tape, in Jenny's own trembling voice, was the saddest thing I had ever heard.

USING QUOTES

I was tempted to fill the story with Jenny's compelling and sensitive quotes from the tape. Instead, I wrote the story in narrative style—telling it as it unfolded. That meant I couldn't use her quotes from the police station about what happened in Robbinsville and on the road. They were spoken after the events of the story were over and would have jolted the chronological flow of the story. Instead, I used her interview as background to tell the story. The only quotes I used were the ones recounting word for word her conversations with Josh and Peck during their journey.

But I couldn't resist her comments completely. So near the end of the story, as part of the chronology, I put readers in the police station with Jenny. Here, I could use her comments about her feelings. My editor, Kristin Gazlay, also suggested it would be the right place to show readers where my information was coming from, since I used very little attribution in the story.

GETTING COLOR

I flew to North Carolina to try to fill in the gaps. Hoping to include details that would make readers feel they were experiencing the odyssey with the runaways, I walked along Poison Branch Trail and peered in the windows of the old science building. I hung out at the video arcade and talked to people close to Jenny, Josh, and Peck who helped me with their family backgrounds.

ENDING WITH HOPE

This was a tragic story with no happy ending. But perhaps there was a hopeful one. I could have ended the story with Jenny's parents taking her home. But I wanted readers to know there was a glimmer of hope for Jenny. Even though she blamed the Lord for the tragedy, I learned that on Sundays, she sings in the church choir. It was just one sentence, but it was a subtle sign of healing, a sign of hope.

David Maraniss
Deadline Reporting

David Maraniss is a national correspondent for *The Washington Post.* The grandson of a printer and son of two editors, he began his career working summers as a reporter for *The Capital Times* in Madison, Wis., while attending the University of Wisconsin. He then reported for WIBA radio before landing a job in 1975 at the *Trenton* (N.J.) *Times.* He joined *The Washington Post* in 1977.

In two decades with the *Post,* he has been a metro editor, projects editor, Southwest bureau chief, and national political reporter. His series on racial integration in American institutions won the 1990 grand medal of the National Conference of Christians and Jews. In 1993 he won the Pulitzer Prize for national reporting for articles examining the events and forces that shaped President Bill Clinton's life and character. He followed that with *First in His Class,* a biography of Clinton. He is on leave from the *Post* to write a biography of legendary Green Bay Packers coach Vince Lombardi.

On deadline, Maraniss constantly seeks details and insights that help him relate the specific news event to universal themes. He crafts stories about national political figures that reveal their humanity in ways that make it possible for readers to better understand them and the news they generate.

—Christopher Scanlan

A solitary figure enters new territory

JANUARY 27, 1996

She arrived in a Cadillac Fleetwood limousine as gray and cold as the winter afternoon. At twelve minutes to two, she stepped out, cloaked in black, and marched across the wide concrete entranceway toward the U.S. District Court building, pausing briefly twice, first to turn and wave back in the direction of scattered hurrahs and jeers, then to speak into a sidewalk microphone, her voice clear and earnest, saying she had to go inside and help however she could. The inevitable press posse pushed close, cameras whirring and clicking, yet she stood utterly apart.

Human beings arrive in the world alone and depart alone—and appear before a grand jury alone. Even the first lady of the United States.

Hillary Rodham Clinton, the best-known woman in America, never seemed more of a solitary figure than at that moment yesterday when she disappeared inside the federal courthouse on Constitution Avenue to answer questions for more than four hours from an independent counsel and 23 grand jurors investigating the swirl of events that have come to be known as Whitewater. A modern woman who burst into Washington determined to take the role of president's wife into uncharted territory, she had now achieved an improbable first: first first lady to be grilled by a grand jury.

After three years, the Whitewater tale remains so dense and foggy that it is hard to see which events associated with it, if any, might be of lasting importance. But what happened yesterday had an unambiguous national resonance all its own. Grand juries are a dark, sacred rite of American life. It is one thing for Alfonse M. D'Amato and Lauch Faircloth, attack dogs of the Republican opposition, to bark out Whitewater conspiracy theories within the political confines of their Senate hearing room, but it is quite another for independent counsel Kenneth W. Starr to get Hillary Clinton behind closed doors and ask her questions all afternoon.

The first lady's appointment in Starr's chamber began at 2 p.m. and continued until long past sundown, interrupted only by occasional breaks during which she could consult with her lawyers in the hallway. The White House plan from the start had been to try to diminish the drama of the encounter, to make it appear as nothing more troublesome for this bright legal scholar than a law school exam.

They called it the "Head Held High" strategy. There would be no furtive comings and goings. Where other grand jury witnesses scurry to a basement exit and escape, heads down, in getaway cars, Hillary Clinton finally emerged from the building at 6:37 p.m., exuding the radiance of a movie star, and stood once again before the waiting microphones.

"Well, you are all still here, I see," she said to the press contingent that had been hanging around the federal building all day. With little else to talk about, the radio and television stations that had been carrying The Hillary Wait live chatted endlessly about what they expected was the main subject of her appearance: questions about Rose Law Firm billing records that had disappeared for two years before they showed up in early January on a table in a reading room in the White House residence. The records offered an account of Hillary Clinton's legal work for one of the Arkansas institutions at the center of the Whitewater investigation, Madison Guaranty Savings & Loan, which was run during the 1980s by James B. McDougal, the original partner of the Clintons in the Whitewater land deal.

The first lady said she was "glad to have the opportunity to tell the grand jury what I have been telling all of you: I do not know how the billing records came to be found where they were found, but I am pleased that they were found, because they confirm what I have been saying."

She said that the grand jury asked her a few questions about other matters, but mostly about the billing records. Then, after handling one of the most penetrating questions in modern political annals—"Would you rather have been somewhere else today?"—with the deft response, "Oh, about a million other places," Clinton said she was tired and heading home.

How the grand jurors felt about the long session is unknown. They are sworn to secrecy, as is Starr. But at least one member of the panel apparently considered this more than a routine day on the job. He brought with him a copy of the first lady's new book, the No. 1 nonfiction bestseller, "It Takes a Village," and asked her to autograph it. She obliged with the inscription: "To Donald, best wishes, Hillary Rodham Clinton."

That is not to say that the first lady is the first famous Washingtonian to end up inside the federal courthouse taking questions from a grand jury. Indeed, one reason her appearance yesterday had such inherent drama is because of the colorful litany of men and women who had made the same walk before her, from the Iran-Contra characters of Fawn Hall and Robert C. McFarlane back to Watergate figures John D. Ehrlichman and H.R. Haldeman.

Though only the harshest Clinton critics compare Whitewater to the earlier Watergate scandal, the two events have a particular ironic bond: Hillary. It was 22 years ago this month that young Hillary Rodham, fresh out of Yale Law School, went down to Washington to work as a junior counsel for the House Impeachment Inquiry staff that drew up the impeachment counts against President Richard M. Nixon in 1974.

Rodham was a favorite of chief counsel John Doar, and spent much of her time listening to the cover-up tapes that helped force Nixon's resignation. Another of her assignments then was to conduct a study of the chain of command inside the Nixon White House, to see who talked to whom about what as a means of determining how and when Nixon would get information.

The Watergate inquiry had a profound effect on Hillary Rodham's political persona. During the years she and her husband, Bill Clinton, were rising to power, she often cited her earlier experience in Washington as a reminder of the abuse of power.

Friends say she has expressed some chagrin, if not embarrassment, that she would now find herself forced to appear before a grand jury in the Whitewater case.

Writers' Workshop

Talking Points

1) Karen DeYoung, one of David Maraniss's editors at *The Washington Post,* says his stories effortlessly convey the larger meaning of each event without belaboring its importance by falling into the conventional newspaper format. Consider and discuss what it is about this story that sets it apart from a more traditional treatment.

2) Maraniss says one of the most important steps for him in the process of writing on deadline is identifying the theme of the story, the larger meaning of the news that takes it from the specific to the universal. The theme of this story, he says, is found in paragraph two: "Human beings arrive in the world alone and depart alone—and appear before a grand jury alone. Even the first lady of the United States." What elements of the story support the theme? How well does he support his theme in the story?

3) Effective deadline writers say that background knowledge is critical to a story's success when time is short. Maraniss is the author of a biography about President Clinton, *First in His Class,* and he puts his deep knowledge of the subject to good use in this story. Highlight the passages in the story that bring historical perspective to this event and that deepen the reader's understanding of Hillary Clinton.

4) In paragraph six, Maraniss writes that "Hillary Clinton finally emerged from the building at 6:37 p.m., exuding the radiance of a movie star, and stood once again before the waiting microphones." Where else in the story does Maraniss evoke this movie star metaphor?

5) Maraniss injects a note of sarcasm in paragraph nine. "Then, after handling one of the most penetrating questions in modern political annals—'Would you rather have been somewhere else today?'..." What's your reaction to this line? Is it fair? Is it appropriate? Is it editorializing? Defend or attack its use.

Assignment Desk

1) Rewrite the lead of this story. Use a summary lead that communicates the news in a single paragraph.

2) The first lady's testimony was widely covered by the Washington press corps. Do a computer search to locate versions from *The New York Times* to the wire services. Compare how other writers handled the story with the treatment Maraniss gave it.

3) Read a half-dozen news stories. Identify the theme of each story and express it in a word, a sentence, and a paragraph.

4) On your next story, identify the theme before you write the lead. Write it down in a word, a sentence, and a paragraph.

5) In your reading, look for ways that writers use metaphors to support their theme and to draw vivid portraits of the people in their stories. Employ metaphors in your own work.

Brown delegation ends with gathering of grieving families

APRIL 7, 1996

DOVER AIR FORCE BASE, Del., April 6—They came out of the back of the big gray plane in flag-draped caskets, one by one, a bitter wind blowing, solemn hymns playing, families, friends and official Washington watching and crying, and 33 shiny black hearses waiting on the cold tarmac to take them away to the mortuary. That is how Commerce Secretary Ronald H. Brown and his trade delegation arrived back in America late this afternoon, four long days after they died on a muddy Croatian hillside on the other side of the world.

President Clinton, the only speaker at a memorial service short on words but deep in symbolic imagery, called Brown and his lost delegation patriots whose lives and deaths served as a "stern rebuke" to the prevailing mood of cynicism.

"The 33 fine Americans we meet today, on their last journey home, ended their lives on a hard mountain a long way from home, but in a way they never left America," Clinton said, his voice choking as the transport plane and hearses framed the scene behind him. "On their mission of peace and hope, they carried with them America's spirit, what our greatest martyr, Abraham Lincoln, called the 'last best hope of Earth.'"

With hundreds of family members and friends gathered inside an open hangar, Clinton noted that the sun was going down and that the next time it rose it would be Easter morning, "a day that marks the passage from loss and despair to hope and redemption." For the 33 men and women who died in the plane crash nearly 5,000 miles away, Clinton said, "their day on Earth was too short. But for our countrymen and women we must remember that what they did while the sun was out will last with us forever."

To Clinton's right sat most of the members of his Cabinet, Brown's former colleagues. Directly in front of him were Alma Brown and her children, Vice President Gore, first lady Hillary Rodham Clinton and the mothers, fathers, wives, husbands, sisters, brothers and children of the dead Americans. There would be private funerals in Washington and other towns around the country next week. There would be many more times to mourn, but this was the one time, the last time, when the 33 would be together, when the totality of the tragedy could be felt in one communal place.

That is what Dover is for, in a sense. It is where the American dead come home. They are sent here because of the military mortuary on the base but the homecoming scene is often more spiritual than medical. No words that the president uttered today had more resonance than the simple sight of the big plane—the very one that the president had traveled in during his visit to Bosnia months earlier—pulling up toward the hangar after the 11-hour flight. When its engines were turned off, the slow, dying whine sounded a haunting, ironic eulogy.

Brown's trade mission to the Balkans, Clinton noted, had begun with a moment of bright optimism. "At the first of this interminable week," Clinton said, "Ron Brown came to the White House to visit with me and the vice president and a few others. At the end of the visit, he was bubbling with enthusiasm about this mission. And he went through all the people from the Commerce Department who were going. And then he went through every single business leader that was going."

The presidential entourage arrived at the air base nearly three hours before the start of the memorial service. Clinton, somber and without topcoat, walked down the steps of Air Force One with Alma Brown at his side. The widow was dressed in black. An unforgiving wind swept her hair in front of her face as she descended, creating the appearance of a dark veil of mourning. Then came the first lady, walking alone, followed by the vice president escorting Immigration and Naturalization Service commissioner Doris M. Meissner, whose husband Charles, assistant secretary of commerce for international affairs, was also among the victims. Behind them were the Meissner children, Christine and Andrew, and Brown's son, Michael, and daughter, Tracey.

Most of the families of the dead traveled to Dover by other means, though at government expense. When they arrived, they were given red-white-and-blue ribbons and taken to Building 704 on the opposite end of the base from the makeshift hangar memorial site. Each family was assigned a small room in which to wait and grieve.

For more than two hours, Clinton, Gore and the first lady moved down the long, bleak corridor, entering one room after another, paying respects and thanks to the survivors of men and women who died in service to the nation. Alma Brown accompanied the consolation party into the rooms of families of Commerce Department aides.

This private procession of despair evoked the same haunting sensation as the sight of the 33 shiny black hearses aligned on the tarmac: Here was the totality of death, an entire hallway full of it, and yet in each room was a different story, a distinct family reduced and shattered and inevitably alone in the loss of one person.

"It was," said White House deputy press secretary Ginny Terzano, who carried her own unbearable weight of sadness as a former top assistant to Brown, "a solemn atmosphere."

Some relatives were planning to stay in this remote Delaware way station for another day or two until they could accompany the bodies of their loved ones back to their home towns for funerals. Officials said it could take as long as 72 hours before military morticians and forensic scientists completed the exacting process of examining and identifying the dead and preparing remains for burial. The obliterating devastation of the crash site on that rocky hillside in Croatia made the task of putting together pieces of bodies difficult and in some cases perhaps impossible.

Because of the mortuary work that still needs to be done, the timing of the funerals is still uncertain.

Sometime in midweek, Brown will lie in repose at the Commerce Department. That evening, there will be a celebration of his life at the Metropolitan Baptist Church in Washington. His funeral will be held the next day at the National Cathedral, where Clinton will deliver the eulogy. At least one high-ranking member of the Clinton administration will attend each of the other 32 funerals.

Perhaps the nation recognized only one of the Americans on the ill-fated trade mission when they were alive, but in death they were honored equally. At the end of his short eulogy today, President Clinton read their names, one after another, in alphabetical order, from Staff Sgt. Gerald Aldrich to Robert Al Whittaker.

The men and women who went on the trade mission with Brown, and who lost their lives on the Croatian hillside, comprised a remarkably diverse lot: 12 from Commerce, 12 corporate executives, six military crew members, two from other federal agencies, one journalist. They were black and white, young and old; some who loved the rambling road of trade and enterprise that the globetrotting commerce secretary followed and at least one who hated to fly but headed off with his boss on every trip anyway.

"Today we bring their bodies back home to America, but their souls are surely at home with God," Clinton said. Soon, one by one, the rear doors to the hearses were closed and they drove slowly out of sight.

Writers' Workshop

Talking Points

1) In his interview, Maraniss describes this story as a "news poem." In that way, the poem form it most resembles is an elegy, a melancholy lament for the dead. Consider the poetic elements—language, rhythm, and imagery—that he employs in this story. What effect do they have on the reader?

2) Increasingly, editors are looking for reporters to bring a voice of authority to their writing. Look for passages in this story where Maraniss makes observations and delivers judgments. Discuss your reaction to these passages. Do you think the writer is overstepping his boundaries?

3) Maraniss says he spent time before the bodies arrived roaming Dover Air Force Base, interviewing officials about the mortuary. The base's public affairs officers also provided him with background material. Notice that he doesn't attribute any of that information to a particular source. Discuss whether the story should include more details about the sources of various information.

4) What is the theme of this story? What elements does Maraniss use to convey that theme to the reader?

Assignment Desk

1) Rewrite the lead of this story. Use a summary lead that communicates the news in a single paragraph.

2) Maraniss says he needed to collect four images to complete the reporting of this story. There are at least six. Identify them.

3) Infuse your stories with images as haunting as the description of Alma Brown, Ron Brown's widow: "The widow was dressed in black. An unforgiving wind swept her hair in front of her face as she descended, creating the appearance of a dark veil of mourning."

4) One of the most moving passages in the story is the description of the Clintons and Vice President Gore visiting

the surviving family members of the other 32 Americans who died in the plane crash. Writers can learn from modeling their prose on another writer's good writing. Study that passage and try to write a description of a scene in a way that matches its power and understanding.

A conversation with
David Maraniss

CHRISTOPHER SCANLAN: You've written series, you've written books. How do you feel about daily deadline pieces?

DAVID MARANISS: I love to do deadline writing. Usually when there's some kind of a major event happening, I either volunteer to help out, or they ask me. I was born with newspapers in my blood, because my dad was a newspaperman and my grandfather was a printer and so no matter what else I'm doing, I always have that uncontrollable urge to write on deadline once in a while. I don't know whether it's a sickness. Even if I'm doing a series, I say, "Look, if you guys need me, I'd be happy to do something."

Do you always say yes?

I try to be in a position to say yes, and I try to volunteer, so that I can have enormous freedom the rest of the time.

I find that so many reporters keep banging away at their editors and having frustrating confrontations about what they have to do or don't have to do. I've always found it much more effective to do what I want to do by doing some things for them.

I like newspapers and love to write on deadline, and so I volunteer. But one of the reasons I do that is so that there's a fair exchange, where they know that I'm always around when they need me, and then in return, I get a lot of freedom the rest of the time to do what I want to do.

What is it you like about deadline writing?

The challenge is to try to write a coherent story, whether it's a lead-all or an off-the-news deadline piece. I get a certain thrill of writing right on deadline. I like to gather inchoate facts and try to make a narrative out of them.

I think a lot of deadline writing isn't very good, so I always like the challenge of trying to make it really good. And also, to be honest, while I am doing all of these other things that I also love to do, I think I'm still part of the newspaper, and so I should help out.

How does most deadline writing fail?

It fails because it just turns into a series of paragraphs slapped together, with no coherent thread through them, no story line that holds the reader all the way through. Sometimes it's the writer's fault. Often, it's the editor's fault for just slapping something into the seventh paragraph and another thing into the 11th, assuming that the reader will read it.

I've always maintained that great writing is impossible without great reporting. You have to have all the facts and try to have more than anyone else, but the one ingredient that's often left out of the whole process is not the writing or the reporting, but the thinking. You have to think your way through the story and how you're going to tell it to the readers first.

How do you accomplish that? How do you think through a story?

There are a few methods I use. I try to always have a plan ahead of time on what's the best possible way I could convey what's happened. And if that plan doesn't work, then I'll change it, but to have a plan ahead of time often helps me do the quick type of reporting and see details that might not seem important to other reporters.

I often try to have an idea, even before I do the reporting, but always with the notion that I'll be flexible if the story takes me in another direction. But I start thinking about the story, and what's the most interesting aspect of it, and how I can present that most interesting aspect, and what sort of structure might do that best, before I even get there to do the reporting.

Are you making any notes in a notebook, or is this a mental process?

It's both. I might write down a note or two. I don't write out the story ahead of time. Before I get to the event, I'm always thinking about one or two larger themes, or just ideas that I might put into the story.

And is the idea the theme?

Often, it won't be, if my reporting develops a different theme that is better.

With Hillary going to the grand jury, I really wasn't sure that I was going to do a story until about an hour before she actually went over there. Because I'd written a book on the Clintons and knew her life, I understood how I would do that story. In the cab over to the federal courthouse I thought, "This is another one of those cases where you have a unique individual, someone that the average reader really can't quite identify with, and she's undergoing something that not everybody does. Everybody doesn't go to the grand jury."

Yet, in essence, it is a humanizing event because it's something that she, at that moment, doesn't have any control over. Once she gets out of that limousine, she's totally on her own, not protected by her press secretaries or all of the apparatus that comes with that high office.

And so that was the image I wanted to convey. It's a case, like most everything that I've tried to do, where I've looked to the specific to relate the universal.

What do you mean by theme?

You don't even have to state it directly in the story, but in a sense, it is a way of letting the reader know that this is more than just another bit of removed news; it is an example of the human dilemma. It's as simple as that, you know?

Every story has some tension to it, and perhaps a lesson. You try not to bang readers over the head with the lesson but use the theme as a way of conveying it.

It's interesting to hear you talk about theme. How long have you been thinking this way about stories?

I think it's something that I started thinking about at a fairly early stage of my career. My dad was a traditional newspaperman, a city editor type, but also a very good writer, and one of the talents he had was writing that was both polished prose and yet storytelling. In other words, you always felt like he was talking to you, even when he wasn't in the story at all.

My mentor at the *Post* was Richard Harwood, who was also both an editor and a great writer, who prided himself on being what they called the lead-all writer. If there was a disaster or a major event, Harwood would take all of the disparate information and write the lead-all for the paper. And both of them were very strong on having a story line and on conveying it in a way that was more than just an accumulation of facts.

There's one step from there to a theme, and that's just my own sort of prejudice in reading. I know that if there is a story line and a theme in a story, I'll keep reading it because I want to follow it. Everything in life has a theme, and newspapers can provide that, and when they do, it gives a story three dimensions instead of two. The trick is to do it in a way that you're not so much insinuating yourself into the story as trying to become the universal observer for all the readers.

You begin "A Solitary Figure Enters New Territory," with a scene: "She arrived in a Cadillac Fleetwood limousine as gray and cold as the winter afternoon. At twelve minutes to two, she stepped out, cloaked in black, and marched across the wide concrete entranceway toward the U.S. District Court building, pausing briefly twice, first to turn and wave back in the direction of the scattered hurrahs and jeers, then to speak into a sidewalk microphone, her voice clear and earnest, saying she had to go inside and help however she could." What were you trying to do there?

I was trying to get the reader right there with me, for that moment, and do it in a physical way that conveyed a whole atmosphere.

So much writing is subconscious, but I think that that paragraph sets up the sense that this was a lonely mission for her, and something that she was trying to buck herself up to do, that was embarrassing, without saying any of those things, just take the reader there.

Why don't you want to say it? Why do you want to take the reader instead?

Because you don't have to say it. It's much more effective to show it through what happened than to just say it point blank. That way, if you don't just say it, then that one moment when you do say something, it has more power.

What about the reporters who say, "My editor would never let me do this? Whenever I try to write anything good, the editor says, 'Wait a minute. You don't even have her name in the first paragraph.'"

Well, that's true. I give speeches once in a while, and that's the overwhelming refrain that I hear. And I don't quite know how to answer that without sounding arrogant, or egomaniacal, because I think the editors will let you get away with it if you do it well enough.

One thing I've tried to learn how to do over decades is satisfy my editor's needs while also satisfying my own thematic and literary and stylistic needs.

How do you do that?

That's not easy. I try to give them almost everything that they need in the classic "Who, What, When, Where, Why, How" sense in the first three paragraphs, without knocking them over the head with it.

I don't know if that specific example holds. I think the more traditional approach is the story about the bodies coming home. That one has some of the traditional news lead in it and some of my thematic stuff.

David Guterson, author of the novel *Snow Falling on Cedars*, says he has to know his theme first and uses it to organize his writing. Is that how you think of using a theme?

Absolutely. And in this case, again, the plane was late, so I had some time to think while we were just standing out there freezing. I actually got pneumonia from that experience.

I was standing there with the rest of the reporters, waiting for the plane, and while we were waiting, one of the families occasionally would walk back from another part of the air base and take their seats. That's when I realized that that was what this day was all about—that realization that here you had 33 people dead, and that's a group, and it moves a tragedy from an individual dying into another level.

And yet for each of those families, it's still an individual dying. It's not mass mourning. It's individual mourning.

That was what I wanted to create as the theme of the whole piece. And so then I found images throughout that would do that, both the individual caskets and hearses and the Clintons moving from room to room in the barracks on the other side of the air base and into each room, where they were entering an individual tragedy.

Tell the story behind that story.

I was working on a piece on Hillary and everything she'd said over the course of four years. And it was an exhausting experience, because I was reading all these documents every day, and trying to compare what she'd said in one year to another.

And when Ron Brown's plane crashed, as usual, I volunteered. For the first several days they didn't need me, and then they said, "Somebody's got to go over to Dover."

It was a Saturday. Most of the reporters were traveling with the president and came on the press plane. I drove up to Dover on my own, and got there about four hours early. I started reporting right then, looking for a lot of details that never got into the story. I went around the base. I interviewed people at the mortuary. I wanted to get a feel for that base and why people come to Dover and what Dover means.

What was your assignment?

They don't say, "Do it like this or like that." They know I'll think of a way to do it.

I try to bring the human spirit into every story. Somehow. And try to develop a voice that doesn't grate on the reader, as "Well, that guy thinks he knows everything," or, "He thinks that, but I disagree." I try to have a voice that is the voice of humanity, or a more universal voice.

Do you think newspapers need more of that?

Sure I do. But there's a fine line between advocacy reporting and having a voice. I don't know how fine the line is, but some people don't see the difference, and I think there is a difference.

When you went to the air base in Dover, did you have a handler?

There were several very nice, young handlers, but they didn't follow me everywhere. They gave me a lot of press releases, which I don't think I used or looked at.

I did have time beforehand, I think, to check the *Post* for Dover stories. I wanted to make sure I wasn't totally rewriting something we'd already done. And we'd done a story in the Style section a long time ago about how all these tragedies come back to Dover.

I read those, but didn't take any notes on them really, and then went to Dover. About two hours before the plane was due, we were corralled into different areas to wait, like the press is whenever the president is on the scene.

There were two places you could wait: where the president's plane would stop and disembark, with some of the families and the president and his entourage, and another place where the ceremony would take place, inside a hangar. And they were a couple of football fields apart, so I would move back and forth between those two, over those two hours, trying to get little details.

It was very straightforward reporting. That's really all you could do, was watch and listen and look for the details that you thought would convey the themes of that day. It just depended on my eyes and ears to see it in a certain way.

What did you do next?

As soon as the plane arrived, it pulled up close to the hangar, and the engine wound down, and the caskets came out, I knew everything I needed to know for the story. There were only about four or five images that will hold an entire story, and I've got them. So then I just had to figure out how to put them together.

You need four or five images to hold the story together?

Well, that kind of story, I thought I did.

What kind of story is it?

Well, it's a poem. A life and death poem, basically, I mean, why else be there? Because it's a universal moment, people dying tragically. It's not news per se. I mean, the news already happened when they died. They're just coming home.

And so any news poem has to have images in it, and I think I found the ones I wanted.

You said "news poem"?

That sounds ridiculous, but that's what it was. It's an elegy. It was my elegy, without intruding too much of myself into it. But what value am I to be there unless I give the readers my eyes and ears and thoughts?

Four images. Do you go in thinking, "I'm looking for these"?

In that specific case I did, because I knew there was no other story. On so many deadline stories, you're not sure what's going to happen. This one, it was pretty much of a set piece.

I spent five minutes before I wrote a lead and just sat down and said to myself, "What are those four or five images, and which one do I lead with, and which one do I end with?"

I didn't order them beyond that. I ordered how I wanted to start it, and how I wanted to end it. Clinton's speech, which I knew I had to put in there for news reasons, whether I wanted to or not, was my one major concession to traditional news reporting. The president was there. He said something that I put fairly high up.

Did you write the images down?

I wrote them down on the back of a press release, probably.

Is that your plan?

It's as close to a plan as I had.

I wouldn't script a whole story before I start writing, anyway, and I don't. But I try to do at least that much.

What do you mean, script a story?

In other words, I'm not going to go through it and say, "Well, this paragraph and then that paragraph." Because once I start writing it, it's like writing a poem. You can't script a poem. You know the idea, but then words come to you.

In the story on Hillary Clinton you write, "Then, after handling one of the most penetrating questions in modern political annals—'Would you rather have been somewhere else today?'" What role does sarcasm play in journalism today?

I try not to do that too often. I just was so struck by that question. And also, I think it's OK to introduce a touch of humor into any story, at some point. I mean, if you can do it appropriately, and in that case, I thought it was.

Let's talk about your background a bit. What was your major in school?

I don't have a college degree, but I studied English.

Where did you study?

At the University of Wisconsin. I got married when I just turned 20, and I became a father and a working guy. I got into writing and never got the degree. It's something I no longer regret, but did for a while, not for any reason other than having to keep saying, "I don't have a degree."

When did you write your first newspaper story?

I started writing in my freshman year in college, covering high school sports for the local paper in Madison.

The Capital Times. **Where your dad worked?**

He was the city editor then. And they had a nepotism rule, so I couldn't really work there. I couldn't be a full-time employee, but I could do Friday night high school sports. And so I did that. And wrote some movie reviews, and then I spent a couple of years working for radio. WIBA.

I covered city hall, but the real value was, on weekends, I would do my own newscasts. It was a neat station, where you could do 15-minute radio news. Instead of ripping and reading it, I would write the whole thing.

I think it had a nice effect on my newspaper writing because I had to read everything I wrote. It had to have a rhythm that could be read.

Do you read your stuff aloud now?

Yeah, sure. Sometimes audibly, depending on how many people are around. If I'm alone, I'll read it out loud.

Do you have a writing philosophy?

Well, just a few things that I go by. One is that I want people to read it, and I want them to read it from the very first sentence to the ending.

Another is that writing is more than just a collection of paragraphs; it has to have a theme, and you have to use the specific to transmit the universal. Everything you write about is part of the human endeavor. It's not just an assortment of facts.

And you can't be a great writer without being a great reporter.

What advice would you give to somebody who wants to write stories on deadline the way you do?

Read as much good writing as you can, and try to study why it is that way.

And think about it a little more. Thinking is the great underappreciated and understated part of being a newspaper person. Take a few minutes to think about the theme and the images before you start writing.

You're on leave now, writing a biography of Vince Lombardi, the legendary Green Bay Packers coach. Do you think you'll be writing on daily deadline again?

Oh, sure. I'm sure of it. Maybe not this year. Can you hold on for a second?

Sure.

(Maraniss comes back on the line.)

That was my editor saying, "We need you." They want me to do a deadline story.

Today?

Yes. I gotta run.

THE WALL STREET JOURNAL

John J. Keller

Finalist, Deadline Reporting

John J. Keller is deputy news editor of technology in the New York bureau of *The Wall Street Journal.* He is responsible for the paper's computer, communications, and online services coverage.

In November 1989, he joined the *Journal* as a reporter in New York, covering the telecommunications beat. Before joining the *Journal,* he was a reporter at *More* magazine, and has been an editor at *Jersey Business Review, CMP Publications, Electronic Buyers News, Communications Week,* and *Business Week.* In 1979 he received the Scripps-Howard Journalism Award. A native of New York City, Keller earned a bachelor's degree in English from Baruch College, City University of New York.

When AT&T Corp. surprised the business world by picking an outsider as its new CEO, Keller spent a hectic day making sense of the news for a sophisticated audience. Facing stiff competition and unrelenting deadlines, he used the skilled beat reporter's tools of sources, background, and insight to produce a comprehensive story that achieved both goals.

Telecom novice handed challenge of remaking AT&T

OCTOBER 24, 1996

Ma Bell has fallen down. Can new leadership help her get up?

AT&T Corp. culminated a much-watched search for a new president yesterday by throwing investors a curve-ball. It didn't choose the star technologist or crackshot consumer marketer that Wall Street was hoping for. Instead, it went with the less well-known chairman of an old-line printer, R.R. Donnelley & Sons Co.

John R. Walter will become president and chief operating officer of the beleaguered telecommunications titan, serving in the No. 2 slot until AT&T Chairman Robert E. Allen retires in January 1998—a full two years earlier than planned. In his apprenticeship, Mr. Walter will have to study the vastly changing telecom business while trying to prop up AT&T's flagging fortunes.

Once the 61-year-old Mr. Allen steps aside, Mr. Walter, 49, will take full command of a company that still labors under too much bureaucracy, internal management strife, uninspired and fragmented marketing and sagging morale. AT&T already has lost several key executives this year—Mr. Walter succeeds Alex Mandl, who quit two months ago to join a startup—and more turnover at the top is likely. Industry executives say several senior AT&T staffers will soon leave, including perhaps AT&T's hard-charging consumer chief, Joseph Nacchio.

The hiring marks a change that many AT&T watchers say was overdue. Mr. Allen's decade of multibillion-dollar restructurings and massive downsizings has been a failure when measured against the revenue, profit and global-market expansion of AT&T's primary rivals, MCI Communications Corp. and Sprint Corp. Investors are fleeing AT&T's stock. A three-way split of AT&T was supposed to ignite growth, but its computer and equipment spinoffs are in high gear while AT&T seems stuck in neutral.

"There is a crisis at the top of AT&T and a lot of inertia throughout the company," says David Shell, senior vice president at Liberty Investment Management, which sold the last of its 700,000 AT&T shares last month. "They've been sailing around rudderless," he adds. "Bob Allen needs to get the hell out."

The new hire is a charismatic manager who coupled teamwork and technology with an iron-fisted focus on profit growth at Chicago-based Donnelley. At AT&T, he must get disparate parts to cooperate better, make the right technology bets, and overhaul and vastly simplify AT&T's marketing to beat rivals. "We're on the fast track," an MCI spokesman boasts. "AT&T's sitting in quicksand."

If Mr. Walter fails, AT&T may never regain the ability to lead the market it created more than a century ago. Other titans, such as Western Union Corp. and International Business Machines Corp., lost their power to orchestrate the worldwide industries they pioneered, once technology changed and management faltered. IBM managed to stabilize and achieve a strong stock comeback. If AT&T missteps, it could end up like Western Union—an erstwhile communications juggernaut done in at the turn of the century by an entrepreneurial, wily startup called American Telephone & Telegraph Co.

Clearly, the new guy has his work cut out for him. Wall Street analysts' reaction to his appointment ranged from lukewarm to almost hostile. In New York Stock Exchange composite trading, AT&T closed at $37.75 a share, down $1.875, on unusually high volume. In his favor are the enormous portfolio assets he will have at his disposal—a powerful brand name backed by a billion-dollar annual ad budget and $60 billion in assets splayed across the communications businesses that will define the 21st century.

AT&T, despite recent travails, remains one of the most financially powerful companies in the world. It is far along in installing some of the major gear it needs to make a big entry into the local phone-service business. It has aggressively targeted some of the high-growth sectors of the Information Age, signing up almost half a million new customers in short order for its Internet-access business—now the nation's second-largest—and owning the biggest wireless business in the world.

But under Mr. Allen, New York-based AT&T has failed to effectively leverage these assets and coordinate the delivery of new services. Its corporate fiefs—from consumer long-distance service to cellular to Internet access—barely cooperate. When a new customer signs up for AT&T long-distance, the company sends out a welcoming letter but neglects to include a pitch for wireless-phone service, or the new WorldNet Web service, or even the DirecTV satellite-television service in which AT&T recently invested.

AT&T unwisely runs the customer-service lines for these businesses independently of one another, forcing a customer to call different 800 numbers to order new services from the same company. AT&T invented toll-free 800 calling, yet it still doesn't offer personal 800 numbers to consumers. That is because the toll-free pitch is overseen by the AT&T unit that serves corporate customers.

MCI, by contrast, offers a personal 800 number and registered a 55% growth in such traffic in the past year. Its unbranded "1-800-COLLECT" service has become a consumer staple.

AT&T also lags behind MCI in marketing to customers of the future. Many youngsters leaving home for new apartments and ordering their first phones were small children unable to even reach a wallphone when their parents lamented the breakup of the old AT&T a dozen years ago. MCI aims special calling plans at college students; it advertises heavily on MTV, and it sponsors Major League Baseball.

AT&T can't even provide something as simple as bundling disparate services into a single monthly statement. MCI has been doing so since the spring. AT&T had hoped to take control of billing for its 90 million accounts, which the regional Bell companies now handle for a fee, but is running two or three years behind schedule.

"AT&T has it all, but it hasn't executed," says Blake Bath, a Lehman Brothers Inc. analyst. "And it's running out of time."

Such basic marketing lapses were survivable when customer loyalty was strong and AT&T held a cozy "triopoly" over the $70 billion long-distance market, its nearly 60% share almost three times the share held by MCI and Sprint. The miscues may be unforgivable in the new telecom wars.

THE HOME MARKET

Consumer loyalty is at an all-time low. Some 24 million households—nearly one-fourth of the homes in America—switched to a new long-distance provider at least once in the last year, up from 19 million defections the year before, says the Yankee Group, a Boston research firm. AT&T has the most to lose, and it relies on consumer service more heavily than MCI or Sprint do. More than half of AT&T's long-distance revenue and two-thirds of its profit comes from the consumer, as opposed to the corporate, market.

Moreover, customers will have ever more choices as they surf for discounts. Some 900 providers and resellers in long-distance are plying a mostly commodity service. They range from fly-by-nights and "dial-around" services, which let customers keep AT&T but sidestep it with six-digit access codes, to middle-tier outfits such as LCI International Inc., which offers a lower flat-rate discount and sells service the Amway way—by pyramids of neighborhood friends.

Such efforts stole away two percentage points from AT&T's market share—and about $1.5 billion in long-distance revenue—in the past year alone. A bigger drain could come with the arrival of giant local phone monopolies. GTE Corp. and Southern New England Telecommunications Inc. have already turned tens of thousands of their local phone customers into long-distance accounts in the past year. GTE says it is signing up more than 6,000 customers a week.

"Soon we'll have seven new MCI-sized rivals, the Baby Bells, coming at us," one senior AT&T executive says. AT&T's internal studies show the Bells could take one-third of the long-distance market within a couple of years.

RIVAL GROWTH

AT&T's two arch-rivals, MCI and Sprint, manage to grow faster in part because they start with a much smaller revenue base. More disturbing, however, is that in the past five years MCI added a bigger net dollar increase in revenues than AT&T could muster, Jack

B. Grubman, a telecom analyst at Salomon Brothers Inc., calculates. MCI added an extra $6 billion since 1991, compared with $5 billion extra for AT&T. MCI, the far smaller and feistier competitor, gobbled up 41% of the industry's revenue growth while AT&T earned only 33%.

"Stocks trade on fundamentals and outlook—and the fundamentals for AT&T's stock are deteriorating," says Mr. Grubman, an outspoken bear for 18 months on AT&T.

As a result, MCI's market share climbed to 20% from 16% five years ago, while AT&T's sank to 57% from 70%. Smaller Sprint is doing even better. Sprint added $257 million in revenue in the third quarter, a higher net increase than the $254 million that AT&T managed to post.

If AT&T and MCI had started from zero five years ago, MCI would be the bigger company. "AT&T has 57% of the market today only because it started with 100%," Mr. Grubman says. "AT&T's core business is decelerating." (Yesterday, Standard & Poor's down-graded about $9 billion of AT&T debt, citing competitive pressures.)

If AT&T's new president has a plan on how to reverse this trend, he wasn't saying yesterday. He did note that AT&T needs to do a better job of coordinating its service offerings. That would require better working relationships among its massive service operations. "I clearly don't underestimate the walls and cultures that exist at AT&T," Mr. Walter says. "We have to make sure we integrate better....Not all our decisions will be right, but hopefully we'll know that before it's too late and move on to something better."

He also indicates he will take a tough approach toward AT&T's future investments, noting that he didn't hesitate recently to shut down a Donnelley plant in York, England, when it no longer made financial sense to keep it running. "We didn't have the scale. We weren't recovering our capital investment. We closed it down and moved the assets elsewhere," he says.

The Baby Bells know Mr. Walter. Donnelley prints their directories and the Yellow Pages. Noting his charismatic, forceful style within the parochial printing industry, one senior Bell executive calls Mr. Walter "a giant among midgets."

But most analysts yesterday were underwhelmed by AT&T's choice. "Walter's relevance to AT&T is questionable," Richard Klugman of PaineWebber Inc. said in his note to investors yesterday. In fact, Mr. Klugman pointed out that in Mr. Walter's tenure as Donnelley's CEO, the company "saw its leadership position in the printing business erode to smaller competitors, and the company encountered losses and restructuring charges for missteps into new technologies," problems Mr. Walter is leaving his successor at Donnelley to fix.

Mr. Walter offers no specifics on AT&T's biggest problem—marketing—or how he is going to quell the feuding among AT&T's major units. AT&T might have been better positioned to win the marketing war in services if Mr. Allen hadn't taken his eye off the ball to focus on his disastrous hostile takeover of NCR Corp., people close to the company say. By late 1994, the beleaguered computer business was losing upward of $700 million a year. Mr. Allen pumped $2.8 billion into NCR to shore up its finances—money that came from the profit of AT&T's core business, one executive says.

"AT&T could have used some of that money to fund its local phone build-out, its new wireless network or Internet," Mr. Grubman notes.

Counters Mr Allen: "We were never inhibited in any of our investments by what we did at NCR." He adds, "AT&T has a strong balance sheet and cash flow."

In fact, though, this became one of the central strategic arguments among AT&T's senior managers last year when the company was also going through the stress of Mr. Allen's three-way breakup. AT&T's communication-services executives regarded NCR as a sinkhole. They argued against harvesting AT&T's core business, throwing good money after bad, to cover NCR's widening losses. A new unified billing system that would allow Mr. Nacchio's group to bundle service was years behind schedule.

Mr. Nacchio, the consumer chief, ended up having to curtail a huge marketing strike against MCI that had begun to cut MCI's gains from its Friends & Family discount service, according to AT&T insiders. Mr. Mandl, then chief of communication services, was forced to make an underfunded drive into the Internet market, hurting AT&T's initial launch. And AT&T had to hold back funds to expand its wireless business, which is now scrambling to pre-empt a spanking new nationwide service from Sprint.

Overseas, Mr. Walter faces other challenges. At Donnelley, he pushed into numerous international markets, acquiring smaller rivals, many of which couldn't afford to stay competitive with the computer-driven systems the company was putting in place. The company's biggest acquisition, its $487.5 million purchase of a big joint venture between Meredith Corp. and members of Germany's Burda family, turned into a headache—and also served to underscore Mr. Walter's readiness to take on regulators.

For AT&T, Mr. Walter may need to act more radically—and fast. While AT&T relies on hundred-year-old ties to state monopolies to cobble together an unwieldy global-communications service for corporations, fleeter joint ventures of MCI's and Sprint's are eating AT&T's lunch. Concert, a global joint venture between MCI and its 20% owner British Telecommunications PLC is posting revenue growth of more than 30% annually. MCI's Mexican network with local partners is ready to offer service in many cities while AT&T is still calling news conferences to announce its Mexican strategy. Sprint's Global One venture with its 20% owners, France Telecom and Deutsche Telekom, is off to a similarly fast start against AT&T's lumbering operation.

Such strategic problems have left investors uneasy for now about AT&T's choice for Mr. Allen's successor. Mr. Allen acknowledges the problem, saying the idea wasn't to go for a marquee name that would give AT&T "a one-day pop" in its stock price. Picking Mr. Walter, he insists, "is an investment for the future."

Lessons Learned

BY JOHN J. KELLER

Reporting and writing a well-paced, informative Page One story on deadline is a cinch—as long as somebody else is doing it.

For the reporter on the spot, it can be a heart-pounding ordeal, more stress-inducing even than losing your reporting notes or having to explain to your editor why you got beat on a story. But several hard-earned lessons about beat reporting carried me especially well through our Page One story on AT&T Corp.'s new president, John R. Walter.

Rule One: Keep your editor informed at all times about potential developments on your beat. This way the two of you can brainstorm better as co-experts. When AT&T Corp. made its big announcement early on the morning of Oct. 23, it didn't come as a complete surprise to me or my editor. The precipitous decline of one of America's great corporate icons had already become one of the hottest business stories of the last decade. I got a tip the night before that AT&T was ready to announce the new guy. My editor, Dennis Kneale, told me that night to be ready in case Page One wanted a story the next day.

I went home that night and hardly slept, thinking about how to map out the next day's coverage. Competition on the AT&T search story had been frenzied for two months. While we were out front on the search itself, the identity of the finalist—the really good scoop—still had eluded me right up to AT&T's announcement. (I'm still sore about this: My source on the night before the announcement refused to identify AT&T's true choice. Such nerve!)

That night I decided to try for a Page One story on the challenges AT&T's new president would face, drawing on months of reporting that I hadn't yet used. Our competitors would focus on what a surprise the finalist was and where he came from. I wrote about the finalist's track record running R.R. Donnelley & Sons Co. in a companion piece the same day. And I got tremendous help on the second piece from reporters in our Chicago bureau and from one of our New York editors who covers management issues.

Rule Two: Prepare well. It helped me to get a fast start on the AT&T story. Only a couple of weeks before the story broke, the *Journal*'s Page One editor had passed on my offer to deliver a quick story on AT&T's problems and challenges. We were mildly disappointed by this, but as it turned out, his rejection left me with considerable string to be used later. It is good to be obsessive about your beat. Keep unearthing data on your prime targets of coverage because you'll have the goods when it counts to turn in a piece of depth and clarity quickly, while your rivals are spinning their wheels in search of an angle and some sources.

Much easier was deciding our angle. AT&T's choice of a little-known captain of the staid printing industry over marquee names stunned the telecom world and the media—negative vibes that could be used to make the story about his challenge at AT&T that much more compelling. I chose not to explore his ability to lead AT&T since there wasn't any way to make that snap call on such flimsy same-day reporting. Better to turn the internal AT&T forecasts and insights from AT&T insiders that were already in my file into a forward-looking story about his challenges.

Following the second rule helped me to execute **Rule Three: Write early**. By the time I left the *Journal*'s World Financial Center headquarters in downtown Manhattan to attend AT&T's news conference at 1 p.m., about 20 blocks uptown, my Page One story to lead the paper was half written as was the companion piece profiling Walter, albeit with a few holes to be filled in later. Obviously this doesn't apply to tornado stories. But with most other breaking majors you can start putting something down right away to frame your story. Flesh it out once your reporting is done. By that time your editor has almost finished smoothing out your first draft, and you can write the rest of your story.

We had to send my complete Page One story and a second sidebar on the new AT&T president to Page One and editors of the *Journal*'s Marketplace section no later than 5 p.m. to make all of the *Journal*'s domestic and overseas editions. By 3:30 p.m. I still hadn't returned to the newspaper's offices from the news conference to write the rest of my stories. I cut things really close that day to do a one-on-one interview with the new president, giving our story more authority.

In the end our Page One story and related profile, which ran on the front page of the *Journal*'s second section, made deadline with time to spare. Our coverage was fair with a fresh AT&T angle for our readers, and our competitors were kept off balance—for another few days anyway. That's the value of **Rule Four: teamwork**.

Los Angeles Times

Sebastian Rotella

Finalist, Deadline Reporting

Sebastian Rotella joined the *Los Angeles Times* as a reporter in 1987, working as a staff writer for the South Bay section, the Valley Edition, and the San Diego bureau before becoming Buenos Aires bureau chief in 1996. He also has worked for United Press International, Lerner Newspapers in Chicago, and the *Chicago Sun-Times*. A Chicago native, Rotella earned a bachelor's degree at the University of Michigan.

Rotella's re-creation of a rebel takeover at the Japanese Embassy in Lima, Peru, is full of vivid details and deft characterizations. His achievement is even more impressive given the fact that the night it happened he was on vacation in Argentina. His deadline account, produced in a blur of on-scene reporting and adrenaline-fueled writing, puts his readers at the scene as witnesses to history.

Terrorists' most effective tool: total surprise

DECEMBER 19, 1996

LIMA, Peru—The target was as tough as it gets: a fancy reception in a well-guarded, high-walled mansion attended by hundreds of diplomats and politicians with bodyguards in tow.

But as witnesses and former hostages recalled Wednesday, the attack on the residence of the Japanese ambassador here was an equally tough display of nerve and skill.

The gunmen of Peru's Tupac Amaru Revolutionary Movement, or MRTA, invaded the fortress-like compound Tuesday night in a sophisticated, meticulous operation with cinematic touches—disguises, bullets hidden in desserts.

And now they are barricaded inside, holding as many as 490 VIP hostages and defying the world.

"It was incredible," said a Spanish bodyguard who identified himself as Paco, his expression mixing awe and anger. "These guys knew what they were doing."

He recalled the attack Wednesday as he stood with other Spanish diplomatic security guards near the cordoned-off perimeter where Peruvian sharpshooters had surrounded the ambassador's residence. The tough-looking security expert wore a sport shirt, medallions on his chest and a semiautomatic pistol on his hip.

On Tuesday night, the bodyguard had accompanied Spain's deputy ambassador to the gala reception in honor of the birthday of Japan's Emperor Akihito.

Because Japan has played a major role in the economic renaissance led by President Alberto Fujimori, the son of Japanese immigrants, the reception was one of the hottest tickets in town.

About 8:15 p.m., the Spanish bodyguard was standing by a bullet-proof Mercedes when a bomb went off, shaking the car. Then withering gunfire erupted from the area of the mansion.

"The bullets were hitting the sidewalk around us, and we didn't know where they came from," he recalled. "Everybody was shooting, and we didn't know who we were shooting at."

Inside, two teams of guerrillas had struck.

One team had gotten past the Japanese Embassy security guards, who have a reputation here for efficiency; the gunmen tricked security forces by posing as waiters and deliverymen setting up for the reception. They smuggled in gas masks, pistols, automatic rifles and ammunition hidden in boxes of panettone, a traditional Italian Christmas cake. Others arrived dressed as doctors in a phony ambulance.

The second Tupac Amaru team set off three explosions—blowing down a wall from an adjacent yard, according to one version. They charged into the midst of the 800 guests on the lawn—looking fearsome with red-and-white kerchiefs bearing the Tupac logo covering their faces—and shouted political slogans.

The firefight with police and plainclothes bodyguards in the street outside went on for half an hour. Miraculously, no one was killed.

The guests spent the next hour lying face down, terrified. Once the guerrillas had established control they strode about, warning their victims not to look up and calling out the names of congressmen, ministers and other powerful hostages. They were confirming that they had caught the roster of dignitaries they had set out to take hostage.

But the poised young men in dark clothes were not vicious. Former hostages agreed that some were even gentlemanly. One guerrilla noticed that foreign correspondent Sally Bowen was choking and sputtering, overcome by tear gas fired by the Peruvian police before they retreated. He dipped his handkerchief in water and helped her dry her eyes.

And when the gunmen announced that they would release the hundreds of women among the hostages—including the president's mother and sister—Bowen, a veteran correspondent for the *Financial Times,* asked for and got a brief interview with the commander of the attack squad. He impressed her.

"He spoke very fluently," said a weary Bowen in one of many interviews she gave Wednesday. "He seemed very sure of what he was about. He had his arguments well-prepared. He was not frightening, because he was very calm."

The guerrilla leader, calling himself Commander Huerta, declared that Tupac had targeted the Japanese ambassador because the leftist, pro-Castro group accuses Japan of meddling in Peruvian affairs and supporting economic policies that have caused poverty and hunger here.

Bowen left with the impression that the government has run up against a daunting opponent.

"They have 250 top people as hostages," she said. "That is the propaganda feat of the century for the MRTA."

Showing its usual flair for public relations, the guerrilla group Wednesday used the media to maximum advantage.

The group let the hostages send out a letter calling for calm and explaining how the gunmen had positioned them as human shields in front of the first- and second-story windows of the mansion.

Though their tone was calm and laconic during telephone interviews, the guerrillas sounded occasionally chilling. They warned that they had mined the grounds with explosives and were prepared to die along with the hostages.

During a tense moment Wednesday morning, a television interviewer asked Huerta if the captives were unharmed. He responded: "Right now they are. But in an hour they might not be."

Lessons Learned

BY SEBASTIAN ROTELLA

One of the things I most like and dread about my job is calls
after 10 p.m. The sound of the telephone at night triggers
memories of exciting and harrowing stories. The sound is a
warning, an invitation, a jolt of mystery and adrenaline.

On Dec. 17, the call came at about 11 o'clock. I was at
home in Buenos Aires, settling into a Christmas vacation
with my family. An editor in Los Angeles was on the other
end of the line. Leftist rebels had just stormed the Japanese
ambassador's mansion in Lima, Peru, and were holding
hundreds of hostages. It was the biggest breaking story in
South America in years.

During a decade at the *Los Angeles Times,* I had covered
some urgent, complex breaking news. At the U.S.-Mexico
border, I had covered political assassinations, drug scandals,
shootouts. I had been bureau chief in Buenos Aires since
April 1996 and had made two previous trips to Peru. But I
was still in the process of learning the beat.

The hostage standoff reminded me of another thing I like
and dread about the job. The challenges change and get bigger. I always experience that surge of anxiety and exhilara-
tion triggered by an approaching deadline. I always learn
something new.

After getting the call on the night of the 17th, I hurried to
the bureau and worked the phones. With the help of the correspondent in Tokyo and the blessing of Pacific Standard
Time, we put together a last-minute first-day story. Then it
was time to catch a 7 a.m. flight. I ran into two other U.S.
correspondents at the Buenos Aires airport. We all had the
same look on our faces.

Four hours later, we hit the ground running in Lima. I
remember speeding to the scene in a taxi, scribbling notes
as a commander of the barricaded rebels gave a phone interview to a radio station. He sounded calmer than I felt.

Breaking stories can be difficult to report in Peru. There
is no real government spokesman other than President Alberto Fujimori. The police had other things to do besides
attending to the press or putting out bulletins.

The coastal mist that perpetually shrouds Lima swirled
with versions, rumors, opinions. The scene was chaotic.
There were so many angles: the international assortment of
elite hostages; the surprise resurgence of terrorism in Peru;

the Japanese-Peruvian connection embodied by Fujimori, one of the continent's most intriguing leaders; and the incredibly daring attack, the biggest publicity coup by Latin American guerrillas in memory.

I developed the framework of a story from news reports and phone calls to diplomatic sources, journalists, experts on terrorism.

But I needed details, voices, first-hand accounts. I went to the besieged neighborhood, where crowds of reporters strained against police lines. I drifted around listening, looking for someone who actually knew something and was willing to talk.

I struck out a couple of times.

Then I noticed several armed men in civilian clothes standing by a Mercedes on the other side of the yellow tape. They looked tense. It turned out that they had been in the thick of the shootout the night before; they were bodyguards for a Spanish diplomat who was now a hostage. After initial refusals, I coaxed them into telling their story. I gathered other first-hand accounts, notably from Sally Bowen, the intrepid *Financial Times* correspondent who took advantage of a few hours as a hostage to interview the rebel leader.

I headed back to the hotel and fired off more calls, gathering context and analysis, the television blaring. I had about four hours to write. My editor, Craig Matsuda, suggested three separate pieces: the main story, a color piece on the attack, and a historical look at the Tupac Amaru Revolutionary Movement.

I groaned inwardly. Three dailies after a night without sleep?

But it was a great idea because it organized the coverage, rather than tossing all the material into a single, amorphous piece.

The article that appears in this book is the color story. It recounts the attack from the street level, trying to re-create the event and plunge the reader into it.

The time constraints and subject matter helped me keep the language hard and clean. The lead set up colliding images of a tough target and tougher invaders. I foreshadowed the kind of details—bullets hidden in desserts—that make a story artful.

With more time I might have avoided the adjective "cinematic," but it was a fast way of communicating this was a real-life action movie.

The first voice in the story was a Spanish bodyguard, a street-level "expert" on violence and terrorism who could talk authoritatively about the spectacular Tupac Amaru operation. The narrative followed the action, starting outside with the firefight and moving inside with the raiders.

Given the lack of an official account, the description of the three-pronged attack was pieced together from the first-hand accounts, diplomatic sources speaking on background, and news reports.

The phony ambulance and the bullets in the Christmas cake had been shown on television, so I was fairly sure about those colorful details. The entry by guerrillas disguised as waiters and delivery men was the most convincing of the multiple and contradictory versions. Making one of many rapid-fire decisions based on sources, logic, and instinct, I went with it. And it was subsequently confirmed.

Next, I turned to the hostages' description of terror and chaos combined with humane treatment by disciplined captors. The incongruous adjective "gentlemanly" worked in the gallant anecdotes of the guerrilla helping a hostage dry her eyes during the tear gas attack.

The closing paragraphs wove in the idea that these were professionals whose propaganda skills matched their military prowess. The final paragraphs were crafted to leave a sense of suspense and danger: The guerrillas had good manners, but they were threatening to kill people.

I always try to close with a strong image or quote; this story culminates with the words of the guerrilla leader, the man with his finger on the trigger—one of the first voices I heard upon arriving. The tone of the writing tries to match his tone, which was all the more threatening because it was calm.

I always prefer to have time to craft and tinker with the language. It is hard to fight off newspaper-speak when you are under the gun.

But in this experience, I learned once again that sometimes adrenaline and pressure make the writing better.

Another lesson: My writing improves when I keep the language simple and bring out details that I would emphasize if I were to sit down and tell the story to a friend one day, starting with the late-night phone call.

The New York Times

Michael Specter

Finalist, Deadline Reporting

Michael Specter is co-bureau chief of *The New York Times*'s Moscow bureau. Specter first joined the *Times* in 1979 as a copy boy. From that time until he left in 1983, he served as a clerk on the news desk and as a clerk for columnist Tom Wicker. He rejoined the *Times* as a metropolitan reporter specializing in the environment in 1991 and became a foreign correspondent in 1994. Before rejoining the *Times,* Specter was a reporter at *The Washington Post* from 1985 to 1991, where he covered local news in Virginia and Washington, national science and medical news, and served as New York bureau chief. He was an urban affairs correspondent for *The Far Eastern Economic Review* based in Hong Kong from 1983 to 1985. Specter received a bachelor's degree in English from Vassar College in 1977 and studied English literature at the University of Warwick in Coventry, England, in 1978.

The day Chechen nationalists retook their capital of Grozny from the Russian military, Specter reported the story first-hand, dodging bullets and shellfire to beat the deadline clock with literary grace. His story conveys the horror and insanity of modern-day combat waged by children with high-tech weapons.

Risky walk in rebel-held Chechen capital

AUGUST 14, 1996

GROZNY, Russia, Aug. 13—There is only one open road left into this city. It is a long series of bomb craters, really, mixed with dirt, mud and occasionally some asphalt. The road starts in the deep woods just southwest of town and runs straight toward the ravaged center.

The road has no name, but it does not need one, because everybody knows what it is there for. It is the last, harrowing route to safety each day for thousands of anguished refugees who have been driven from their homes here in the capital of Chechnya by war and death, and it is the best entry route for the secessionist rebels who now reign over most of the city.

Winding through twisted trees, past ruined houses and down the middle of one of Russia's largest—but long unused—oil refineries, the path has become a surreal Chechen version of the Ho Chi Minh Trail.

The right side is filled with pathetic, broken cars edging through the mud, piled high with boxes and always waving white flags ripped from sheets.

The left lane is for the separatists, often walking in groups of less than 10 or driving in flatbed trucks like those used by many refugees to flee the burning city.

Today, a walk from the nearest village, Alkhan-Yurt, into Grozny was a treacherous journey, with helicopter gunships hovering in the distance, Russian planes screeching across the steel-gray skies and a column of tanks to the west firing rounds at random. But the rebels moved along it, seemingly unfazed.

"They can't touch us here," said Imran Agimel-zoya, 16, carrying a gun almost as large as he was and wearing a Chicago Bulls cap, as he made his way along the muddy path toward Chernorechye, the southwest part of Grozny. "The Russians have tanks at every other entrance to the city, but they really can't stop us here."

It is now clear that the Russians are losing badly in their second battle for Grozny in the last two years.

What began as a rebel hit-and-run intended to humili-
ate President Boris N. Yeltsin for his failed promises
of peace has turned into something like a conquest.

Chechen commanders here say they originally
planned to teach Mr. Yeltsin a lesson by showing the
vulnerability of a city that has been a Russian redoubt
since early last year, and then withdraw after they
made their point.

But now, they say, having captured Grozny and
other Chechen cities so easily in the last week, they
have no intention of pulling out, and plan to hold on
until the Russians withdraw from the republic.

"This is our city," said Akhmed Zakayev, the national security adviser to the separatist government
and one of its top commanders. "Why should we
leave it again?"

Although the two sides announced a cease-fire to
begin on Wednesday—the latest in a series of such an-
nouncements, none honored for long—today the fighting continued in the center. Jets and helicopters
unleashed their assault on the Chechen separatists who
stormed the city a week ago and have taken effective
control of it. Yet there are no Russian soldiers wandering the streets of the city; only the Chechen fighters
dare to do that.

Under the overall command of Shamil Basayev,
who led the infamous raid last year on the southern
Russian city of Budyonnovsk, the separatists have
split Grozny into five parts. And they appear to be running all five.

Mr. Zakayev agreed to speak to a reporter today in
his temporary headquarters, a graceful former old-age
home in the leafy Chernorechye section. For two days,
Russian bombers have attacked the neighborhood, in
part because they know Mr. Zakayev is there.

In the West, Mr. Zakayev, a former Chechen Culture Minister, is not well known. But for more than a
year he led the fighting for the mountain village of
Bamut, generally considered to be among the fiercest
battles of the war.

Now he has 1,000 hungry and forlorn Russian troops
surrounded in their barracks only 500 yards from his
office. Mr. Zakayev said his orders from Aslan

Maskhadov, the Chechen military chief of staff, were to keep the Russians pinned down but not to attack.

"When they come out and surrender, we will put them to use," Mr. Zakayev said. "Until then we will keep them surrounded." One of his lieutenants, looking slightly uncomfortable, added, "They are starving to death like flies."

Mr. Zakayev's headquarters resembles a school for wayward boys. Scores of heavily armed teen-agers are constantly running in and out of the base. They play with grenades and rocket launchers as if they were baseballs and lacrosse sticks. But they always do exactly what they are told.

Mr. Zakayev said he had great "military" respect for Aleksandr I. Lebed, the Russian national security adviser who returned from a quick trip to the region on Monday full of praise for the rebels' tenacity and scorn for the way the Russian Government was waging the war.

"That is nice," Mr. Zakayev said. "But we lost hope long ago in the Russian side. They have never fulfilled a single treaty or promise. So I was happy to hear that Lebed says we are brave and that his soldiers are badly treated. I am not sure, though, he can do anything to solve our problem."

The Chechen separatists are still well armed and seem extremely well organized. They say they never permit their soldiers to fight for more than a few days in a row, and routinely rotate troops.

Mr. Zakayev used a new-model Motorola radio, decorated with a sticker of the wolf, the symbol of the Chechen people, to communicate with his staff. During the interview he received word that one of the Russian-installed leaders of the Chechen government was trying to escape the city on the back of a tractor. He quickly issued orders to have him picked up.

Despite the talk of a truce and the fact that the fighting, while continuous, was less intense than yesterday's, separatists said a truce was unlikely. None of the residents fleeing the burning city held out much hope of a halt in the war.

"You look at that," said Andrei Usayov, who with his family of six was walking the path to Alkhan-Yurt, as he pointed at the huge black plumes of oil and smoke shooting into the sky above his city. "I have seen everything in Grozny I want to see. They can never bring peace to a place like this."

Lessons Learned

BY MICHAEL SPECTER

Who could sum up the lessons available to someone stupid enough to take a long walk on a hot day into a hellish battle zone? My first instinct is to say, "Don't try this; life is too short." My second instinct would be to rush right out and do it again.

And I would. In general, I'm not the war correspondent type. But there is a simple—if ugly—reason that this type of story becomes so compelling. People at their best—and worst—are incredibly interesting to write about. They are also easy to write about. When you see an entire family fleeing its hometown for the fourth time in a year, you cannot help but be moved by the agony and senselessness of it.

That day we walked along an old passageway into the city. I was with two British journalists, and we were amazed by the mass of humanity fleeing. It was surreal—a little like a war film—with helicopters hovering overhead and tanks shooting off the occasional round. There were snipers in the city, and we didn't know where. Nobody every taught me how to avoid being shot; it's something you pick up as you go along, unfortunately.

My own take on writing this type of story is that the little details—Who is wearing what? Is the girl carrying her teddy bear or a kalashnikov? Is there water? Are people in tears defiant or resigned?—those are the things that make this type of story work. Everyone is going to see mass destruction on television. Bombs are scary, but I don't think newspapers are the best place to make that clear.

What we can do, as writers, with stories like this one, is look at how a battle rips apart lives, and to do that I think it's easiest to start with the simplest things. I was amazed to see mail boxes standing—no houses, no roads, certainly no phones—but mail boxes. I opened a couple. Yep, mail. When I got to one of the Chechen leader's positions, I saw young soldiers in his brigade playing soccer, then I saw old women trying on boots in the central market.

I hate to be boring, but if I learned anything that day, it was to keep my eyes open for those mundane events that form daily life. There may be places where less embellishment was needed than in Grozny last year, but I certainly have never seen them. And come to think of it, I hope I never do.

Reporting with kick, writing with punch

BY KAREN F. BROWN

Years ago, when my sons began to outgrow me, I decided to join them in learning karate. I learned to *rei*, bowing low to the *sensei*. I practiced punches and kicks, earned a few belts, and got over my fear of dogs.

Lately the voice of my *sensei* has returned to me as I read newspaper stories or listen to news reports. I hear his teaching, but applied to powerful newswriting. Here's what I hear:

Some news stories don't have a target. They are full of good information but leave readers or viewers wondering about the point. Many stories find the target but don't hit with power. The information is there, but not in a way that causes readers to think, talk, or move to action.

The best journalists know a better way. Their stories offer lessons in writing with more kick and more powerful punches. Here are six principles of karate writing:

SEE THE WHOLE

Stance is important for a martial artist. Not only must the combatant be balanced and positioned to attack in any direction, the fighter must be able to see the whole of the opponent. Stand too close, and you miss the attack coming from the side. Stand too far back, and your attack will not reach effectively.

Too often journalists are too close to subjects: to politicians, public figures, or the heartbroken. Or they are too distant, reporting by phone from windowless offices. They are so far away they can't see enough of the story to compel others to read.

Rick Bragg of *The New York Times* is always looking for the perfect distance. Instead of saying "She spent almost nothing," or "She is a Bible reader," Bragg describes a woman who binds her "ragged Bible with Scotch tape to keep Corinthians from falling out."

PRACTICE THE KATAS

It's funny about martial artists. They prepare for any test by practicing the same *katas,* day after day. A *kata* is a dance-like series of moves designed to prepare one for fighting multiple enemies. It doesn't take long to learn, but a true martial artist will practice *katas* for a lifetime.

The martial artist thinks: Is my fist tight; is my block aligned correctly with my body; are my knees bent; as I punch, am I relaxed? The idea is to keep perfecting each move, because in real combat a properly executed move could mean the difference between life and death.

Writers at *The Miami Herald* often hear the voice of their *sensei,* Gene Miller, as they prepare to write. Miller offers advice such as, "Get as much detail as you can possibly get.... You may not need it, but get it in your notebook. And don't just tell them it's ice cream; tell them what flavor of ice cream."

Part of the journalistic *kata* is to learn from teachers, editors, and writers and to regularly practice key lessons. Part of the job of editors and coaches is to constantly present a few key messages that will speak to writers when they need them.

GET IN, GET TO THE HEART, AND GET OUT

The traditional stance in fighting was for two opponents to stand in fixed positions, facing each other, and exchange punches. That doesn't work any more in any form of combat. A fighter needs to get close to an opponent, deliver a well-aimed blow, and move away.

Journalists, too, must make an impact with their writing and get out. Here are three moves:

- Find the appropriate hook.
- Tell the reader where you're going.
- Make your point and get out.

VARY THE ATTACK

Imagine that you have one of the great front punches of our time. Your form is perfect, you strike with power, your punch is respected by opponents. Now imagine that is your *only* weapon. You have two problems. First, you are predictable, which means you're not only vulnerable, but also boring. Second, you are ill-equipped for situations that require something other than a front punch.

You could vary your attack to something more dramatic, say some kicks. But that requires greater skill: You must be able to balance on one leg, pull your toes back, and strike with the ball of the foot. It also puts you at greater risk. For instance, the spinning kick, seen in movies, looks good, but most sane martial artists wouldn't use it. It requires you to be in the air with your back to an opponent; the risk isn't worth the possible impact.

Journalists face similar dilemmas. Many stick with a safe, solid, predictable, and boring style of writing regardless of the story. Some go for dramatic risks that aren't worth the likely impact.

REMEMBER THE LAST-SECOND SNAP

The natural approach to a punch is to throw the fist out, palm down. The approach in Wado-Ryu karate is to launch the fist with the palm up, then quickly turn it over just before it lands. The snap adds power.

Many news stories run out of energy near the end. Trained in the inverted pyramid and rushed to make a deadline, many writers put all the good stuff near the top and string together everything else to the end. They don't really have a kicker, just a swamp of information that readers can barely wade through.

Reporters need to see the end from the beginning. A powerful ending won't come from the story's leftovers. Writers need to plan stories, saving a special snap for the end.

KEEP STRONG IN COURAGE

I expected to practice endless repetitions of punches and kicks when I took karate. I expected a new vocabulary and new skills. I hadn't counted on sparring. More specifically, I wasn't prepared to be repeatedly punched in the face while *Sensei* hollered, "Open your eyes. Keep your eyes open."

For me, sparring required courage.

Courage means different things to journalists. About 100 years ago the courage to speak out against lynching cost Ida B. Wells her newspaper and nearly her life. A Memphis mob, following the advice of another newspaper, came after her. She had fled to New York, so they settled for burning down her newspaper office.

Today, courage might mean going to a neighborhood considered unsafe. It might mean taking on tough interviews of important people. It might mean writing in ways that challenge the traditions and cynicism of a newsroom. Like karate, powerful writing requires skills, but ultimately it requires commitment and courage.

Newsday
Team Deadline Reporting

When a jetliner bound for Paris exploded and crashed over the Atlantic Ocean off Long Island, most *Newsday* staffers had already left the office. In a fortunate irony, a large crowd of reporters and editors had gathered in a Queens restaurant for a reunion to commemorate the closing a year earlier of *New York Newsday*.

At the restaurant, Miriam Pawel, an assistant managing editor for Long Island news, parceled out assignments. "Within an hour and a half, there were reporters on boats, at makeshift morgues, at the command center, and at the airports," *Newsday* editor Anthony Marro said. "Librarians got out of bed, and photographers came back from vacation." Back in the newsroom, the night staff scrambled to get the story into the last edition. Ultimately, the presses were stopped and the paper produced an extra edition. By Friday morning, less than 36 hours after the plane fell from the sky, the newspaper produced a 24-page special section. For its coverage of the explosion of TWA Flight 800, *Newsday* also won the Pulitzer Prize for best local reporting of breaking news.

Nearly a year later, the crash of TWA Flight 800 remains a puzzle. While frustrating to investigators and families of survivors, the lingering mystery testifies to the integrity of the paper's coverage. Resisting the impulse to rush to judgment, the paper combined saturation reporting with critical analysis. The result was competitive coverage that touched all the bases but didn't overreach for unwarranted conclusions.

—Christopher Scanlan

Some of the *Newsday* reporters who won the 1997 Jesse Laventhol Prize for Team Deadline Reporting are pictured with some of the staff who also worked on the winning stories. Those in the picture, listed alphabetically, are: Michael Arena, Al Baker, Deborah Barfield, Bill Bleyer, Rita Ciolli, Matthew Cox, Carol Eisenberg, Martin C. Evans, Ken Fireman, Mitchell Freedman, Craig Gordon, Katti Gray, Isaac Gúzman, Joe Haberstroh, Carol Hernandez, Adam Z. Horvath, John Jeansonne, Glenn Kessler, Robert E. Kessler, Chau Lam, Jerry Markon, Alex Martin, Matthew McAllester, Phil Mintz, Geoffrey Mohan, Elizabeth Moore, Samson Mulugeta, Soraya Sarhaddi Nelson, Ching-Ching Ni, Miriam Pawel, Liam Pleven, Sidney C. Schaer, Paul Schreiber, Andrew Smith, Stuart Vincent, Beth Whitehouse, and Olivia Winslow. Others who worked on the stories but do not appear in the picture include: Sylvia Adcock, Emi Endo, Ford Fessenden, Tom Incantalupo, Jessica Kowal, Earl Lane, Ken Moritsugu, Shirley E. Perlman, Jordan Rau, Knut Royce, Gaylord Shaw, Michael Slackman, Patrick J. Sloyan, Lauren Terrazzano, James Toedtman, Robin Topping, Alan J. Wax, Steve Wick, Paul Vitello, Ellen Yan, and Steve Zipay.

Tragedy on Flight 800: 229 perish in jet crash

JULY 18, 1996

A TWA jetliner bound for Paris with 229 people aboard exploded in midair last night just after taking off from Kennedy Airport and plunged into the Atlantic Ocean south of Moriches Inlet, and the Coast Guard said no survivors had been found.

Trans World Airlines Flight 800 had climbed to approximately 13,800 feet when federal aviation officials lost radar contact with the Boeing 747-100 about 8:45 p.m., just as witnesses on the South Shore reported seeing a bright fireball light up the darkening sky.

"I looked at the bay and saw a reflection on the water, then I looked up and I saw a big orange fireball falling into the ocean," said Robert Siriani, who was outside his parents' home in Mastic Beach. "I'd say it was one hundred feet wide and a couple of hundred feet long, the whole thing was flames, the flames were so bright I didn't see anything else."

The flaming wreckage then plummeted into the dark waters about 9½ miles south of the Suffolk shore, triggering a massive search over five square miles of debris in the open ocean.

"Bodies are being recovered. There are no signs of survivors at all," said Chief Petty Officer John Chindblom of the Coast Guard office in Moriches. Professional and volunteer rescuers found mostly body parts strewn among the torn seat cushions and mangled metal.

At the Coast Guard base in East Moriches, rescue workers—armed with latex gloves and body bags—began bringing in the bodies of the dead. A police official said that a boat with about 20 bodies sat outside the inlet, which was too narrow for it to enter. Workers transferred the bodies—many of which were burned and not whole—into smaller boats, which brought the dead to the shore.

At Kennedy Airport, frantic family members were scrambling for information and searching for solace. Jose Fermin of Brooklyn was running around, trying to find out if there was any chance his brother, Alberto, might be alive. "My mother wanted to come with me," he said. "She's crying and crying."

Alberto Fermin of Manhattan had been working two jobs, saving money for his long-dreamed-of vacation to France as a 28th birthday present to himself. "I didn't see him very often because he was working almost seven days a week," said his sister, Maria, while waiting for news at her mother's Brooklyn home. "He had been saving money for this vacation."

The cause of the crash was still not known last night, and officials cautioned against jumping to conclusions. Speculation focused on the possibility of a terrorist attack two days before the opening of the Olympic Games in Atlanta.

A top Clinton administration official said late last night that no warnings were received from any group, and there is no evidence at this point that the attack was from a terrorist bomb. But James Kallstrom of the Federal Bureau of Investigation's New York office announced at 1:25 a.m. that the bureau is taking over the investigation under the aegis of its joint terrorism task force with the New York Police Department.

Sources familiar with the investigation said agents are poring over the passenger manifest to see if there were any suspicious people or potential terrorist targets on the plane, and questioning pilots who were flying nearby at the time. In addition, agents were contacting informants—"everybody we know"—around the world to see if they have any information on threats against TWA or U.S. citizens.

In addition, U.S. Transportation Secretary Frederico Peña and FAA Administrator David Hinson are expected to arrive at Long Island-MacArthur Airport in Islip this morning at 7 to help with the investigation. And the federal Bureau of Alcohol, Tobacco and Firearms, which has expertise in explosives, was sending agents to help in the investigation, said John Pitta, the head of the ATF Long Island office.

Officials with the Federal Aviation Administration said the plane had arrived in New York from Athens as Flight 881 about three hours before it left for Paris. The plane was a 747-100, which has been flying since the 1970s and is the oldest series of the model flying, according to officials.

TWA said the plane was bound for Charles de Gaulle Airport outside Paris with 212 passengers, 14 flight attendants and three pilots. The passengers included some who had been scheduled to leave for Rome on an earlier flight that had been canceled.

Avrohom Hakeller of Crown Heights, Brooklyn, came to Kennedy Airport because his friend, Joseph Cohen, was on the flight.

"I was driving in the car and then over the radio I heard the news," Hakeller said. "My reaction when they said the flight number was that I was just shocked."

Cohen, 29, of Flatbush, was a science student who was traveling to Paris on vacation until September, Hakeller said.

Kennedy officials brought the families of relatives on a bus into the Ambassador Club in Terminal 5 to talk to TWA officials and chaplains.

James Devine, the Kennedy airport chaplain, said the airline was putting the families at a hotel overnight but was not able to tell them whether their friends and relatives were on board. "They haven't told them anything as yet," he said shortly after midnight.

Rabbi Alvin Poplack, the Jewish chaplain at the airport, said, "Some were in really bad shape, but others were hopeful. You can imagine what kind of questions they're asking."

Robert Wingate, spokesman for the American Red Cross, said the agency has mental health counselors coming in from around the country. Some were already talking to the 40 to 50 family members at the terminal last night and early this morning.

Information available to families and friends in France, where the flight was due to arrive at 8:15 a.m. local time, was sketchy. But the airline later set up an information center at the French airport, north of Paris.

The extensive search began immediately after the first reports of the explosion. State Air National Guard aircraft on maneuvers off of Moriches Inlet spotted the explosion, and the Coast Guard immediately launched a search that grew to 40 to 50 boats, including some pleasure craft, as well as six helicopters.

Other agencies also responded, including a New York City Police Department helicopter and the Air National Guard. About six Suffolk County Police boats were also searching the area. Coast Guard Lt. John Heller just after midnight said that four other large cutters that had been on fisheries patrol off New England were en route along with additional small patrol boats from the Long Island stations.

"We've recovered bodies and debris but not survivors," Heller said. He said crews of the helicopters were using night-vision goggles to help spot bodies or debris. "The winds and visibility are good for a search," Heller said.

In East Moriches, the hundreds of tense rescuers began turning their attention to finding enough refrigerated trucks to hold the mounting number of corpses.

The initial morgue was set up in East Moriches but was scheduled to be moved to Hangar B at the Air National Guard base in Westhampton. Coast Guard officials said that any survivor in the water could last more than 12 hours before hypothermia would set in.

"Whatever this explosion was, the debris was what you would pick up with a sink strainer," said Capt. Chris Baur, a helicopter pilot with the Air National Guard's 106th Rescue Wing in Westhampton who was on a training mission, saw the explosion directly in front of him and was the first rescue person to arrive.

Heller said a C-130 patrol plane would join the search at first light. The Coast Guard had set up security zones to keep unofficial aircraft and vessels away from the search area.

Suffolk officials sent deputy sheriffs, town and village police and military personnel in 30 to 40 four-wheel-drive vehicles intended to patrol the beach near the crash site today to discourage sightseers and to watch for bodies. Suffolk also sent flood maps to the command center so workers can figure where the tides are most likely to wash bodies up.

"Everything is part of a potential crime scene," said Suffolk County Executive Robert Gaffney. "I'd hate to think that anyone might pick up a piece of evidence."

National, state and local officials responded with reassurances of an ongoing search. "The president was informed about the reports we were getting shortly before 10 p.m.," White House spokesman Mike McCurry said. "He is deeply concerned."

State officials said the State Police and the state
Emergency Management Office had also been acti-
vated to respond to the crash and Gov. George Pataki,
who was in New York City yesterday, was staying in
touch with emergency officials and would be going to
the scene today.

New York City Mayor Rudolph Giuliani said, "The
mood at the rescue site is very serious and very somber. They have recovered bodies and they are bringing
them back to shore."

The explosion startled many onlookers, who were
unsure what to make of the small flash of light, followed by a large explosion and then a trail of flame
plunging to the sea. But a former National Transportation Safety Board official said the sequence may not
be meaningful.

The official, Ira Furman, said the fireball cited by
witnesses could just be an engine flameout that followed another problem—"a symptom, not a cause."
Such an explosion could also have ignited the aircraft's fuel but would still give no clue to the initial
problem with the airplane.

Of a bomb or mid-air collision, he said, "I don't believe either is the first thing to come to mind."

'A huge ball of flame, it was unbelievable'

JULY 18, 1996

By Craig Gordon

As a languid summer day gave way to night, witnesses turned their eyes upward—from fishing boats, surfboards bobbing in the waves, even other planes in the sky—to watch a disaster play out before them.

At first, there was a slow-motion quality to the descent of TWA Flight 800, a number of witnesses said—just a spot of brightness out over an ocean horizon, a light that some said looked like a flare from a distant boat.

In a horrible instant, though, that curious flicker exploded into a mass of flame that lit up the sky and sent a streamer of fire toward the ocean below.

"It was such a huge ball of flame, it was unbelievable. I've never seen anything like it," said Lake Grove resident Tom Erikson, who was at Smith Point State Park with several friends.

"It went down like a long tube of flames," said Erikson, one of the many startled witnesses who saw the explosion from the shore. "It looked like fireworks falling back to Earth."

Capt. Chris Baur, a helicopter pilot with the New York Air National Guard in Westhampton Beach, was flying a routine training flight when he saw the explosion and flame.

Dipping as close as 20 feet above the water, he and his crew saw two bodies. Soon they saw more, 50 to 60 in all, some in clusters, some by themselves. None had life jackets, he said.

Three men were surfing in the waters off Smith Point Park, scanning the horizon for the next big wave, when David Mueller's eye latched on to the glowing spot.

"I just saw this tiny little ball falling," said Mueller, who lives in Coram. "That fell for a couple of seconds, then all of a sudden it just exploded into a huge fiery ball, and then it hit the ocean."

Added his brother, Steve: "This thing turned from a little fiery ball in the sky to this humongous explosion. We knew it was an airplane, because it was just too big to be anything else."

For the three, even the noise had a delayed-reaction quality to it—about 20 seconds later, they heard a sound like the clap of distant thunder.

Distance at first also minimized the impact of what some witnesses now realize they were watching. "It definitely didn't look as big as it was from where we were. It seemed like it might be a small plane," said Chris Conley, a bartender at John Scott's Raw Bar in Westhampton Beach who was sitting on a deck outside the restaurant when the plane went down.

Conley and his 10 friends then ran across the beach to get a closer look. "All we could see was a puff of smoke, no flames or anything," he said. Farther east, people in homes on Dune Road in Westhampton Beach said they felt what they believe was an explosion from the plane's destruction. "It felt like someone dropped something on top of the house," said Christine Sildar.

Frank Sessa was miles away in Wading River, closing his store, and to him, the flash was the size of a dime. "That plane was up there for a long time, 10 or 15 seconds after the flash. I was a good 30 miles away and I saw it. It was a big bright flashing light."

And some witnesses reported seeing the fireball as far away as Connecticut.

Vic Fehner's first thought also was of a small plane. "It was just kind of hanging, coming down very slow," Fehner said. "Then it burst into a tremendous amount of flame."

For witnesses, the moment of recognition—when they realized it wasn't just a flare but far worse—was frightening.

"Was I scared?" said Steve Mueller. "I don't know what I felt, it was just, I don't know, I'm speechless. My heart was pounding, I can tell you that."

Stuart Vincent, Jerry Markon, Liam Pleven, and Molly McCarthy contributed to this story.

How '90 crash compares

JULY 18, 1996

By Robin Topping

While last night's plane crash was Long Island's second major air disaster—coming six years after the 1990 Avianca crash in Cove Neck—there are major differences in how the tragedies took place and how emergency services responded.

Last night's crash of a TWA 747 taking off from Kennedy Airport occurred apparently from a higher altitude than the Avianca flight, after what witnesses said was a fiery explosion. Also, the TWA jetliner fell into the ocean south of Moriches Inlet.

There were no immediate reports of survivors, and the freshly fueled plane erupted into flames when it went down at about 8:40 p.m. The emergency response was made easier because the weather was clear, allowing for a good view of the scene.

The Avianca flight crashed at 9:34 p.m. on a foggy winter night and the aircraft plunged from a low altitude as it ran out of fuel and crashed, ending up in a tiny Cove Neck enclave, where there was just one road leading to the rescue area. Of the 158 passengers and crew aboard, 73 died in the crash or soon after and 82 were seriously injured, with three receiving minor injuries.

Because there was little or no fuel left, there was no smoke or fire surrounding the Avianca crash, said Dr. Joseph Greensher, chairman of the Nassau Emergency Medical Services Committee. "That's why we had so many survivors," Greensher said last night from his home.

Greensher said that in 1990 the biggest challenge to those responding to the Avianca disaster was setting up a triage area for survivors, treating them and getting them to area trauma centers.

"In this [yesterday's] case, there appears to have been an inferno and anyone who was in the middle of it had very little chance because all the oxygen is being consumed by the fire...it makes it very difficult to survive," Greensher said.

"With Avianca, the plane came in at a low altitude, there was no explosion, there were large pieces of the plane intact and there was no smoke or fire.... [Yesterday's crash] appears to be some kind of a midair explosion," Greensher said.

The emergency response to the crash scenes were also different. In 1990, the scene was overwhelmed by emergency vehicles, and later it was determined that the combination of an over-response and very limited access may have contributed to delays in transporting victims.

Last night, as of 11:30 p.m., Nassau Fire and Rescue Coordinator Peter Meade said that since neither Coast Guard nor federal air officials had requested assistance from the county, emergency crews were standing by but not responding.

"If we haven't been called, we're staying home," said Meade, who helped run the response to the Avianca crash. "We're not going to do what was done to us six years ago," he said.

Meade said the biggest challenge for emergency officials at the scene would be recovering and identifying bodies. "The biggest job will be the recovery and then establishing a family care center for the relatives," he said. "They have a very big job ahead."

Because the disaster occurred on water, the U.S. Coast Guard is in charge of the operation, along with any federal officials.

Boaters brave dark sea

JULY 18, 1996

By Martin C. Evans and Steve Wick

Following the traditions that bind together those who work the sea, scores of volunteer boaters headed out in their crafts yesterday, braving darkness and the flames of burning jet fuel in a futile search for survivors.

The flat, black sea looked like a floating city of lights near the downed plane, as small craft mingled with Coast Guard cutters during the search, and helicopters churned overhead.

"There are so many bodies. There are so many bodies," one boater was overheard saying on a marine radio frequency.

Pete Scopinich of Hampton Bays piloted a fishing trawler within 100 yards of the flames, where a wing section floated on the surface.

"Oh my God, I've never seen anything like this in my life," he said. "This is unbelievable."

A rescue helicopter hovered above a partially submerged life raft, searching for signs of life.

"I'm going down lower to see if there is anything under it," the pilot was overheard saying on radio. Other rescuers radioed for extra body bags and plastic gloves.

Lt. Kevin Dunn, the U.S. Coast Guard officer in charge of the scene, said about 40 to 50 vessels were searching for survivors, including pleasure craft who had volunteered to help. "We've got vessels of every type," he said.

Flames were still shooting 10 feet in the air more than four hours after the crash, fed by a fuel slick that stretched more than 50 yards wide and 100 yards long. Fumes from the flames added to a low fog.

The inky sea, lighted to an eerie glow by the burning fuel, was littered with debris from the downed aircraft. In a swath that went for miles, shredded seat cushions and other items bobbed in the waves.

Light from the flames actually helped rescuers in their grim search. Helicopters also dropped flares that illuminated the water surface.

Dunn said officials would not begin collecting wreckage or diving for bodies until today. He said Coast Guard helicopters had dropped data buoys in the water so that a computer search area could be set up based on the tides and currents. Shortly after 2 a.m., Suffolk officials urged the private boats to leave the area, after reports that some were plucking pieces of wreckage—and even body parts—from the crash scene.

Ralph Lettieri, a firefighter from Hagerman, said he responded to a Coast Guard appeal for help, riding in his small boat for more than an hour across the placid bay.

"If anyone survived, it's a miracle," he said. "You couldn't tell it was a plane."

Just after 9 p.m., Bryan Kerns, who lives on Tuthill Point Road across from the Moriches Inlet, sailed out in his 19-foot boat to what he estimated was about eight miles from the reported crash scene. In the darkness, he said he saw burning debris spread over about 1,000 feet on the water, while scores of other boats, including Coast Guard vessels, headed in the direction of the scene. "The boat traffic was incredible," said Kerns, a 29-year-old car salesman. "Spotlights were everywhere."

But with his small craft, Kerns figured he would interfere more than help. "If we were in a better position to help...then we would have done anything we could," he said. "We were hoping that we would be able to help."

The crew of about six people, including neighbors and friends, spent about a half hour on the water before heading back.

"At this stage of the game, we weren't going to trek eight miles out [to sea]," Kerns said. "We didn't feel we could help. There wasn't much more we could do.

"It's a horrible thing."

Deborah Barfield and Mitchell Freedman contributed to this story.

Probers focus on possibility of bomb or missile; toll at 230

JULY 19, 1996

The swiftness of the jumbo jet's mid-air destruction, the broad swath of the Atlantic Ocean littered by debris and the absence of any emergency call for help has led investigators to focus on the possibility that TWA Flight 800 was knocked from the sky by terrorists.

Even as they cautioned against premature conclusions, federal, state and local investigators were exploring every scenario from whether a bomb exploded in the plane to whether a missile fired from the ground picked it from the air. If confirmed, it would be the deadliest terrorist attack in American territory ever.

But the prospect of a catastrophic mechanical failure also remained. Evidence culled from the gruesome retrieval of more than 100 bodies and wreckage from the waters off the South Shore also puzzled investigators because initial inspections turned up no telltale signs of shrapnel or powder.

All that was clear was that all 230 people on board the Boeing 747 bound for Paris perished in the explosion or by drowning in the water below, spreading grief among friends and family across at least two continents.

"It's just a senseless waste of two people," said Richard Hammer of Long Beach, whose wife, Beverly, 59, and daughter, Tracy Anne, 29, were on the flight. "You can't make sense out of it. You take two people at the top of their game and literally wipe them out. I'm stunned."

Stunned too were officials at all levels of government. For part of the day, the National Transportation Safety Board and the Federal Bureau of Investigation struggled for control of the case, and New York City Mayor Rudolph Giuliani wrangled with TWA officials. Gov. George Pataki flew over the crash site and later hugged victims' families, then said, "It's the worst thing I've ever seen."

On a placid summer sea, meanwhile, a small navy of boats dispatched by federal and local authorities continued throughout the day and into the night the grisly task of filtering the wreckage and human remains still floating in the water.

As debris drifted slowly east with the current, divers had to pick through everything from a red TWA flight bag to a child's purple backpack emblazoned with Barney the Dinosaur. Investigators were using radio waves to seek the plane's "black box," which could indicate if an explosion ignited the fireball.

The Coast Guard was able to recover plane debris ranging from hundreds of small parts to a 30-foot piece of the wing, which could prove critical, officials and aviation experts said, because the markings on the metal could confirm whether the plane was blown up, and if so, with what type of bomb.

The pieces were being brought to the former Grumman facility in Calverton for examination. Experts who helped collect evidence after a ValuJet plane went down in the Everglades May 11 and after a Pan Am flight was blown up over Lockerbie, Scotland, in December 1988, were brought in to help with the search.

Government officials, both civil and criminal, said they were seriously examining the possibility that a missile struck the plane, because of an apparent blip on the screen before the explosion. The blip, if not a meaningless shadow, could conform to what some investigators said were accounts of a flash rising from the surface before the blast.

But electronic clutter on the tapes is making a determination difficult, the officials said. And the plane was believed to be outside the range of most shoulder-launched missiles. As one intelligence official said, "We can't rule anything out at this point. But the missile wouldn't be all the way up there on the probability list."

White House press secretary Mike McCurry said investigators were "trying to clarify any abnormalities" that turned up on radar screens. Asked about speculation on a missile, McCurry replied, "There's no American official with half a brain who ought to be speculating on anything of that nature. There's no concrete information that would lead any of us in the United States government to draw that kind of conclusion."

Officials were also quick to caution that the circum-
stantial evidence of an attack does not rule out a mechanical failure. In both 1991 and 1992, an early
model 747 jet had crashed shortly after take-off when
an in-board engine fell off the plane and then tore off
the outboard engine on the same wing.

"I wouldn't be surprised if it turns out this has been
a horrible accident," one source familiar with the investigation at the site said. But sources conceded that
they may not have recovered those parts of the plane
or the bodies that could show blast damage.

In the absence of explanations, theories abounded.
One focused on a fax sent Wednesday to an Arabic
language newspaper in Beirut warning of an attack.
State Department and CIA officials confirmed they
had received copies of the fax yesterday.

The message said "tomorrow morning we will
strike the Americans in a way they do not expect and
it will be very surprising to them," according to one
official. A counterterrorism source familiar with the
fax said that it was sent at 11 a.m. New York time
Wednesday, more than nine hours before the bombing.
But a CIA source said that the agency "does not attach
too much significance" to the fax.

Another key sign that investigators were looking at
yesterday was whether the metal in the wreckage was
twisted outward, which would suggest an explosion
like one caused by a bomb from inside the plane, or
twisted inward, which might suggest that an engine or
a missile had exploded outside.

"If there was an explosion, there will be very specific, telltale signs by the way it explodes, the damage
to the airplane, and the residue left," said Dick Stone,
who heads the Virginia-based International Society of
Air Safety Investigators.

Recovering bodies also remained a top priority. By
last night, remains of 140 of the 230 people TWA officials said were on the flight had been fished from the
water. The bodies were placed on Coast Guard cutters
whose decks were stained with blood, then brought by
smaller boats to a makeshift morgue at the command
center in East Moriches.

The remains were often badly burned and mangled
beyond recognition. One was just a charred torso with

no arms, legs or head, another's clothes and hair were burned off, and a third was a woman still wearing a black dress and a gold necklace.

"I was telling the guys these aren't people anymore, they're just bodies. The people are gone," said John Rich, 28, a Coast Guard petty officer. "Some of the guys out here are pretty young, 19 or 20 years old, and they've never seen anything like this. I told them to just mentally block it out. They handled it pretty well. But I'm sure when it's all over, that's when it's really going to hit them."

When the bodies first arrived at the morgue, investigators opened each body bag only long enough to take photographs and note identifying characteristics or jewelry before they were moved to refrigerated trucks.

Officials said X-rays will be taken of each body to search for shrapnel or other evidence of a bomb. "We're looking for things like that, missiles or projectiles that are embedded in a body," said Dr. Charles V. Wetli, the chief medical examiner for Suffolk County.

But Wetli said the first 20 autopsies turned up no evidence of any kind of explosive, nor any powder residue. Some of the victims had drowned, he added, though they were believed to be unconscious when they hit the water.

Yet many more corpses still remained in the ocean late yesterday, and divers and emergency workers on the boats described the search in waters 120 feet deep and about 10 miles from shore as gut-wrenching.

"It's a grim task," said Raymond Tremer, a diver with the New York City Fire Department team at the scene. "We aren't sure what we are going to find. We suspect that the passengers are seat-belted into the fuselage. It's a difficult situation because you have to enter the fuselage. There are cable and wires there."

By evening, there were also scattered reports that sharks might be in the area, and the search is likely to get harder still as clear skies are replaced by thunderstorms and showers today.

For the families awaiting what seemed almost inevitably negative news yesterday, the day was worse still. After a restless night during which top TWA officials were hard to find at Kennedy, the families sought news at daybreak.

But for hours, TWA refused to release the full list of people on the plane. The airline revised the number of people said to be on the plane twice during the day before settling on the figure of 230, including 212 passengers, 14 flight attendants and four crew members in the cockpit.

Mark Abels, a TWA spokesman, said the airline wanted to notify all the families before releasing the list. But even after relatives gathered at the Ramada Inn near Kennedy yesterday afternoon, no list was released, and Giuliani engaged in a nose-to-nose shouting match with one TWA official about the delay.

Frank Capozza, a New Jersey man waiting at Kennedy who had put an 11-year-old French exchange student on the plane Wednesday night, erupted at the wait. Capozza, who wanted someone to call the child's parents in France, walked over to another TWA employee standing nearby and said, "This is wholly out of control. Don't you have a system? You have people here that don't know anything. Talk about a low-rent airline."

Although TWA released the list at 8:24 p.m., the clash raised anew questions over whether airlines—which face liability and public relations threats after an air disaster—are equipped to deal with families after plane crashes or whether government entities should assume control. But TWA officials defended their handling of the incident.

"Like...[Giuliani], we regret that the notification process took so long," said Abels.

During the day, most family members and friends at Kennedy and elsewhere were more subdued. Many concluded that almost everybody expected to be on the flight—people such as Eric and Virginia Holst of Manorville, who were headed to a family wedding in France, and Jacques and Connie Charbonnier, married flight attendants happy to work the same flight—must have perished.

And TWA did release the names of the cockpit crew early in the day, including that of Capt. Steven Snyder, 57, of Stratford, Conn., who had been with TWA since 1964.

Friends said Snyder was a "master pilot" who had just paid for a complete overhaul of his own single-engine Cessna.

"He called it his pet," said Stanley Logan, a fellow small-plane flier. "He got more of a kick out of the little one than the big one."

A small number of families unexpectedly heard good news yesterday. On Wednesday night, Jose Fermin was running frantically through Kennedy, saying that his mother was "crying and crying" because his brother, Alberto, of Brooklyn, was booked on Flight 800, headed for a French vacation. Yesterday, however, the Fermins were euphoric after learning Alberto had taken a Tower Air flight to Paris instead.

Eileen Remce of Appleton, Wisc., was also marveling at her good fortune. Her connecting flight from Chicago had been delayed, and even though she arrived at Kennedy about 15 minutes before Flight 800 departed, officials refused to seat her.

"I guess I cheated the grim reaper," said Remce, who called her family, and told her younger daughter that she had missed the plane. But Remce nonetheless planned to get another TWA flight to Paris last night. "Is that stupid or what?" she said.

As the day wore on yesterday, officials and experts increasingly devoted attention to the possibility that the explosion on the plane was caused by a bomb.

The practical reason for arriving at that conclusion was the fact that Flight 800 disappeared from FAA screens suddenly and without warning, according to officials close to the case. Even in the ValuJet crash, the crew had time to transmit calls for emergency aid.

"Either something happened quickly, like the wing tore off and exploded—which has never happened—or a device went off...airplanes do not blow up suddenly in flight," said one official.

Many other explanations were dismissed by aviation experts. Weather was not a factor, because the skies were clear. As it climbed to about 13,800 feet, there were no mountains or other physical barriers the plane could have struck. And a collision with another plane would be unlikely, considering the sophisticated navigation equipment on planes.

Nor did the plane's crew indicate any problem to the three traffic control centers that handled the flight between the time it left the runway and it disappeared from the screens of controllers in Nashua, N.H. "When a controller sees [an airplane] disappear on the screen, you know either you have a radar problem or you have a disaster on your hands," said an FAA spokesman.

If terrorists did down Wednesday's flight, it would not be the first such attack on a plane within American territory, with previous episodes dating back to 1933, when seven people died after a bomb exploded on a plane in Palm Springs, Calif.

But if terrorists are responsible, they caused more deaths than any other such attack within U.S. territory. The terrorist act currently considered the nation's deadliest was last year's Oklahoma City blast, which killed 169.

In the morgue, somber tasks

JULY 19, 1996

By Sidney C. Schaer and Ellen Yan

There was a business-like grimness about the Suffolk Medical Examiner's Office yesterday, the kind that follows refrigerated trucks full of bodies.

With long-tested methods, including a borrowed digitized X-ray machine for quicker dental identifications and a line of pathologists autopsying plane passengers on stainless steel tables, forensic experts began the task of identifying the bodies and mutilated parts from Wednesday's fiery crash of TWA Flight 800.

"We have a large amount of what appears to be virtually heavy blunt force, some drownings and also postmortem burns," Dr. Charles Wetli, Suffolk's medical examiner, said between autopsies. "Once we see the injury pattern, we will have a better idea of the cause of the death. We look for certain patterns on how to develop an answer for what appears to be a large jigsaw puzzle."

Victims' fingers will be shriveled after hours in ocean water, making it harder to get good fingerprints. Their teeth, the most durable part of the body, may be blackened by fire, requiring dental experts to clean them before comparing them to records. Preliminary results indicate death for some was "close to instantaneous," Wetli said. He said he believed those who drowned were unconscious when they died.

Identifying the human remains of the TWA crash will in several ways be a much easier task than the recent ValuJet crash in Florida waters, forensic experts said. In Florida, the water temperature rose to about 100 degrees, speeding up decomposition, unlike the ocean off Suffolk's South Shore, which has been about 65 degrees. "If you recover most of the body parts, you can identify most of the bodies," Ray Blakemey, director of operations at the Oklahoma State Medical Examiner's Office, said in a telephone interview. The office identified each of the 168 dead victims in the 1995 Oklahoma City explosion.

Moreover, most of the 140 bodies recovered off Long Island by late yesterday afternoon have been largely intact.

Wetli and his team worked into the night yesterday, bringing in the bodies one by one from huge trucks backed up to the loading docks. First, each one is weighed. Then each is wheeled to the photo room, where cameras record the condition of the body. In an intelligence room, literally wallpapered with data and X-ray information, each body is numbered. The forensic experts keep trying to build up an intelligence record so they can make an exact identification. Finally, the body is placed onto a steel table, where an autopsy records in detail the characteristics of the person and the injuries. A full autopsy takes about two hours.

Forensic and criminal investigators have been trying to determine what caused the jet to explode.

"I believe the dead giveth us tales," William Maples, a forensic anthropologist who investigated the ValuJet crash, said from his office at the University of Florida. "If you don't ask, you don't get tales. Comparing the seating plan and what happened to that identified body, you can find out the exact placement of the explosive device or part and really reconstruct the events of those last few minutes."

Basic rules guide forensic experts in the chaos following disaster as their key tools become X-ray machines, fingerprints and comparisons of body part sizes with bodies.

After the Oklahoma City explosion, the Oklahoma state medical examiner set up stations in the morgue in a sort of assembly line compelled by the number of fatalities. Each focused on a different subject. One station collected the clothes, jewelry and personal items found with each body. At another station, specialists fingerprinted the remains, sometimes peeling off the skin to get good prints. Dental experts sat hunched at another station, using toothbrushes to clean dental remains.

But throughout it all, one person stood by each victim through all the stations. "That escort takes it from station to station," Blakemey said. "That way, you don't lose bodies and you don't lose paperwork."

The clues to a person's identity lie not just in the fingers but also in the teeth and tissue. Each set of fillings, gaps and tooth shapes helps experts make identifications. DNA tests are usually a last resort, when only "atomized" remains have been recovered. Those tests sometimes take up to two months.

But sometimes, teeth and DNA tests may be all but useless without data such as dental records for comparison. In the TWA plane, which was headed for Paris, some of the passengers may have been French nationals, making record collection harder.

"You get a bachelor who isn't in close contact with his family, and people just don't know he's getting on the plane to Paris," said forensic anthropologist Thomas Holland of the U.S. Army Central Identification Lab, whose job is to identify the remains of those killed in war or in military accidents. "I would be surprised if everybody is identified because there are going to be some people you don't have records on."

By yesterday afternoon, the Suffolk County pathologists had finished about 20 autopsies but had not made any definite identifications.

"With a bit of luck," Wetli said, "it will all be completed by the end of the weekend."

Private hopes, public deaths

JULY 19, 1996

Beverly Hammer was terrified of flying, but overcame her fear to join her daughter, Tracy Anne, on a "mother-daughter bonding trip" to Tours.

Jacques and Connie Charbonnier shared their lives as flight attendants and tried to work the New York-Paris route as often as possible.

Vera Feeney was taking her only child, Dierdre, with her on what she said would be the last of her annual pilgrimages to Ireland to visit her terminally ill mother. She planned a detour to Paris first.

Eric and Virginia Holst, married six years, were off to a family wedding.

And producer Jack O'Hara had a pink slip in hand, en route to covering the finale of the Tour de France bicycle race for the last time as an ABC Sports executive producer. O'Hara hated flying and traveled by car or train whenever possible. His wife, Jane, and daughter, Caitlin, took the flight with him.

They are names on the manifest of TWA Flight 800 to Paris, strangers who came together in the broad fuselage of a 747 arcing toward France, full of private thoughts, private hopes, all shattered by a wrenching public death.

At the departure gate in Kennedy, Beverly Hammer's eyes were bright with pride in having passed her stockbroker's exam little more than a week ago. The 59-year-old mother had visions of touring medieval castles while her daughter, Tracy Anne, a 29-year-old doctoral student at Michigan State University in East Lansing, was looking forward to presenting a veterinary-science paper in Tours.

"Everything was perfect," said an exhausted Richard Hammer, standing by the telephone in the living room of his Long Beach condominium and talking about the wife and daughter he lost in Wednesday night's fiery crash off Long Island's South Shore.

"The trip was in the planning stages for four months. It was planned right down to the last detail," said Hammer, an advertising sales consultant. "The ironic thing is, I said to Tracy, 'With my schedule being loose, maybe I can move something around and we could all do the trip together.' She said, 'But you're not invited, Dad. This is a mother-daughter thing.'"

Mother and daughter were high achievers, with restless intellects and voracious reading appetites. Tracy Anne had a lifelong love of horses and would have finished double doctorates in veterinary science and microbiology in May.

"She had tried to get her mother to fly several times," said Hammer. "Beverly had been terrified of flying her whole life. Not just scared, terrified."

When the Hammers went to their vacation home in Naples, Fla., they drove the 1,375 miles. When Richard Hammer won an all-expenses-paid trip to the Canary Islands, he took it in cash instead. When Beverly got her passport to accompany him on a business trip to Madrid five years ago, she balked at the last minute.

But Beverly got over her phobia with the persuasion of Tracy, whom Hammer described as a replica of the strong-willed TV character Murphy Brown.

Surely they would do fine by themselves in Paris, he thought as their departure time approached.

"We walked over to gate 27 where the plane was and they posted the new departure time, 7 p.m. I gave them a fistful of francs and a fistful of American Express travelers checks. Then Beverly said, 'You know, I'm really feeling good about this. I'm really going to sit back and relax.'

"I'll never forget it. Her eyes were just brilliant. She was all pumped up about this. I've never seen her so pumped up. She was really looking forward to this trip.

"Shortly after 6 p.m., I said, 'I'll leave you international travelers to bond.' I gave them a kiss and a hug and walked away."

A short time later, Richard Hammer called his son, Andrew, 27, in the Hamptons. Your mom and sister got off just fine, he told him. The telephone clicked. Call waiting. It was Beverly's mother from California. In a shaky voice, she asked what flight Beverly and Tracy Anne were on. Flight 800, he said. "Turn on the television," she said. "It crashed."

* * *

Jacques and Connie Charbonnier of Northport met as flight attendants 21 years ago, fell in love, and worked the New York-to-Paris route as often as five times a month, a former TWA attendant and friend recalled yesterday.

Their love was obvious to passengers and crew members, said Annbeth Reyman of Roslyn. "They almost only flew to Paris," she added. "That was their route, Flight 800."

Jacques, 65, who managed the cabin attendants, and Connie, 49, one of his crew, loved to work flights together—they met working on a flight 21 years ago, other friends said.

"They had what I would call an ideal relationship, they came from love. They were very positive, very passionate about life. They were the world to each other and it was evident in everything they did," said Reyman.

Connie also had another love: water-color painting, which she displayed at the Lamantia Gallery on Main Street in Northport. She was a frequent visitor; each month she'd offer something new she had painted for display, a stunned gallery staffer said yesterday.

* * *

Going to Ireland was an annual journey for Vera Feeney, 56, a home-care nurse from New Hyde Park. Her husband, John, who has worked in TWA's baggage department for 42 years, stopped accompanying his wife five years ago, when his parents died there.

But 17-year-old Dierdre Feeney, who graduated with honors from Kellenberg Memorial High School in Uniondale last month, gladly accompanied her mother.

Brian O'Hara, a friend, woke John Feeney with word of the crash late Wednesday.

"When he heard the news, he didn't want to talk to anybody," said O'Hara. "He got up and got dressed and went and sat in the living room. I sat with him and watched the news. We haven't discussed much."

* * *

Eric and Virginia Holst of Manorville were in their early 30s, married six years, and eager to attend the wedding of Eric's brother Troy in France.

Eric, 32, was a dentist, and proudly displayed his soft spot for children in a Yellow Pages ad for his dental partnership, Moriches Dental Associates: "We love children." Virginia, 31, ran a merchandise distribution business from their home at Hampton Vista Condominiums.

"They were just a wonderful loving, caring couple," said Vivian Kramer, a neighbor. "I lost my husband two years ago and there are just certain people who are there for you. And that's the way she was."

Luz Mari Pelaez, mother of Virginia Holst, said the couple were going to Paris for about 10 days.

By coincidence, Rosemary Everett, manager of an office next to Eric Holst's, was out on a boat with her husband near the site and saw the smoke. She didn't know it was a plane crash until she saw the 11 p.m. news. She didn't know it was a man she saw every day until yesterday morning.

"I thought, 'Oh, my God, this is a real person. One of those bodies they're talking about, this is a real person and you're never going to see him again.'"

* * *

As executive producer of ABC Sports, Jack O'Hara journeyed far and wide to supervise the network's telecasts of *Monday Night Football, Wide World of Sports,* the Kentucky Derby and college football games. But he made no attempt to disguise his dislike for air travel.

"You're on planes all the time in this business, but more than anyone else I know, he was fearful of flying," ABC Sports spokesman Mark Mandel said yesterday. "Jack went out of his way to drive or take a train whenever he could."

On Wednesday night, O'Hara, 39, boarded TWA Flight 800 en route to Paris to oversee the production of the final stage of the Tour de France for this weekend's *Wide World of Sports* show. His wife, Janet, and 14-year-old daughter, Caitlin, accompanied him. Their twin 12-year-old sons, Matthew and Brian, stayed in upstate Irvington in the care of Jack's parents.

The assignment was to be O'Hara's final one for the network after 14 years: he and Dennis Lewin, a senior vice president of ABC Sports for 30 years, were fired Tuesday by former ESPN President Steve Bornstein, who assumed control of ABC Sports in April.

"He and Janet had planned to take this trip for a while. He was combining it as business and a vacation," said Larry Kamm, a longtime friend and former ABC colleague who spoke with O'Hara by phone Wednesday.

"I had called to offer some support because I heard about the situation at ABC," Kamm said from Atlanta yesterday, where he is coordinating director for Turner Sports. "Jack was upbeat. He said, 'You know something, Larry? Janet and I are going to Paris. Twenty-four hours from now we're going to be sitting on a boulevard drinking a very expensive French wine.' He said we'd talk when they got back."

* * *

A combination of work and family obligations kept Brooklyn State Supreme Court Justice Michael Pesce off TWA Flight 800, but sadly his fiancée and her mother went ahead with their plans and were among those on the doomed flight, according to a friend.

"He delayed his departure for a week for a combination of work and family," said Tom McMahon, a friend of the judge. After Pesce heard television news reports about the explosion, McMahon said, the judge spent Wednesday night and yesterday trying to confirm whether his fiancée, Bonnie Wolters, 44, of Brooklyn, and her mother, Betty, were on the plane.

"We got official word from police department sources and New York State officials. How do you take something like this? He's in shock, very upset, [and] reflecting," said McMahon.

* * *

Luke Capozza, 14, tried to savor every last moment with Ludovic Chaunce, an 11-year-old French exchange student who was headed home on Flight 800. At the gate, a flight attendant had to separate the two, who had become fast friends during the past two years of summer exchanges.

"He invited me to stay with him next year," said Luke, of Mendham Township, N.J., who went with his father to the Ramada Inn at Kennedy Airport after the crash. "We were going to send mail back and forth. He shared any secret with me. We were like brothers. He was a real good friend."

Ludovic liked pistachio-flavored ice cream and American sports, Luke recalled. "He really liked baseball and basketball, and always said Michael Jordan was the best. He loved the Bulls."

* * *

Dan and Stephanie Gaetke, both 32, of Kansas City, Mo., were traveling to France with Stephanie's cousins, Brenna and Chrisha Siebert.

Married for about six years, the Gaetkes made good friends when they settled into their neighborhood three years ago, helping their neighbors by baby-sitting, watching pets and offering gardening advice.

"They were just the dearest neighbors you could hope to have," said Judy Spaar, who lived near the Gaetkes in Kansas City. Neighbors said Dan Gaetke taught art at an elementary school, and the couple ran a landscaping business called Earthworks.

"Their yard is like a park," Spaar said, describing the well-tended flowers and the Japanese goldfish pond with lily pads and fountains.

Another neighbor, Paula Sterner, said, "They were really excited about the trip—most excited about seeing the gardens and landscaping in France."

Sisters Chrisha Siebert, 28, and Brenna Siebert, 25, who were traveling with the Gaetkes, planned to hit Paris with brio. "They were going to tour as much of France as they could," said Lynn Peters, a close family friend.

Theater was the motivating force in Chrisha's life. A technical director for Rockhurst College in Kansas City, she designed the sets for their theater and musical productions for the past two years.

Brenna, an assistant at the West Side Veterinary Clinic in Jefferson City, recently bought a house in Holts Summit, Mo., where she lived with her two dogs.

* * *

Kyle and Amy Miller, of Andreas, Pa., were going to visit a friend Amy met as a college exchange student in France.

Although TWA officials had not confirmed that the Millers were aboard the flight by yesterday afternoon, "We're sure they were on it," said Todd Miller, Kyle's brother.

Kyle, 30, was the "family clown," Todd Miller said.

Amy, 29, "will be remembered as the exact opposite of him—very professional, very meticulous," he said. The couple, married five years, "complemented one another very well."

Kyle Miller, who enjoyed woodwork and fixing up old houses, worked in his family's hardware store as well as their plumbing and electrical business. Amy Miller was the secretary for the hardware store.

"We as family members have placed our faith and hope in Jesus Christ and know that Kyle and Amy are in his presence," Todd Miller read from a prepared statement yesterday. "We know God will see us through this tragedy."

* * *

Stevenson, Ala., is a close-knit town of just over 2,000 people, and the loss of five hit hard—Brenda Privette; her son, Thomas Weatherby; Michael Scott; his wife, Barbara; and their 13-year-old son, Joseph.

"The initial shock is beginning to wear off and the reality beginning to set in," said Bettye Jackson, city clerk in Stevenson. "In Stevenson everybody is related by either kinship or friendship. It's a close-knit town. Both Brenda Privette's family and Michael Scott's family have lived in the area for a number of years.

"But now for Michael Scott's elderly mother—her whole family is gone."

* * *

Luc Bossuyt, 52, the director of international technology in the medicines division for Bristol-Myers Squibb, was traveling on business.

Bossuyt, who has two adult sons, lived with his wife, Myriam, in Trumbull, Conn. His eldest son, Stephen, 27, of El Paso, Calif., was flying in to be with the family. His other son, Francis, 26, is studying rain forests in Peru, where officials with the pharmaceutical company were trying to contact him.

"It's dreadful," said Alison Olivieri, a family friend. "He traveled a lot but you never expect this. He traveled all over the world."

* * *

Flight attendant Paula Carven of Bel Air, Md., also traveled all over the world. On Wednesday, she was on Flight 800 as a passenger with her 9-year-old son, Jay.

"This was a special trip for her son," said Jean Gregonis, who lives across the street from the Bel Air home Carven shared with her son, mother, Ann Carven, and brother, Sean Carven.

Gregonis said Carven was traveling with her friend, another flight attendant, who was bringing her two children.

"I was shocked. She had a lot of friends here," said Gregonis, a neighbor who has known Carven for 16 years. "It's hard to believe, but it will sink in eventually. It's been a very trying day."

* * *

Tenafly, N.J., lost a resident in the Pan Am Flight 103 blown up over Lockerbie, Scotland, in 1988. Now it has lost two more to an air crash: Robert and Elizabeth Miller.

"My children told me when I got home that they were passengers," said neighbor Donna Sack, whose comments were punctuated with sobs. "They saw it on the news. I'm still in shock, I can't really relate to it personally. These are the first tears I've shed over it. We've been neighbors for 20 years."

The Millers have a daughter, Kristina, but Sack said she hadn't talked to her yet.

Elizabeth, known as Betty, was a teacher and Bob was active in local government, said Sack.

"We all have to rethink the values we hold and where we intend to travel. I went to London in February and was a block away when a bomb went off there. I didn't think about the reality of it until the next day when we saw the police lines."

Small town grieves 21 dead

JULY 19, 1996

By Ken Moritsugu

MONTOURSVILLE, Pa.—They knew them as the girl who spilled the fries in the car. Knew them as the boy who shot baskets and lighted the candles at church. Knew them as the girl who wrote poetry and played the piano.

In this small central Pennsylvania town they knew them all, knew them as the kids who sold them pizza or a hoagie or washed their cars to raise the money for a trip to France—a trip that ended in tragedy, when TWA Flight 800 exploded, taking the lives of 21 people from this tight-knit community.

"Everybody knows everybody," said Ron Paulhamus, a print shop owner.

And now everybody grieves. Sixteen dead high school students, five dead adults. Twenty-one dead friends.

"There will be very few people not affected by it," said Paulhamus, whose 16-year-old son, Ross, attends the local high school.

Ross's mother, Ginger, said her son is devastated. "These are kids he grew up with and he's known and pals around with everyday.... Everybody you know has either a friend or a family who's been affected."

Ginger and Ron Paulhamus attended a hastily called noontime prayer vigil with other community residents at Bethany Lutheran Church for members of the high school French club and their adult chaperones who boarded the fatal TWA flight to Paris Wednesday night for a 10-day trip during summer break. Some victims were high school athletes. Others, musicians. One was an acolyte at the Methodist church.

They left behind sisters and brothers, girlfriends, boyfriends and best friends.

The crash was like a knife through the heart of this central Pennsylvania community of about 5,000.

"I'm still shaking," Michelle Follmer, 19, told friends outside the high school late yesterday morning.

"Brock lost his girlfriend," Josh Lewis, 17, told her, speaking about a mutual friend.

Follmer already knew: "She was in my car Tuesday night. She spilled her fries all over my seat," Follmer said, forcing a laugh.

They were talking about Michelle Bohlin, 16, a swimmer who had just finished her sophomore year. They recalled how excited Michelle had been about the trip. And the others: Jody Loudenslager, a distance runner on the girl's track team. There was Rance Hettler, the church acolyte and a basketball player, and Wendy Wolfson, who played the piano and wrote poetry. The airline had not released their names, but several residents and friends identified people they knew who had taken the trip.

And then there were the adults: Judith Rupert, a secretary at the school practically since she graduated in 1961. Rupert was asked to join an overseas school trip for the first time after enthusiastically helping so many classes with fund raisers. French teacher Debbie Dickey and her husband, Douglas, a salesman. The couple left behind two children, ages 5 and 7. Two others include a former school board member and a mother of one of the students on the trip.

BrenDena Trick, 27, an assistant girls track coach at the high school and a 1987 graduate, heard the news on the radio as she and her husband drove to work. "I just couldn't talk. I felt like someone punched me in the stomach," Trick said. "We went on to work. We were just a wreck. We were in tears."

By the afternoon, a somber mood had descended on this community, just east of Williamsport, where many residents work. There was a holding out of hope, with many of the bodies not yet identified, of someone miraculously surviving the crash. There was disbelief. And there was shock.

Experts said it was a lull before the full outpouring of grief that will undoubtedly come.

"It's been eerily quiet in there," said Dan Chandler, the high school principal. "You almost think too quiet. It's early in the process, we're told, and I think there will be much more grieving later."

"We really didn't believe that all was lost," said Gary Hettler, whose younger brother, Rance, was aboard the plane. "We never really gave up hope and we still haven't given up hope yet." As of yesterday afternoon, Hettler said his parents still had not received the official confirmation from the airline that Rance had been killed. "I just couldn't believe it happened to such a perfect role model student as my brother. He was the epitome of a role model."

At the high school, which has 800 students for grades 9 to 12, counselors talked to grieving students and adults as the media hovered outside. The flag was at half-staff, and students tied red and white ribbons and blue and gold ribbons around the flagpole and nearby signposts. A few bouquets of flowers were left outside the entrance.

Downtown, walking distance away in this compact community, the mood also was subdued. At Turkey Hill Minit Markets, a gas station and convenience store, clerks said they had bought a sympathy card for their manager, who had a niece on the plane. One customer said his cousin was a passenger. And a worker from the tire shop across the street said his friend's wife also was aboard. "I don't know anybody in this town who isn't thinking about it," said Tanya Kelley, one of the clerks.

The students were described almost universally as an outgoing, fun-loving crowd, the types who never hesitated to raise their hands to volunteer for this or that project. The trip cost $1,200 to $1,500 per person, Chandler estimated, and the students paid for it with their fund-raising and family contributions. None of the money came from the school.

"They are an amazing combination of talent," Chandler said. "We look at them as real leaders, both in our school and in our community."

Fourteen of them were still in high school, and two had already graduated. The French Club tries to take a trip to France every three or four years, so each student has a chance to go during his or her high school career.

The community pulled together for the victims and their families. Clergy planned to hold another prayer vigil in the high school gymnasium last night. A local bank offered to set up a relief fund and a memorial fund. Local hospitals sent psychotherapists to the school to work as counselors.

The crash followed an unusual number of tragedies for the community this year. A January flood caused $1.5-million in damage and took eight lives in the surrounding county. One high school student dropped out and committed suicide. Another died in a car crash on an icy night. And a third-grade student was killed by a school bus.

"Stuff don't happen just in the big towns," said Josh Lewis, a 17-year-old student. "It happens in Montoursville."

Olivia Winslow contributed to this story.

Terror darkens 'City of Light'

JULY 19, 1996

By Matthew McAllester

PARIS—The elderly lady in the charcoal gray suit gazed up at the airport monitor in Charles de Gaulle Airport, wondering why the screen announced that TWA Flight 800 that should be landing had been canceled.

She was puzzled but not scared until an official quickly came over and led her to a trauma center set up for those meeting the New York flight that went down into the waters off Long Island.

The arrivals gate at Terminal One is usually a scene of happiness, where every day thousands of people walk through the automatic frosted glass doors with expectant faces that are met by the smiles of waiting friends and relatives. Yesterday, it was turned into the site of horror for about 30 people who came to meet the passengers of Flight 800. None of the 230 passengers and crew pushed trollies through the doors. None felt the excitement of reaching a new country. None felt the comfort of arriving home. Relatives had no one to meet.

"Help us," called out a teenaged girl in jeans and a black T-shirt after throwing herself for comfort into the arms of a woman who appeared to be her mother. Others cried as they entered the futuristic concrete building, having heard the news on breakfast radio shows as they drove to the airport.

Still more moved in stunned silence as police fixed red adhesive labels to their lapels and handbags as identification tags and led them to an enclosed lounge where a team of about 100 counsellors and medical experts stood by to provide care.

Gilbert Dennemont, a TWA spokesman, said that most of the people who turned up at the airport at around 8 a.m. yesterday were French and that a few were American. "Every family member has been assigned a trauma team specialist," he said.

As the day wore on the distraught family members came and went from the trauma center, their faces blotchy from crying. Michel Clerel, chief physician for the Paris Airports, said that some relatives had held out hope during the early part of the day that their loved ones might still be alive.

"We have to put them in a mental state of waiting ...before eventually confirming to them the loss of a loved one," he said. "We get them to talk and discuss their feelings with specialists, then we leave them alone for 10 or 15 minutes and we speak to them again."

At the airport one man was living a nightmare of doubt. "It's a brother of ours," said Jean-Claude Bindikou. "He was supposed to be on a two o'clock flight from New York but we're told he might have been on the eight o'clock flight."

As relatives wrestled with their grief French government officials visited the trauma center, which was closely guarded by police.

French President Jacques Chirac, on a visit to Africa, sent President Bill Clinton a message of sympathy saying he was "deeply shocked and dismayed."

And French Prime Minister Alain Juppe said he was saddened by a tragedy that "is even more horrible as it occurs a few days before the opening of the Olympic Games. But at this moment we cannot yet say if it was an attack."

But the focus in Paris yesterday was on those affected by the tragedy.

By the evening all of the 30 friends and family members had left the airport, which returned to its normal business. Children laughed as they chased each other around the check-in lines. The circular building with its trademark crisscross automatic walkways was bustling with people from all over the world as they crossed paths on their way to their destinations.

One American man stood talking to a friend on a pay phone. The man had been traveling for more than 24 hours and had not heard the news.

"I'm shocked," said J. Schroeder, 28, a law student from Portland, Ore., on his way to an old college friend's wedding in Paris. "I just heard from friends."

Especially upsetting to Schroeder, a graduate of the University of Pennsylvania, was the thought that nearly 20 students from the area were killed in the crash. "That gets a little close to home," he said.

Schroeder may have had a near-miss himself. A storm in Chicago, where he was making a connection from Portland, caused some airlines to exchange seats on flights. He missed a plane to Paris by 20 minutes, ending up in Frankfurt. He wondered if that saved his life. "There are only so many flights to Paris," he said. "I suppose I should ring the folks."

Special correspondents Eric Nagourney and Julian Nundy contributed to this story.

Flying was his job and pastime

JULY 19, 1996

By Deborah Barfield and Chau Lam

Only days ago, TWA Capt. Steven Snyder stopped by a small airport in Bridgeport to check on the single-engine plane he loved to fly over the Connecticut countryside.

"He called it his pet," corporate pilot Stanley Logan, one of Snyder's flying buddies for 15 years, said yesterday at the airport. "It was his pride and joy. He got more of a kick out of flying the small one than the big one."

Snyder was a captain aboard the TWA jumbo jet that exploded and crashed off Long Island Wednesday, killing him and 229 others aboard the flight.

News of Snyder's death shocked the community of Stratford, where he lived. "The first thing on my mind was I hope it's not Steve," said Selma Baker, a neighbor of 14 years. "We all will miss him very much. It's been a shock because we saw him pick up the mail a couple of days ago."

Snyder, 57, was one of two veteran captains on Flight 800 headed to Paris. Others in the cockpit were Capt. Ralph Kevorkian of Garden Grove, Calif., flight engineer Richard Campbell of Ridgefield, Conn., and flight engineer Oliver Krick of St. Louis.

Friends and neighbors describe Snyder, who was divorced and lived by himself at Oronoque Village, as a quiet "gentleman" who liked to golf and loved to fly his Cessna, which he had completely refurbished nearly a year and a half ago.

The plane, which sits at a local airport, had a new paint job, new avionics, a new engine and new interior, Logan said.

When Snyder wasn't flying TWA planes to Europe, he was checking his plane or flying it across the state, Logan said. "He loved TWA and he loved to fly."

When he wasn't flying, he could be found on the golf course at the Oronoque Country Club. Pro shop manager Dawn Kusznir remembers him with pipe in hand leaning across the glass at the pro shop.

"I was terrified of flying. He would reassure me about how safe the planes were. He said he was never afraid," Kusznir said. "He said these planes were so well taken care of.... He would say, 'I wouldn't be flying if I thought something was wrong with my plane.'"

Snyder had more than 30 years with TWA, where he logged more than 17,263 flight hours. As captain he had logged 2,821 hours.

Although quiet, Snyder won over people with his friendly and pleasant manner, friends said.

John Korolyshun, a golf pro at the country club, recalled Snyder joking about his golf game. "He hit two balls in the water on the third hole and did not hit the green," Korolyshun remembered. "He told me he can control a plane better than he can control a golf ball."

Campbell, the flight engineer also from Connecticut, leaves behind a wife, Margie, who is a schoolteacher, and two sons.

"He always had a smile and a good word," said William Mayr, a family friend and pilot for TWA. "He was a super nice guy. He's really going to be truly missed."

Campbell, a former Air Force pilot, was hired in 1966 at TWA and had 18,527 flight hours. "He was a dedicated professional pilot.... And he loved flying," Mayr said. "This is not a job you do because it's a job, you do it because you love it."

Michael Arena contributed to this story.

Footage too sad to televise

JULY 19, 1996

By Rita Ciolli

For more than a day, the world has seen dramatic television footage live from Moriches Inlet, but amid the floating debris and personal items there have been no images of the worst of the crash: the bodies.

WNBC News Director Paula Walker told the pilots of Chopper4, whose state-of-the-art cameras provided the most gripping images of the fiery wreckage on Wednesday, not to zoom in on any of the human remains floating in the ocean.

"I told them, 'Don't go too close,'" said Walker, who described the images as "very sad and disturbing." She also put out an electronic message to all her producers instructing them not to broadcast any pictures of bodies. "We don't need to show everything we've got to tell the story," said Walker.

Both WNBC Channel 4 and Cablevision's News12 also had footage from staff members who had joined the flotilla of private rescue boats in the dark hours after the crash.

"Our cameraman shot 40 minutes of video, but only four minutes made it on the air," said Janet Alshouse, assistant news director of News12. "It was very gruesome and disturbing; there was no purpose to airing it," she said.

The frantic rescue effort and its location also turned some reporters into participants. WNBC's crime reporter John Miller had taken a day off when he was paged by his office. He rushed to his 24-foot Boston Whaler at a marina on Shinnecock Inlet, but realized he was still a novice at navigation. Just then, Tony Villareale, the owner of Hampton Watercraft and Marine, arrived in response to a Coast Guard call for private rescue craft and joined him. Miller also took his home video camera along.

"I got a couple of shots of other boats spotting bodies and pulling them in," said Miller, who was also filing live audio reports to Chopper4.

But then he also had to put his camera down. "When we spotted bodies, we left to get the county police boat. At another time, we would shine our lights for someone else pulling in bodies."

"It was kind of like wearing three or four hats at once," said Miller, who had also served as New York City deputy police commissioner. "This wasn't my first plane crash or even a plane crash in the water. And I saw a lot of bodies with the police department. But this included some sights that will show up in a couple of nightmares, I am sure. I saw things I never saw before." Little of his graphic video was televised.

Local News12 had the first live report from the scene Wednesday when it went on at 10:15 from inside the gates of the Coast Guard station. "When we first heard of a plane crash, we sent a truck immediately. They called us and said it is a very, very, very big plane," Alshouse said as she described the beginning of News12's live coverage throughout the night with reports from the scene. Most of the New York City-based stations stopped their live reports during yesterday's early morning hours.

And city stations' recent practice of basing reporters and crews on Long Island also paid off with fast, aggressive coverage.

WABC Channel 7 reporter N.J. Burkett and a news van pulled into the Air National Guard headquarters at Gabreski Airport. "It was literally two minutes to eleven," he said. "I climbed up on top of the truck and went live."

During one of his live broadcasts, the crews of a National Guard C-130 plane and helicopter who had been practicing a routine night refueling landed. The pilots turned out to be witnesses to the explosion and told of the fireball and swooping down to 100 feet to see clusters of bodies in the water and no signs of life.

"It was the first actual description of what it was like out there," said Burkett. "They described the bodies in the water."

Writers' Workshop

Talking Points

1) In its main story, "Tragedy on Flight 800," *Newsday* employs a summary lead that attempts to condense an entire story into a single paragraph. By definition, the summary lead is very selective. List the elements contained in the first paragraph of the story and discuss why each was included. Are elements missing that you would have used?

2) In "A Huge Ball of Flame, It was Unbelievable," writer Craig Gordon deliberately used a more leisurely approach in his lead to recreate the scene of a summer night off Long Island as TWA Flight 800 exploded over the Atlantic Ocean. Such "color" stories rely on the senses to convey the experience of the news event to readers. What other senses does Gordon use, besides vision, to communicate what eyewitnesses described?

3) "Boaters Brave Dark Sea" is based largely on the eyewitness account of reporter Steve Wick, who motored to the crash site with a *Newsday* photographer and filed his observations via cell phone to a writer back in the newsroom. Debate whether the piece could have been written in the first person. What are the arguments for and against such an approach?

4) *Newsday*'s second-day story on the crash of TWA Flight 800 presents two possibilities for the tragedy: terrorism or mechanical failure. Decisions about which theory to emphasize occupied *Newsday* editors throughout their coverage. In hindsight, their conservative approach paid off since the cause remains a mystery. Compare the newspaper's lead with stories written by other news organizations that day. Did others take a less conservative approach?

5) The extensive details and authoritative voice that mark "In the Morgue, Somber Tasks" might lead readers to believe that reporter Ellen Yan and her colleague Sidney Schaer were inside the Suffolk Medical Examiner's Office. Like all the other reporters in Long Island, they were kept behind yellow police tape. Study Yan's comments in Recalling Deadline to learn how the pair produced such an informative piece.

6) "Private Hopes, Public Deaths" is a gut-wrenching portrait of many of the victims of TWA Flight 800, produced in a single day of reporting and writing. Notice how the first five paragraphs illustrate the theme of the story, found in paragraph six: "...private thoughts, private hopes, all shattered by a wrenching public death." Study how the story returns to tell in greater detail each of the cases cited in the lead.

7) Good writers vary the length of their sentences for effect. Short sentences, even sentence fragments, used judiciously, slow down the reader and deliver powerful information with a punch. Long sentences can take the reader on a journey of space, time, and emotion. Study the effect of the length and style of sentences in paragraph four of "Small Town Grieves 21 Dead" by Ken Moritsugu.

8) The public often views the media, especially on disaster stories, as vultures eager to prey on the misfortunes of others. How does Rita Ciolli's story, "Footage Too Sad to Televise," portray television news directors and reporters? What is your view of the ethics of reporting tragedy? Does this story change your mind?

9) The story "Terror Darkens 'City of Light'" employs a single-instance lead, focusing on an elderly woman who arrives at the airport in Paris only to learn that the plane she had come to meet had crashed. It's a gateway approach that "uses one example to illustrate a larger topic," says Jack Hart, writing coach at *The Oregonian* and editor of *Second Takes,* a monthly newsletter on writing. "A mainstay of magazine writing," single-instance leads have "spread rapidly into newspaper writing." Look for other examples of single-instance leads, and discuss whether criticism that the device is over-used is valid.

Assignment Desk

1) *Newsday*'s deadline coverage of the TWA Flight 800 crash combines saturation reporting with clear and vivid writing. The main story alone relies on more than 20 different sources, ranging from officials to family members of those on the plane. Identify the sources and discuss what each one contributes to the story.

2) To find potential eyewitnesses to the TWA crash as well as locate neighbors and friends on deadline, Deborah Barfield and other *Newsday* reporters made extensive use of a

reverse telephone directory, which lists a community's residents and their phone numbers by street address. If you've never used this research tool, consult one in your library. Familiarize yourself with its resources by finding your family and neighbors. Build a list of names and numbers to call.

3) *Newsday* reporters and editors say that a culture that demands an abundance of information ("overreporting" in their words) is the key to the success of the newspaper's coverage and the richness of the writing in its prize-winning package. Look for examples—details, analysis, anecdotes —that you think are the product of "going the extra mile" in reporting. Review your own reporting methods. Do you generally overreport?

4) Good reporting makes good writing possible. Using four stories from *Newsday*'s coverage reprinted here ("Tragedy on Flight 800," "A Huge Ball of Flame," "How '90 Crash Compares," and "Boaters Brave Dark Sea"), write a single 750-word story on the crash of TWA Flight 800 for an out-of-town newspaper.

Recalling deadline with
Newsday

Deborah Barfield, social issues reporter

I was supposed to try to find out as much as I could about the TWA pilots. The library was working with us, especially with names and addresses and phone numbers to call neighbors. I knew somebody who used to work at TWA. He told me that one of the pilots had a license for a small plane, and he was able to give me the name of the airport and the number. They connected me with somebody who had just seen him the other day. I found out that he was a golfer. Some of his neighbors didn't want to talk on the record, but they led me to the golf course. I called there and the manager was able to give us a lot more color. I learned to tell people that I just wanted to let folks know about this person they cared about. Simply asking, "Tell me a little bit about him. What did he wear? What did he do? How often did he come in? And what was he doing when he came in?" People wanted to share that, especially with somebody they liked. As one person was talking about it you could tell she was smiling. And I smiled and laughed right along with her, and got her to open up. By the time I was asking stupid questions, like, "What color?" or "What kind of pipe?" it wasn't like I was asking a stupid or personal question. By then she was telling you about somebody that meant something to her.

Rita Ciolli, media writer

It dawned on me as I was watching all the television coverage, at some point in the middle of the night, that although I was hearing talk of bodies, we weren't seeing any bodies. The next morning when I got into the office, I started calling around to news directors about how they handled it. People are always saying television shows too much. It's too graphic. Too violent. And what was so compelling about this was that you had reporters making the judgments on the scene or back in the studios that "We just can't show this to

people. This is a horrible tragedy, and we're just not
going to do it."

Craig Gordon, business reporter

We were as careful as we could be in the short amount
of time we had to use anecdotes and witness accounts
that were consistent. We could be confident that we
were actually telling a story about what people really
did see, and not stuff that was altered by what they
heard on the news. You've got one crack at these
people, and you need it in a big hurry, but you know
that you have to keep walking them through. "Start at
the beginning. Where were you? What were you doing? What did you see? Then what did you see?" It's
the reporting that allows you to tell the story in a well-
written way.

Adam Horvath, deputy Long Island editor

We're so used to needing to sort out information that,
in this case, where there was little official information,
we just naturally went on our instinct of, "We're going
to have to do a really big job of analyzing what to take
from people and what to throw away." In this story it
turned out that nobody was authoritative, that the authorities were fighting with each other and back stab-
bing each other. There were people in positions of
authority willing to say things that were not based in
fact. Our drive to overreport always seemed to give us
some contradictory information that sent up a red flag,
that made us say, "Hey, wait a minute." It turned out
to be a great strength.

Alex Martin, Long Island day editor

You've got to have a lot of people available in the office: to make phone calls, take feeds, funnel to the writers. You need people in the office, as well as people out
in the field, especially on the larger stories. There's so
much information coming in: you've got your reporters
calling in, you're reading the wires, watching TV, you
have people listening to the radio, phone calls coming
in from citizens. You've got to sort it out. We estab-

lished a computer queue for all the feeds to go in. Assistant managing editor Miriam Pawel reads the feeds, so you're not dependent on just the rewrite person for the selection of what's important. When the editing of the story comes up, you can have Miriam reading back on it, and she's saying, "There's a great quote from Joe Blow that really would go well at the top; let's try to get it in." We keep enriching the piece with our best information. And sometimes that means substituting quotes, sometimes it means adding quotes from the large stockpile of reporting.

Ken Moritsugu, reporter

You take a step back, and say, "What is the point of the story? What are you trying to say?" The thing that struck me, when I got to Montoursville, and as I started talking to people, is how small this community was. A tiny, close-knit community. Homogeneous. Everybody knew each other. It wasn't like Long Island or New York City where, if 20 kids died, they'd be from all over the place, and down at the gas station they would never have heard of them. Here everyone you talked to literally knew somebody on that plane. Once I had that concept in my mind, that's what I wanted to relate in the story. It's the story of how this one community was hit by this plane crash.

Miriam Pawel, assistant managing editor

When there is breaking news, we have tended to have a culture where we just go all out. So if it's a small plane crash and two people are killed, you run with it. We have a lot of reporters who are trained to think that way. So when something like this happens, it's no big deal, in a sense. They went out and did what they do every day. It's just that the story is a national story, instead of a page 38 story.

At *Newsday,* the copy desk is fairly small. They set the rules about deadlines and presentation. They were extraordinarily helpful. Particularly for the first two weeks, when there were news conferences at 8 o'clock at night, we couldn't start writing the main story until then. We couldn't get to sources until after the meetings to filter through all of the information to try to figure out what we could actually say. Their ability to adjust to that, and to give us leeway, and to help in the whole presentation was very important. They're unsung heroes.

Liam Pleven, Suffolk County political reporter

I started writing the first edition eyewitness sidebar about six paragraphs down, at what would be the start of the narrative. This was the first time that I had ever tried to write a story without writing the top first, and it's worked since. I wrote from that stage down to the end before I did the first six or seven paragraphs. There were certain anecdotes that I spent more time on because I felt they were so compelling, like the woman who missed the plane. It was the kind of story that would give somebody a little bit of relief. This was not a conscious thought; that's the effect it had on me.

Then I said, "OK, you've just spent 1,500, 1,700 words to describe this situation. Now distill that into five, six, seven paragraphs, and make what the body of your story has described as compelling as you possibly can. Take one small detail to illustrate each point. Make each paragraph focus on only one idea or one aspect of the story, and then try to get one or two really strong quotes."

Robin Topping, staff writer

I felt I could be most useful by putting together a comparison between the Avianca crash and the TWA crash. There were many, many differences, it turned out. One of the main differences was that there were many survivors of the Avianca crash, and there were no survivors in the TWA crash. I was very lucky that night. I happened to get the chairman of the Emergency Services Committee who had written the report critiquing how emergency services responded. I was the lucky one, because I had a clear focus. I knew what the theme of the story should be. I was able to get my information quickly. I didn't have to wait for other reporters to bring me information. I had everything at my fingertips.

Steve Wick, staff writer

Another reporter, a photographer, and I found a boat to take us to the crash. We headed out about 11 p.m., and it took us an hour to get to the site. It looked like the sea was literally burning. Behind the flames a sea of lights, hundreds and hundreds of boats. In the sky, C-120s from a nearby Air National Guard base, dropped parachute flares into this black sky. As these flares slowly descended, the ocean lit up as if it were the middle of the day, bright enough to read under. For miles the ocean was covered with debris, seat cushions, insulation, big pieces of metal, a section of a wing, luggage, backpacks. An empty baby bottle floated by. The debris was so thick you could not see the water.

You could hear the traffic between the Coast Guard and the civilian boats; it was quite clear that there was just a hellish array of bodies and body parts all over the place. All you could think was, two hours before, a 747 filled with happy people heading for Paris blew up right over our heads. I had my arm wrapped around this pole for dear life. And all I was thinking was, "I have got to give great notes." This is one of these intensely dramatic moments in which a reporter has to be observant and describe what he sees. I felt a tremendous sense of sadness for the people. But the job that night was to inform our readers that something really horrific had happened.

I had a cell phone, and every 15 or 20 minutes, I would call in to dump notes on a writer, Martin Evans. The value was that 600,000 people on Long Island awoke to an eyewitness account the next morning. It was light before we came back. John Williams took a remarkable photograph that ran in *Time* magazine, showing this burning ocean. It was a terrible thing to see.

Ellen Yan, criminal justice reporter

By luck and morbid curiosity, I had toured the Suffolk morgue weeks before the crash. I'd gotten blood splattered on my dress during an autopsy, and the division chiefs there spoke to me like they'd been in solitary confinement for years. That tour, expected to be two hours, took up a day. On the second day of TWA coverage, I thanked my stars for all that. I could set the scene with word pictures: the steel tables in the autopsy room, the overhead camera across the hallway, the weight station, and the refrigerators with gurneys of the dead. I could also inject what I learned about forensics, the whodunit detective of sciences, from years of covering crime. I knew I might not get a whole bunch of details from the busy Suffolk morgue, so I focused on what had happened in other man-made disasters. Right away, the ValuJet crash in Florida and the Oklahoma City explosion came to mind.

The spokesman for the Oklahoma state ME's office was great, describing a morgue that had been reorganized into a sort of mass assembly line to put back together humans as if they were jigsaw puzzles. Getting names of other experts from experts, I reached folks who had worked on the ValuJet crash and other challenging cases. Often, it takes time to interpret science jargon, but in this case, the scientists responded in everyday terms, eager to make sure a lay person understood.

That day, from all the people I spoke to, there was a sense of trying to help those connected to the TWA disaster. It was as if a nation were trying to grapple with the uncertainty of why the plane went down, and everyone hoped understanding a small part of the tragedy would make them feel less lost. I felt indebted that day to my sources, who did all they could for me. Their accommodation was like a balm for me in covering a disaster.

Deadline Tips:

Leave no stone unturned. Tap into as many resources or sources as you can: the neighbor, the teacher, the golf course. There's always somebody who can add little details to the picture. Share them with the reader.
—Deborah Barfield

Preparation is nine-tenths of everything, either what you know from your experience, or having all those private numbers for people whom you can plug into at the last minute to give you the kind of information you need. On a media story, it has to ring as true for you as it would whether you're covering politics, or business, or anything else. And resist the temptation to give your buddies the benefit of the doubt. Ask some of the hard questions, too. **—Rita Ciolli**

You don't have time to get bogged down in your notes. Go back through the notes, but try to write as much of the story as you can without looking at them. Your brain will do the work for you. Think about what you know you have in your head, and put it together in a way that makes sense and tells the story.

—Craig Gordon

You need to have one person who does nothing but read all the feeds and direct traffic, making sure the right things go in the right place. You need to communicate to the people at the scene what stories you're trying to do. They need to know where they fit into the big picture. If you don't tell them, you're not going to get what you need. **—Adam Horvath**

You have to have somebody a step removed to really work the feeds and to have a field marshal idea of where the troops are and the information that's arriving. That way there's somebody with a breadth of knowledge about what you've gathered. **—Alex Martin**

There's no magic formula. You just have to hit the ground running. As quickly as you can, orient yourself. You have to find out where you are, where things are happening. When they're going to happen. Ask a lot of questions very quickly to figure out what's there and where you can get it. Get a phone book. Use city hall, use the public library. And always be thinking: what's your lead and what is the point of the story.

—Ken Moritsugu

Plan ahead as much as possible. If you're running the story, force yourself to break away and delegate, so that you can keep getting ahead. If you're just thinking about the next deadline, you're always going to be behind. **—Miriam Pawel**

The most difficult thing about doing rewrite is trying to describe to the reader in vivid terms something that you very likely haven't seen yourself because you've been in the office. So when you're reading the feeds, when you're talking to people, try to immerse yourself in the situation, imagine it, visualize it.
—**Liam Pleven**

Breathe, and I'm serious about that. It's very easy to sort of start panicking. When you panic, you get this huge writer's block. So write one paragraph at a time. Get the lead done. Then the second paragraph, then a quote, then some background. If you have to follow a formula to get done, do it. If you have to write a little outline for yourself, if it helps you focus quickly, just do it.   —**Robin Topping**

Be prepared for all contingencies. You can't sit and wait for everything to line up perfectly, you've just got to go. And in this case, we witnessed history. And don't forget: the story's not about you. It's about what you see, not what you do.   —**Steve Wick**

Keep names and numbers of people you think you'll never talk to again, because you will. When I have the chance, I try to escape from the office. Ride along with a cop or a legislator or take a tour of a state prison. In this job, I'm always learning how stupid I am, and sometimes that's fun.   —**Ellen Yan**

Chicago Tribune

Chicago Tribune

Finalist, Team Deadline Reporting

Cardinal Joseph Bernardin was no stranger to the readers of the *Chicago Tribune,* but when he died last November the stories that filled the paper the next day brought readers a wealth of information about his life and beliefs and deepened their understanding of the man and his times. Ellen Warren, a veteran reporter, bolstered by reports from staffers and interns, including Cathleen Falsani, produced a touching portrait of the devoted followers and friends Bernardin left behind.

 Ellen Warren has been a local, national, political, White House, foreign, and war correspondent. She also has been a feature writer and columnist, and the first woman legman for Chicago's legendary columnist Mike Royko. She has covered fires, murders, Chicago City Hall, NATO, arms control, the Lebanon civil war, the Middle East, and opening day at Wrigley Field. She started her career with the City News Bureau of Chicago and joined the *Chicago Tribune* in Chicago in 1993—after 17 years in Washington, including five years as White House correspondent. Her most recent award was induction in the Chicago Journalism Hall of Fame.

 Cathleen Falsani was a metro desk intern in the fall of 1996. She was born in Connecticut and is a graduate of Wheaton College. In 1996, she earned a master's degree from Northwestern University's Medill School of Journalism and will receive a master's in theological studies from Northwestern in 1997. She has worked for a women's theological journal and written for the Religion News Service, *The Capital Times* in Madison, Wis., and designed the religion content for the *Tribune*'s Internet site. She won the 1996 National Stoody-West Fellowship for Religious Journalism.

Thankful for the memories

NOVEMBER 15, 1996

By Ellen Warren and Cathleen Falsani

The children arriving at Blessed Sacrament School in North Lawndale, giggling and goofing around, knew immediately that something important had happened.

Bundled lumps of mittened energy watching their breath turn to fog, the youngsters entered the main hallway Thursday morning, but all was dark. And quiet as a church.

Clutching daddy's hand, they wondered in big, audible whispers—what was going on?

The only light was the unreliable flicker of a single red candle on a table in the hall, and soon the children knew the news. On the table with the candle, they spotted a framed photograph of Cardinal Joseph Bernardin.

Throughout the day, pairs of students in blue and white uniforms took turns in a silent vigil, watching over the tiny makeshift shrine.

You could almost call it a miracle: quiet in the hallway of a busy, bustling grade school.

Nearby, principal Sabrina Roy clutched a tissue and said softly, "He was just a strong supporter of Catholic schools, especially in the inner city. He just believed in Catholic education for all children."

Cardinal Joseph Bernardin talked to presidents and potentates. He communed with God. But sometimes it is the smallest moments, the quiet footnotes that tell the most.

The patience of listening, a lit candle, a gentle touch, an unexpected Christmas phone call, silence where there had been raucous noise.

These are the grace notes of a life that will be long remembered:

There was education-made-flesh at St. Sabina Academy on the South Side, where first graders in Colette Flynn's class were talking about the cardinal's death, and death in general.

"He's an angel now and he's watching over us," she told the children, amusing themselves by poking their tongues into the holes left behind when a tooth or two fell out.

"Do any of you have a relative up with God?" Flynn asked the class.

Every kid had a hand in the air.

"I've got two there," trumped Darry Wilson, 6.

"Is the cardinal sick any more?" the teacher asked.

"No," they said.

Then this epitaph from Charles Jackson, 6, standing near a wall covered with construction paper owls: "He's happy and he's in our hearts."

A DIVINE SENSE OF HUMOR

Those who knew Bernardin speak of his approachability, hail his humanity. What is not so widely known was here was a guy with a sense of humor.

Maynard Wishner, past president of the Jewish Federation of Chicago, traveled to Israel with the cardinal in March 1995 as part of the first official Catholic-Jewish delegation visit to the Holy Land.

During their meeting with Palestine Liberation Organization leader Yasser Arafat, the PLO leader kept calling the cardinal, "Your Holiness."

After their meeting, Bernardin poked Wishner in the ribs, eyes twinkling: "I just got a promotion in there," Bernardin said.

In the world of Catholic protocol, only one man on Earth is called "Your Holiness." That would be the pope.

CHURCHES, UNITED UNDER GOD

Seven fancy church steeples poke into the sky above southwest suburban Lemont, a town of fewer than 11,000 souls along the Illinois and Michigan Canal.

This town dominated by steeples seemed dominated by sadness, too, on Thursday as the people of Lemont learned that the cardinal had died.

Joseph Ricken, 52, stood outside St. Alphonsus Church, a red brick building 130 years old where he had bowed his head in a well-worn wooden pew to pray for the cardinal.

Twirling like a compass, Ricken pointed here, then here: "There's a German Catholic church over there and a Polish church over there, and an Irish Catholic Church down the hill.

"He taught us to be one community and not to think about our ethnic divisions."

A PERSONAL TOUCH

Patty Crowley, 83, has long disagreed with the teachings of the Catholic Church on the issue of birth control. She and her late husband were part of the Christian Family Movement, a grassroots social justice group, and in 1964, they were asked to be part of the Papal Birth Control Commission.

The Crowleys, and others on the commission, viewed the issue one way. The pope disagreed.

Years later, when Bernardin took over from the more conservative and traditional Cardinal John Cody, he invited those who had been hurt or offended by the church to write to him.

Crowley took him up on it.

But Bernardin sent a form letter in reply. That was in 1982 and she felt offended all over again.

Nearly 15 years later—just this past January—out of nowhere came a call from Bernardin. Could he come to her house to visit, he asked.

Crowley was stunned. "Sure."

For an hour, over tea and cookies, Patty Crowley told him her story of a wound that had not fully healed in 32 years.

She was profoundly moved by the visit: "The fact that he came and listened, to me, was remarkable."

A PLACE ON THE MANTEL

On Thursday, another family photograph was added to those that crowded the altar at Providence of God Church in the largely Mexican neighborhood of Pilsen—that of their brother, Joseph.

It is a tradition that has followed the parishioners from Mexico to the West Side of Chicago where, during November, photos of the deceased are propped amid the votive candles, for special remembrance and prayers.

With patterns of red and blue from the stained glass shining on their sad faces, two dozen prayerful members of the church's senior citizens club listened as

Rev. Robert Perez remembered Bernardin at mass Thursday morning at the church.

"He has helped us look at the ways death can be a friend," said Perez. "In this case he has befriended death. He has not made death such an enemy."

Showing us how to die, that is one of the lessons of Bernardin's battle with cancer.

In city and suburbs, from Catholics and those of other faiths, the words rang out over and over, that the cardinal—through his own public dying—had taught them lessons of reacting to their own mortality.

Charline Aycock learned of the cardinal's death as she awakened—for no reason—in the early hours of Thursday and heard the news on the radio at 3 a.m. Earlier, she had attended the opening of a music club.

"I was lying there listening to all his friends saying all these great things about him and I felt so comforted," said Aycock, who practices no formal religion.

"It was such a contrast to come back from the opening of the House of Blues. As I stayed there [in bed] listening, it occurred to me what is really important...

"I think he removed some of the fear of death," she said. "I think he made the path easier for us."

LESSONS FOR THE LIVING

But if Bernardin showed us the way to die, he showed us how to live, too.

At the Loyola medical complex where the cancer center was recently named in his honor in west suburban Maywood, Bernardin was remembered at the daily mass.

Hospital patient Janet DiVecchio of Joliet, recovering from hip replacement surgery, sat quietly in her wheelchair in the back of the chapel.

A nurse herself at University of Illinois medical center, DiVecchio said, "I know I've learned patience from him. I've learned to look at humanity a little differently and I hope to bring some of that to my job."

A word of caution. A reminder from Rev. William O'Shea of Naperville's St. Margaret Mary Church not to forget the lessons the cardinal taught. "His openness about death helped us illuminate the mystery of our own existence. I think he helped people deal with their own illnesses, their own losses," he said. "But we need to share the reality of our lives. When we stop being private, we become more human."

LENDING HELP, SHARING HOPE

There were favors, large and small, efforts great and greater during his 14 years in Chicago. Bernardin "tried to do the impossible," said Rev. Ted Stone.

Stone ought to know. In 1971, with church sanction, Stone left the priesthood to marry. Ten years later, Stone's wife committed suicide and he was left to raise his two small children, ages 5 and 7, one of them handicapped.

In 1984, Stone asked for Bernardin's help to be reinstated as an active priest. Over many years, the cardinal interceded repeatedly with the Rome church officials for Stone's reinstatement.

"He kept going back and back, trying to get the authorities to allow it."

After seven years they agreed. During that long and difficult time, said Stone, "He always radiated such hope himself...that I never had a bitter moment. His hope was contagious."

Today, with great thanks to the efforts of Joseph Bernardin, Stone is pastor of Mary, Seat of Wisdom, Park Ridge.

GENTLE, EVEN IN PRIVATE

"I'm not a very religious person. I'm a lawyer," said John O'Malley, by way of explaining that when he took on Bernardin as a client, he wasn't prepared for what he got: A man every bit as honest and decent in private as he seemed on TV.

O'Malley and attorney Jim Serritella worked on the cardinal's legal defense after Steven Cook accused him of sexually abusing him as a teenager in Cincinnati in the 1970s. Cook recanted the charges and Bernardin ministered to him before Cook died of AIDS.

After days of rumors in a media feeding frenzy over the Cook charges, O'Malley was with Bernardin when he took his first look at the accusations listed in Cook's court filing.

"The man you saw on TV, the man of integrity, the gentle man...is the person we saw and dealt with in person," said Serritella.

A MAN FOR ALL PEOPLE

To hear members of his flock speak, Bernardin seemed to have touched every corner of the archdiocese. Almost everyone, it seems, has a personal story to tell of their time with the cardinal.

Sister Joseph Marie Zenda, president of a retirement community run by the Franciscan Sisters of Chicago in Lemont, remembers the cardinal's habit of touching a person's hand or arm when he spoke with them.

"You felt as if he was talking to you and only you," Zenda said.

For Buddy Bulow, father of four young boys, it was the voice at the other end of the phone. Bulow was dying from cancer at home in Orland Park, the phone rang and Buddy's wife answered and handed him the phone.

"Buddy's whispering to us it's the cardinal. We started laughing, thinking he had too much medicine in him," his wife said.

But it *was* the cardinal, said his wife, Kathy.

"He called three or four times. It was comforting to my husband just to think he would be praying for him.

"Just to have somebody like him, somebody important like him take the time to do what he did. He even called Christmas night just to wish him a Merry Christmas.

"And my husband passed away Jan. 15."

Tribune reporters Lisa Black, Teresa Puente, and Carolyn Starks contributed to this article.

Lessons Learned

It was no secret that Chicago's beloved cardinal, Joseph Bernardin, had terminal cancer. This man of near saintly stature had been dying in public, with painful dignity, for months. He had told the city that he prayed for the courage to be an example in dying, as he tried to be in life.

So, faced with what surely would be one of the biggest stories of the year—his death—what's a big newspaper to do? Plan. Plan. Draw up a plan.

I was part of the Plan, a "team leader" no less. My job would be to write the page one "color" story the day he died. A react/man-on-the-street, though they aren't called that any more.

The challenge was to make it interesting, telling, emotive. To capture the mood of the city and suburbs in a way that went beyond the expected, the predictable. In short: to tell a compelling story worthy of this extraordinary man.

I've always believed that in the newspaper business, Planning can be dangerous. You can get so wedded to the Plan that you can't make room for the unexpected, the delightful, the *news*.

But I was in the Plan up to my ears.

First, as enforcer of one part of the larger strategy, I had to figure out what to do with all the reporters—a number of them enthusiastic interns—I was to dispatch for reaction to Cardinal Bernardin's death.

What we were after was what my friend Susan Bennett, now an editorial writer at *USA Today,* calls "Gates of Graceland." As a UPI reporter in Memphis, whenever anything huge happened, anywhere in the world, she'd run over to the front yard of Elvis's house and grab a cross section of the universe to react to it.

We, too, wanted a cross section that would represent different parts of the community.

"No detail is too small," I told my crew as we worked out the logistics, designed to catch people as they got the news of the cardinal's death.

"Pretty writing," I heard myself saying over and over, "can't make up for bad reporting."

Meanwhile, as we learned the cardinal was failing fast, intern Cathleen Falsani and I started tracking down people the cardinal had touched, who genuinely had been affected by him.

This was for backup, in case the stuff we turned up after he died was the flat, predictable, "He was a good man. A holy man. I'll miss him." That might be heartfelt, but doesn't say much.

Falsani unearthed a batch of people whose stories about the cardinal had never been told before, and so did I. Her interview notes were so good that a number of the people she found—a prominent Jewish leader, an octogenarian who disagreed with the Catholic Church on birth control—made it into the story. One of my interviews fit as a sweet, sad kicker for the piece.

The cardinal died in the early morning hours, and the city desk called me around 6 a.m. Before the coffee kicked in, I remember calling one of the reporters on the team and declaring, "The pope died," as I sent her off to her own Gates of Graceland assignment.

The reporting ranged from the predictable to the terrific. Unloading notes from the young reporters, I kept asking for more detail. Not just quotes. Take me there. What color was the candle? Were they paper owls or paper penguins on the bulletin board?

A critically important function performed by a reporter who got no byline this day was Flynn McRoberts's role as the Organizer of the Notes.

With 40 or 50 files from at least 30 reporters coming in from all over, Flynn printed out, photocopied, and distributed the stuff to the appropriate writer, crossing out passages that were clearly a waste of time, highlighting the good stuff, and writing a two- or three-word summary atop each.

(I told him to save the best for me!!)

The Plan probably wasn't a bad idea. At least everybody knew what they were supposed to do and where to go. It gave us some ethnic and geographic range we might not have had otherwise.

That said, I'm happy to report that the lead of my story came from somebody not listed on the Plan at all, editor Byron White, who was one of the few *Tribune* staffers not working on the cardinal story that day. He called in some notes from Blessed Sacrament School after he dropped his kids off there that morning.

It renewed my belief that in journalism, nothing beats initiative, good luck, and—who knows?—divine intervention.

Lessons Learned

BY CATHLEEN FALSANI

My pager sounded at 3 a.m., wresting me out of the fitful sleep I had endured since arriving home from the newsroom two hours earlier.

I knew what it meant: Joe was gone.

My first response was excitement for the opportunity to cover such a historic moment as a reporter just starting out, but then I began to cry. At the time I chalked it up in part to exhaustion—I had been working nearly around the clock for days—but in retrospect I believe they were tears of joy that Cardinal Bernardin was finally at peace, but also of deep sadness, that such a magnificent soul was no longer with us.

An hour later, I found myself standing in the frigid darkness of Holy Name Cathedral, waiting for the first mourners to arrive at the parish that Cardinal Bernardin called home, where they called him pastor, father, and friend. The moments of solitude gave me the opportunity to reflect on how I had spent the previous day.

After being assigned to "Team Ellen," a group of young reporters under Ellen Warren's leadership who would construct the "color" piece the day Bernardin died, I had spent hours on the phone collecting stories from people who knew the cardinal, not best, but in unique and telling ways.

The cardinal had been gravely ill for more than a week, and the *Tribune* had run many stories already talking to his closest family and friends about what he was like and the hole that his passing would leave in their lives. This piece had to be different. My editors wanted to hear voices that hadn't been listened to before: non-Catholics, non-religious folks who had had personal encounters with the man Chicagoans of all creeds referred to as "our cardinal."

Their stories easily could have been overlooked: a Jewish man who had traveled with Bernardin to Israel and who choked back tears as he told me story after story of his "brother Joseph's" dry sense of humor and tender heart. There were the lawyers—hardly the place to go looking for spiritual reflection and tales of personal transformation. But the stories Jim Serritella and John O'Malley shared painted a picture of a man who, even in his darkest moments, lived what he believed and touched those around him with a profound trust in his Creator.

Then there was Patty Crowley, a feisty, straight-talking woman whom many consider to be the grande dame of Chicago's liberal Catholic renegades. In one of the many calls I made that day, another source told me that Crowley had a great story to tell, if I could get her to tell it. She didn't trust the press. After more than an hour on the phone the evening before Bernardin died, she did. Although it may never stand alongside Bernardin's meetings with powerful religious and secular leaders in the history books, her story, to me, was among the most revealing I heard that day and in the days to come.

Confined to a system that was both spiritual and political, Bernardin could not always say everything that was on his mind. But he had a long memory. Three decades after one woman was offended by that system and those politics, Bernardin took the time to try to heal her wound. He came alone to her home, sipped his tea, and listened. Crowley said the remarkable encounter made an indelible impression, that it changed her.

Grace. That's the best way to sum up all of the stories I heard that day. That's what was on my mind as I typed a dozen sets of interview notes and shipped them to Ellen. That's what comes across in the piece we ran, and in the stories that didn't make it into the final copy. Cardinal Joseph Bernardin was, for fellow clergy, for his Catholic followers, for chance encounterers, and for the thousands who knew him only by reputation, a vehicle of grace.

The 48 hours that Team Ellen worked on our piece were draining and invigorating. For me, they were also some of the most memorable and profound I have experienced both professionally and personally. How do you describe what grace looks like? You can't, but I think we came close.

Sun-Sentinel

Sun-Sentinel

Finalist, Team Deadline Reporting

After a disgruntled former city worker opened fire early one morning on a group of co-workers, the staff of the Fort Lauderdale, Fla., *Sun-Sentinel* produced a powerful and complete package of stories that helped readers understand this latest manifestation of urban horror. From its murder mystery opening to the kicker's irony, John deGroot's deadline portrait of the only person to escape the bullets fired by an enraged former co-worker puts readers on the scene. His tools: telling details, the playwright's sense of drama, and an ear for how people really talk.

 John deGroot is a senior projects writer for the *Sun-Sentinel* and a writing coach who has conducted seminars at newspapers and journalism centers throughout the United States and Europe. He has won numerous national and regional writing and reporting awards. He is also the author of *Papa,* a one-man play based on the life of Ernest Hemingway.

Out the back door, she flees unharmed

FEBRUARY 10, 1996

By John deGroot

Death wore a light blue sport coat.

"He was all dressed up in this nice jacket with a shirt and tie," Nancy Ellers said. "And he was holding a gun and pointing it at us with both hands. I think he was dressed nice because he knew he was going to die."

A moment later, Cliff McCree opened fire on Nancy Ellers and her co-workers in the trailer on Las Olas Boulevard, killing five of them, wounding one and killing himself. Only she escaped unhurt.

Nancy hadn't seen Cliff since he had been fired from his job as a Fort Lauderdale beach worker.

"I heard it was because he'd failed some kind of drug test," Nancy said. "He was always OK with me, but all the other guys said he had a real short temper and couldn't get along with anybody. Several of them said Cliff told them he was going to get even after he lost his job."

All that happened a year ago last December.

Friday morning, Cliff McCree walked into the trailer where Nancy Ellers and her fellow workers were drinking coffee and getting ready for another day cleaning the beach and making everything nice for the tourists.

It was shortly before 5 o'clock—at least an hour before the arrival of the morning's first joggers, dog-walkers and surfside treasure hunters armed with their metal detectors.

"We always get together for a coffee in the trailer before we start our day," Nancy said. "All those guys were really good friends."

The sky was dappled with stars and a breeze whispered in from the Southeast. The temperature hovered in the mid-60s and the sea was a cool 71 degrees.

All in all, the night and the air gave every promise of another immaculate South Florida day at the beach.

"We were all sitting there talking and then Cliff came in with this gun. He was real wild-eyed."

Nancy was seated close to a back door when Cliff began shooting.

"I jumped up and ran for the door and felt this bullet go *whoosh* between my arm and my side. Then the bullet put a hole in the door in front of me.

"I got through the door and kept running because there were more shots coming from the trailer."

Nancy raced to the pool of light that bathed the parking lot in front of the 7-Eleven on State Road A1A just south of Las Olas Boulevard.

"I called 911 and told them there was this guy shooting my friends," she said. "And then I stayed there until this police officer came. I was afraid to leave. I didn't know if Cliff was still out there walking around with his gun."

The sky was breaking purple and pink when a police officer drove Nancy back to the trailer.

The police told her four of her friends and co-workers were dead and two others gravely wounded. After shooting her six friends, Cliff had turned the pistol on himself to finish the job.

"I stayed outside," Nancy said. "I didn't want to go in there and see what he'd done."

Later, they took Nancy down to the police station where she told the detective what she'd seen.

"After that, I just wanted to go home," Nancy said.

Nancy Ellers is a solid, round-faced woman with gentle eyes and the pale, freckled skin of the Irish. Her maiden name was Gallagher.

Nancy lives with her husband, Paul, in a new suburban Tamarac home. Head west another mile or so and you're surrounded by the silent expanse of the Everglades.

"We came out here to get away from what's happened to Fort Lauderdale," says Paul, who retired a few years ago.

"It used to be real nice," Paul says of their old neighborhood in southwest Fort Lauderdale. "But then the neighborhood changed. Friday and Saturday nights you'd hear gunshots going off all the time."

"Don't say anything bad about the city," Nancy warns Paul. "I been with them 10 years and they been real good to me."

"Well, it's not just Fort Lauderdale," Paul says. "Things have gone bad all over. Look how they're killing each other at the post office."

"None of it makes any sense," says Nancy. "I don't go to church. But after this morning, I think I better start."

You ask about her job.

"It was the best job you could ever have," she says. "And we were all really good friends.

"Being out on the beach with the sun coming up every morning—it was so peaceful, with all the colors in the sky and the ocean and all."

It has been Nancy's job to paint over the graffiti and the Rollerblade skid marks the young people leave on the pristine white wall the city built between the sand and the sidewalk along A1A.

Nancy, 42, has been with the beach crew for three years.

"Before that, I worked at the cemetery. That was real peaceful, too."

It's then that the irony hits you.

Nancy Ellers spent seven years surrounded by death as she mowed the lush grass covering a city's worth of dead at rest in Fort Lauderdale Memorial Gardens.

She did her job well—learning to keep the blades of her mower away from the trees and shrubs among the graves and to make sure the machine's roar did not disturb the silent group of mourners clustered around another gleaming coffin suspended above another freshly dug grave.

But during her years at the cemetery, death came with quiet dignity, borne by a shiny black hearse before a parade dressed in black.

"Then they contracted out the maintenance job at the cemetery," Nancy says. "And that's how I got to the beach."

Lessons Learned

BY JOHN DE GROOT

Here in South Florida, as in so many urban regions across the nation, violence has become the elevator music for the approaching millennium.

The true horror is that our culture has made white noise of pain and suffering.

The electrocution of another killer in Florida is buried inside the A section—unless flames shoot from the condemned man's hood as they put the juice to him.

A domestic killing in a low-income neighborhood makes a brief on 3B—unless the man hacks off his lover's head with a machete and runs naked and bloody down a busy city street, screaming obscenities about the devil.

So for me, the real challenge as a tribal storyteller is to capture the desperate reality of violent crimes.

I think this is Edna Buchanan's great talent as a Pulitzer Prize-winning crime reporter for *The Miami Herald.* In an Edna cop story, the reader experiences the true context of most violence: Something horrible has happened to one of us—and it doesn't make any sense.

This was the logic behind my lead for a story about a woman who survived the sudden shooting death of five of her fellow workers by a disgruntled former co-worker.

"Death wore a light blue sport coat."

True, the fact that the killer wore a dress shirt, necktie, and light blue sport coat was a detail that came far into my interview with the still dazed woman on her front doorstep.

But for me, the light blue sport coat was THE telling detail and metaphor I needed to let the reader experience the real horror (and context) of more senseless death.

After all, light blue sport coats are what cologne-laden high school kids wear to the spring prom. But the costume of a crazed killer who strikes in the soft pink of dawn?

Oh, yes.

What really made this detail work was the fact that is was a *light* blue sport coat. A mere blue or dark blue sport coat wouldn't have been the same thing.

And I must confess to choosing "sport coat" over blazer.

It's what Mark Twain was talking about when he said there's a hell of a difference between lightning and lightning bugs.

After opening my story with an irony-tinged seven-word sentence, I shoved the reader into the scene with a truly powerful quote. (To help make my point, I've underlined the words that give the quote its remarkable power.)

"He was all dressed up in this nice jacket with a shirt and tie," Nancy Ellers said. "And he was holding a gun and pointing it at us with both hands. I think he was dressed nice because he knew he was going to die."

The quote wouldn't have the same power without "dressed up" and "dressed nice." Once again, the words heighten the tragic irony of what had happened.

Truth is, words (and facts) are all we have as writers. So our job is to become aware of their connotative power. As in the difference between *ocean* and *sea*. Or *cry* versus *weep*.

Which is why it vexes me to hear some sad newsroom burnout bemoan the lack of creativity in the newspaper business.

I had a lot going for me when it came to the structure of my story about this Fort Lauderdale beach cleaner who escaped death at her work place. It was a sidebar and part of a package. So I was able to concentrate on telling a story. Thanks to all the information in the headlines, photos, maps, and other stories that made up our packaged coverage. Which allowed me to focus in on a series of stark details and startling quotes laid out in more-or-less chronological order. Which made my job fairly easy. Because telling a story in chronological order is a lot like sex; once you're into it, the whole thing pretty much takes care of itself.

One final thought.

Most of us like to have a "model" to use in shaping our stories—which is why God made the inverted pyramid.

I stole my favorite story model from the movie *E.T.*

Remember how the little boy trapped the tiny alien in his back yard? He did it by laying down a trail of candy-coated bits of chocolate peanut butter.

E.T. picked up the first piece of candy, sniffed it, ate it, and loved it. Which led him to move on to the next piece of candy. Which he picked up, ate, and loved. Which led him to the next piece of candy...and so on.

Which is what storytelling is all about.

Only as journalists, the bits of candy we use to trap our readers must be facts.

But the dynamics remain: Be it trapping E.T., or luring the reader, the trick is to carefully select and arrange the most tasty morsels.

And therein, as Mr. Hamlet once mused, lies the rub.

The Boston Globe

Eileen McNamara
Commentary

Eileen McNamara began her career at *The Boston Globe* in 1976 as a secretary. She used the position to listen and learn. She brought to her job a splendid education, which included a degree from Barnard College and a master's degree from the Columbia University Graduate School of Journalism. In spite of her New York education, she thought she was destined to return to Boston, her birthplace, to work for the *Globe,* even if it meant starting as a secretary.

She gained valuable experience between 1977-79 as a Boston reporter for UPI. The *Globe* hired her as a general assignment reporter in 1979, a job from which she ascended to a variety of beats: state house reporter, congressional correspondent, special projects reporter, Sunday magazine writer, and columnist.

She brings to her columns a distinctive voice that always sounds like her, but can be used to express admiration, respect, righteous anger, empathy, or a sense of place. Never the armchair columnist, McNamara practices the skills of her earlier experience, using the eyes and ears of a curious neighbor, the feet of a dogged reporter, and the heart of an Irish storyteller.

In 1997, her commentary won not only the ASNE Distinguished Writing Award, but also the Pulitzer Prize.

—Roy Peter Clark

Waiting room awaits us all

MAY 22, 1996

It is church quiet in the Waiting Room when the woman in the knit pantsuit pulls out the jigsaw puzzle.

"If we all work on this together, we'll be done by the end of the day," she says, dumping 1,000 cardboard pieces of "The Beech Trees" onto a circular table in the center of the room.

Her no-nonsense tone, crisp and authoritative, confuses many of the dozen people waiting in small knots or all alone for word of relatives fresh from, or still in, surgery.

Who is this woman? Not a hospital employee—no ID badge. Not a volunteer—no pink smock. "Come on now," she coaxes, her good cheer jarring in a room thick with anxiety and exhaustion. "I had more takers last week."

This is her sixth week in the Waiting Room. It has been that long since her 85-year-old mother was wheeled into the Intensive Care Unit deep in a coma after open-heart surgery.

Now she is the Veteran, the self-appointed recreation director for the Waiting Room, a one-woman entertainment committee devising ways to fill time between the 15-minute visits permitted on even-numbered hours between 10 a.m. and 8 p.m.

It is the Veteran who instructs newcomers that the pay phone takes incoming calls, that the wall clock in the Waiting Room is three minutes slower than the one inside the ICU.

It is the Veteran who steers newcomers away from the coffee in the cafeteria and toward the cappuccino from the pushcart outside Radiology.

The windowless Waiting Room where the Veteran holds sway is in a university medical center but, with its French Impressionist prints in pastel frames, its day-old newspapers and its gray carpeting blackened by coffee stains, it could be in any hospital, anywhere.

The room is dominated by middle-aged women suspended between their children at the end of the pay phone and their parents at the end of their lives. Some of the women come and go during the day; most just stay, adhering to their own routines, until it is time to return home or to a motel nearby.

The Napper curls up on the too-short, too-hard couch and manages to sleep. The Reader moves too quickly through Jane Smiley to Sue Grafton. The Weeper stakes out a corner chair, where her sobs are as quiet as her cheeks are damp.

There is no privacy here. Every emotion is on display, especially when someone in blue surgical scrubs enters. The silence and the tension hang heavy until he or she alights.

Everyone eavesdrops, measuring their own fortunes against the good or bad news being delivered to someone else in the Waiting Room. The Veteran always hovers then. Over the weeks, she has learned to read the room, figuring out who needs a hug and who needs to be left alone.

She keeps a box of tissues at her elbow while she works the puzzle. The box comes in handy the night the surgeon tells a woman that a large blood clot, dislodged from her father's chest during surgery, has come to rest in his brain.

It is depleted after a nurse explains to a Russian immigrant that her husband's disorientation and paranoia is temporary, a consequence of narcotics and too much time in the netherworld of the brightly lit ICU, where day is indistinguishable from night.

When it is time for a visit, it is the Veteran who leads the group through the automated doors, past the nurses station where they separate, heading off to mothers on respirators, fathers on morphine.

Visitors go alone or in sometimes awkward pairings. The newly minted ex-wife meets her husband's lover in the ICU. He has had a massive coronary. His prospects are grim. The two women work out their respective positions silently. The younger woman moves from the side to the foot of the bed, giving 20 years of shared history their due.

It is church quiet late in the afternoon when the doctor slips into a chair at the blond oak table where the Veteran is hard at work piecing together "The Beech Trees."

"Did she wake up?" she asks, startled after so many weeks of benign neglect to find herself the focus of interest.

"No, she didn't," the doctor responds quietly, leaving unsaid what the room knows. The Veteran's wait is over.

The Napper brings her the tissue box. The Weeper folds her in an embrace.

When the Veteran has gone, those who remain in the Waiting Room pull their chairs up to the table and set to work on the unfinished jigsaw puzzle.

Writers' Workshop

Talking Points

1) The author describes the characters in her columns as types: the Veteran, the Napper, the Reader, the Weeper. Discuss the effect of this technique.

2) The term "microcosm" means a little world that represents a larger universe. In that sense, Earth is heaven's waiting room, a recognition of our own mortality. Study how the author moves us from particular moments to universal themes.

3) The first phrase, "It is church quiet," foreshadows the final dramatic scene, where the phrase is repeated. Discuss the effect of this technique.

Assignment Desk

1) In the interview, McNamara reveals that she was in the waiting room, not as a reporter, but as a person concerned about a loved one. She decides to keep this from the reader. Write two versions of a column. In the first version, feel free to use the word "I." In the next version, take the "I" out. Consider and discuss the differences.

Neighbors bid a fond farewell

NOVEMBER 13, 1996

The Lady Next Door has died.

To her grave, she takes her fierce intelligence and her unsparing judgments of those of us she leaves behind.

With her death, she deprives a neighborhood of one of its central characters: its scold and its conscience.

She lived next door to me, but she also lives on every city block, in every suburban subdivision, in every small town.

The Lady Next Door was leery when the young couple with two obstreperous boys and a wailing baby moved into the wreck of a house behind her back fence. She had hoped for a family with the means to clean up the place overnight. What she got, instead, was repair and renovation on the installment plan.

The Lady Next Door was a master of indirection. Upon return from a weekend trip, she would gaze across the fence: "Is it my imagination or did that forsythia have a growth spurt while we were away?" (Translation: "Trim your hedges.")

"I know how hard it is to find workmen in a new town. I've taken the liberty of making a list for you. Our painters' names are at the top." (Translation: "Paint your garage.")

She was attracted and repelled by the chaos on our side of the cedar stockade. Boys batting softballs into her gutters, kicking soccer balls into her front yard and, on their retrieval missions, snapping branches off her ornamental shrubs.

The Lady Next Door endured in silence a noise level that was often cacophonous. Barking dogs. Screaming infants. But she did not hesitate to reprimand the culprits if salty language from a soccer scrimmage carried to the screened porch where she entertained on warm afternoons from April through October.

Chances for good relations looked especially bleak when she traced a sneaker imprint in her well-tended flower bed to the foot of her new, 3-year-old neighbor.

He shrank from her withering glare, but he watched his step thereafter.

The children took their cues from their mother, who never, ever called The Lady Next Door by her first name. There was in her manner the sense of absolute authority she must have projected when she was a mathematics teacher so many years ago.

The children sensed it, too, becoming uncharacteristically polite in her presence. The Lady Next Door was grown up in a way that their own parents were not. She provided a model of adult behavior and expectations only hinted at in their own household.

She wagged her finger but she gave them gifts they are now too young to appreciate—the soothing strains of Chopin through an open window on mild nights, the rickety clack of a hand mower across the grass on Sunday mornings.

Long after they have forgotten the face of The Lady Next Door, they will remember those sounds of summer, how much more gracious they were than the thump of rock music and the sputter of the gas-powered lawn mower in their own back yard.

They will remember that the first seedling in their first garden was a gift handed across the back fence.

They will remember the smiley faces she took to drawing on their wayward kickballs before tossing them back.

The Lady Next Door was a snow bird with a reverse migratory pattern. She flew home each December for the holidays. Christmas in the desert was unthinkable for her, a Canadian native.

Six months ago, she came home from her winter retreat in an ambulance.

In one of life's cruel ironies, her hospital bed in the front parlor sat opposite the piano she could no longer play.

The stroke had rendered The Lady Next Door speechless, a condition that never beset her in life.

She had opinions about everything and everyone. She was especially confused, as older accomplished women often are, by the laments of younger women about the burdens of juggling a career and a home.

Hadn't she juggled, too, at a time when there was little enough tolerance for women with careers and none at all for career women who complained?

Through the summer, her husband pushed her wheelchair around the block, letting her drink in the familiar sights of a life that was slipping away. It was awkward to meet them. She had so much to say and, suddenly, no way to say it.

The other morning, the hearse came for The Lady Next Door. We had been expecting it, but were saddened nonetheless.

Our sadness was tinged with relief. We had raked the yard the day before. All was in good order for the last trip through the neighborhood of The Lady Next Door.

Writers' Workshop

Talking Points

1) This column begins and ends with the same phrase: "The Lady Next Door." Discuss the effects of that circular structure.

2) The author describes a particular person, her next-door neighbor, but also tries to make her an emblem for a type of person. What techniques does she use to universalize her neighbor?

3) Most journalists write about neighborhoods from the outside in. Eileen McNamara writes from the inside out. Consider and discuss the difference.

Assignment Desk

1) Create a brainstorming list of other central characters in American neighborhoods. Using this column as a model, try writing a description of such a character. List characteristics that mark the person as an individual; the qualities that mark the person as representative of a type.

2) Look through the "neighborhood" sections of a daily newspaper over a month's time and clip out the best feature story you can find about a neighbor. Make a list of the ways in which the writer brings this character to life.

Draft pick from an ugly lineup

APRIL 24, 1996

Attention Bob Kraft: Christian Peter might be a little late for training camp this summer. With any luck, he'll be in jail.

The University of Nebraska defensive tackle just drafted by the New England Patriots is due in court for sentencing May 21.

The senior co-captain for the two-time defending national champion Cornhuskers faces three months in jail and a $500 fine for grabbing a woman around the throat while hassling her and other women in a bar after a football banquet last month.

This is nothing unusual for Peter, 23, a 290-pound, 6-foot-3 very Big Man on Campus.

It has only been three months since his probation expired for sexually assaulting Natalie Kuijvenhoven, a former Miss Nebraska whose crotch he grabbed repeatedly in a packed bar while spewing obscenities and telling her how much he knew she loved it.

That was in 1993, the same year Melissa DeMuth filed a police complaint that Peter invited her to his room and then pinned her down and ejaculated on her face in front of his friends. DeMuth remains convinced authorities never prosecuted the nose guard because he was a college football star.

It was Peter's star status that a 21-year-old Colorado woman says intimidated her from filing criminal rape charges in 1991. Last summer, frustrated by university inaction on her complaint and bolstered by therapy, she filed a federal sex discrimination suit against Peter and the school.

Peter denies the rape charges, but they are supported by a dorm mate to whom the plaintiff confided at the time. Her dorm mate wasn't surprised. She says Peter tried to expose himself to her after getting drunk at a campus party.

"She came forward because she realizes he is never going to change and more women are going to be hurt unless this guy is held accountable for his actions,"

Larry Trattler, a Denver attorney for the alleged rape victim, said yesterday.

Trattler's civil complaint against Peter and the university runs to 15 pages. It takes almost that long to enumerate Peter's arrest record beyond the sexual assaults: disturbing the peace, trespassing, urinating in public, refusing to comply with the order of a policeman, threatening to kill a parking attendant, possessing alcoholic beverages while under the age of 21.

All and all, you can see why New England Patriots owner Bob Kraft and coach Bill Parcells want this guy on their team.

Only last week, Parcells waxed philosophical about the off-field antics of his potential draft picks. "This league isn't all choir boys," he said. "You've just got to do your homework and hope you get the right kind of players on your team."

Well, either the dog ate their homework, or he and Kraft have very different hopes for this team than many Patriots' fans.

Kraft was too busy to talk yesterday, but Don Lowery, his spokesman, said the Pats are not reconsidering their offer to Peter, who will earn a six-figure salary if he makes the cut.

"The issue we face in drafting him," Lowery said, "is whether his basic character is so flawed that he is incapable of conducting himself properly in his personal and professional life in the future. We don't feel this is the case."

Now that's odd, because it wasn't too long ago that Kraft himself said he would never draft Lawrence Phillips, Peter's Nebraska teammate, because Phillips was convicted of assaulting his girlfriend.

What's the difference between Phillips and Peter? "I don't know, to be honest," said Lowery.

That's because there isn't any difference.

They are both thugs who graduated from a college football program distinguished by its tolerance of violence off the field, particularly violence against women. (In addition to Phillips and Peter, four other Huskers have been charged with everything from attempted murder to assault in recent years.)

Nebraska coach Tom Osborne's idea of discipline? After Peter pleaded no contest to sexual assault, Osborne suspended him from practice for a week and from one irrelevant spring game.

The Patriots player personnel director, Bobby Grier, concedes the Patriots did not know the extent of the charges against Peter, did not talk to his victims or their lawyers and did not go beyond the usual interviews with his coaches and agent. "We did talk to him about this," Grier said. "We think he's sorry."

I'm so glad.

If the past is prologue, Christian Peter won't be getting any jail time in Nebraska. Can't you just hear him now, telling the judge he's got a good job at good wages all lined up in New England?

Writers' Workshop

Talking Points

1) What words would you choose to describe the voice of the writer in this column? Do the same for her other columns. If there were no bylines on these columns, what clues would lead you to conclude they were written by the same person?

2) After reading this column, what advice would you have for Bob Kraft on what to do? What evidence weighs most heavily for you?

3) The author uses the real names of two victims of sexual assault. This is a controversial practice. Describe the effect of these names on you as a reader. Do the names strengthen the writer's argument?

Assignment Desk

1) McNamara uses graphic language to describe two sexual assaults. Try to rewrite these passages with less graphic detail. Discuss the effects of your revisions. Do they change the column for the better?

2) Research what has happened to the athlete described in the column. Write a story or column updating the public.

What the hell were her parents doing?

APRIL 12, 1996

Grief and anger compete today after the death of Jessica Dubroff in the crash of the plane the seven-year-old girl was piloting cross country.

Anger wins.

Anger at the parents who put a child in that cockpit.

Anger at the flight instructor who let them.

Anger at the cult of celebrity that has systematically killed off common sense in America.

We talk a lot about rights versus responsibilities in this country, but we almost always have the poor in mind when we do.

When flames engulf a tenement apartment we are quick to ask: "How could that mother have left her children home alone to run to the store for milk?"

When a child is shot dead on a summer night on a city street, we ask: "What was he doing out at that hour?"

This morning it is impossible not to ask about the ambitious middle-class parents of a precocious little girl: "What the hell were Jessica Dubroff's mother and father *thinking*?"

They certainly had a right to strap their little girl into a pilot's seat at Half Moon Bay Airport in California and point her toward the East Coast and 15 minutes of fame. But, just as surely, they had a responsibility not to.

Jessica was 4-foot-2. She weighed 55 pounds. She needed a booster seat to reach the control panel and leg extenders to reach the rudder pedals!

Her death was no accident. This child was put in harm's way.

Whether through a twisted sense of adventure, or a more base impulse toward self-promotion, Jessica's mother and father forgot that the first responsibility of parents is to protect their children.

"I don't want this to mean to people that you should hold your children down, that you don't give them freedom and choice," Jessica's mother, Blair Hathaway, said upon learning of her daughter's death.

"And, God, that was what her beauty was. She got to choose."

Oh, Mrs. Hathaway, I know you are in shock, but what in heaven's name are you talking about?

Seven is old enough to choose which sweater to wear with what skirt, to choose, at least for a while, to hate broccoli. But it is nowhere near old enough to choose to risk life and limb to become the youngest person to pilot an airplane across America.

Even the idea of such a record is obscene. That's why the *Guinness Book of World Records* eliminated the youngest pilot category years ago, knowing it had the potential to encourage such dangerous flights.

It's not just Jessica's parents who lost their moorings. The whole state of California seems to have taken leave of its senses.

Forrest Storz is a flight instructor at the airport south of San Francisco where Jessica had taken 30 hours of instruction in the last four months.

"Whatever happened was beyond their control," he said yesterday. "Some day your number is up."

What?

Have we gone so far down the road of evading responsibility that we blame *fate* for the crash of an airplane being piloted by a seven-year-old?

I understand that Jessica was a very, very bright child and that she really, really liked to fly. But I also know what she said about flying during the pre-flight publicity: "I enjoy looking out the window. But you have to concentrate on flying."

What she enjoyed doing and what she had to do to accomplish her goal—or her parents' goal—were two different things.

On any given day, my 7-year-old would really, really like to try his hand at any number of adult-sized challenges. He even has the skills to accomplish some of them. But what he lacks, and what Jessica lacked when she got behind the controls in that cockpit, was not the skill but the judgment that comes with maturity.

Seven-year-olds might know that thunder is nothing more than the violent expansion of air that has been heated by lightning, but that doesn't stop them from hiding under the covers.

They don't lack knowledge; they lack maturity.

The cross-country flight was all his idea, Lloyd Dubroff said the day before he, his daughter and her
flight instructor climbed into that four-seat Cessna
177B Cardinal. "I'm the culprit," he boasted.

May you rest in peace, Mr. Dubroff, but you were
right about that.

Writers' Workshop

Talking Points

1) Persuasive writers often use repetition as a drumbeat in a story. Discuss the repetition of the word "anger" at the top of the column, and "choose" in the middle. When does repetition work? When does it become redundancy?

2) Discuss the effect of directly addressing the dead father in the final line of the column.

3) Writers use quotations for many different purposes. Discuss McNamara's use of the parents' quotations. What effect does she create?

Assignment Desk

1) Imagine writing a column celebrating the effort of Jessica Dubroff and her family. It would run next to McNamara's at the same length. Sketch out the argument you might make. Try writing the lead.

2) Write a letter to *The Boston Globe* agreeing with or arguing against McNamara's column.

A conversation with
Eileen McNamara

ROY PETER CLARK: How long have you been doing the column now, Eileen?

EILEEN McNAMARA: I started in July of 1995.

Has it gotten easier or harder?

I find it really hard every day. It's gotten easier in the sense that I now know that an empty space won't run in the paper twice a week, that something will occur to me or something will happen in the world that will elicit a response from me. I didn't know that at the beginning.

I was panic stricken when I started that I would have nothing to write about. I know now that that's not the case. I worry more now about whether I have anything intelligible to say.

Where do the ideas come from?

Well, I've never lacked for opinions about anything, so that part's never been a problem. But I really think columns ought to be off the news a lot of the time. And since I write a local column, I pay pretty strict attention to what's going on here in Boston and try to find a different wrinkle to write about. I leave the headline stuff to the news reporters, but I try to find some way into a story that maybe somebody hasn't thought about.

I'll give you an example. We have an *au pair* here charged with shaking a baby to death and she's facing first-degree murder charges. So the front-page stories have focused on the criminal charges, on the family, on the training provided by *au pair* agencies to these girls who come to the United States to be caregivers. And I wrote a column about this. I tried to write from the parents' perspective. As the mother of three small children, I've had *au pairs*. And I wrote about how you hold your breath as you pull out of the driveway every day when you leave your children in someone else's care. So I try to find a way into the story that's maybe a little more personal and a little different.

Is this a perspective that you developed as a columnist or is it something that you used to bring to your reporting as well?

I think it's always something I've done as a reporter. You know, I've covered the traditional beats here and I've covered the statehouse and I went to Washington and I covered Congress, and I never found any satisfaction in simply conveying the news. I was always looking for a way to tell a narrative story in a way that made sense to people in their own lives.

A lot of my neighbors and friends who aren't in the newspaper business tell me that they've given up on newspapers because they don't see their own lives ever reflected there. Now this is a middle-class perspective, obviously. But we do tend to write about the extremes. We write about the poor and we write about the rich.

And we write about the dramas in life, the drive-by shootings and the lottery winners. But when do we write about the average person in a way that they understand and they relate to?

You seem much more connected to the patterns and rhythms of everyday life than most journalists I know. Does that sound like an odd observation?

No. You know what I think it is? I think we're all connected to those patterns because we all have lives. I take my life to work. And I think a lot of us have been trained to edit ourselves out of this job, in part because of the professional standard toward objectivity, which I certainly subscribed to as a reporter and believed in and tried to live up to. But even as I did that, I realized the folly of pretending that there was not a human being holding that note pad and that part of what I would even decide was a story was based on my own biography. You know, the subjectivity doesn't start when you sit down and start typing the story; it starts when you choose the story.

And I knew what was driving me to choose stories. I don't think it was an accident that I was eight months' pregnant when we published a series of stories on infant mortality that I wrote. I think your life leads you to certain preoccupations with issues at certain times. And that's not a bad thing.

There are a lot of traditional inhibitions against doing that, aren't there? Don't write about your friends, don't write about anybody you know. Don't write about yourself.

And I don't. You'll notice in these pieces, I'm disguised in some of them because I have a very strong repulsion towards writing the pronoun "I." I'm one of the characters that I described in "The Waiting Room." My mother had just had heart surgery.

But when I sat down to write about it, I was fighting that impulse you just described, which is that we can't write about ourselves and we can't write about our own experience. But I knew that almost everyone I know has been in that waiting room and that they have met the characters I met in that waiting room. And I wanted to find a way to say that this is every waiting room.

So I did not write it in the first person because then, it's just my experience. I wanted it to be everyone's experience. And it was. I mean it hit a chord with readers who have parents who are going through what my mom went through.

This is a metaphor for something very big. "The Waiting Room" is Earth, right?

Right, right, right. We'll leave it to the philosophers to decide why we're here on Earth and what the meaning of it all is. But the experiences that we have that we think of as mundane or routine, sitting in the waiting room, are actually some of the most profound experiences of our lives, not because we're sitting there, thinking profound thoughts, but because we're going through something.

You're writing about people who are sort of thrown together, in a sense. You're talking about neighbors, right? You're talking about the people who wind up living in the same rooming house with you

and the people who wind up sitting in the waiting room with you.

So you have the people in the waiting room and the lady next door as kind of universal characters. But what about the other two columns, where you seem to be going after "villains."

In both of those columns, the villain is us, the villain is this culture that created a Christian Peter, tolerated him, advanced his career, despite his behavior. And it's a culture that creates a 7-year-old pilot taking off into a storm so she can beat a record.

Yeah, so she can get on TV.

So she can get on TV or, worse, her parents can get on TV. And we're part of that culture—the media—we help create that. I mean my indignation in both of those columns is about us as much as it is about the particular people in those columns. What have we become that we offer Christian Peter a chance for an NFL career and a million-dollar salary?

When I quote that poor mother in that column, I'm not trying to pick on the mother, but what was she thinking of to talk about her daughter dying in joy? No 7-year-old child who dies in a plane crash is dying in joy. I just don't believe that.

You really seemed angry, outraged, you know, and your voice was heated up in those two columns.

Oh, indignation is a marvelous fuel for a columnist, and I often feel it, and the best columns I write are when I'm righteously indignant. What you don't want to be is sanctimonious and what you don't want to be is self-righteous. But, God, indignation has its place, it does.

What makes you feel indignant?

Injustice, or cultural stupidity, which I felt in both of these columns. The Jessica Dubroff case is interesting in how that came about. It wasn't my day to write. And my colleague was asked to write on this topic because it was obviously what everybody in America was talking about. And she filed a column celebrating Jessica's choice and I saw it in the queue.

I mean I had been fuming about her death ever since I'd seen it move on the wire. And the editor saw me over here, banging things, and someone came over and said "What's the problem?" I said, "You go ahead, run that, just run that in isolation and the readership is going to go nuts because I don't believe that's how people really feel." Some people feel that way. Clearly, this columnist feels it and is entitled to feel it. It was a beautiful column, it was an absolutely beautiful, evocative column about freedom and choice and looking heavenward and seeing this girl's face in the clouds. But all I could see was the burned plane on the runway.

And it enraged me. And I said, "Well, I wasn't going to write about this for tomorrow because I'm a local columnist, and I'm not supposed to write about this, but I dare you not to print it." And I just sat down and I banged out that column and I banged it out in reaction not just to her mother's quotes, but to this beautiful celebration of this child's life, which is just so opposite of what I was feeling and what I just knew in my gut a lot of people were feeling. And I said, "You should twin them, you should run them side by side."

I think it's important to be fueled by your emotions. People live by their emotions; I mean we're altogether too rational most of the time. And when you feel something deeply, it's connected to something else, something bigger. And the chances are that if you do feel something that deeply, other people do, too, and maybe if you write it, you'll connect with them.

Columnists and other writers talk about the concept of voice. They say they hear a voice in the story or in the column. Does that word have any meaning for you as a goal or as a strategy or as an effect of your writing?

I guess it's always my voice, but my voice has all kinds of inflections. Sometimes I'll write a column and I'll read it back and I'll realize it's too angry. And I'll think that's not what I want to convey here. I want to convey the fact of the injustice. I often break news in this column, so I'm often telling people things they don't know about. A lot of times I need to get my anger out of the way just so that I can let them know something's happened that's not right.

So I think the voice is really, really important. The other reason that I think it's important to realize that you have more than one voice is so you can choose which voice to speak in. Otherwise, your column becomes so predictable that, you know, you're the angry feminist, you're the blue-collar lunch pail guy. And I think that's just not useful for anybody because I don't want to write just for people who agree with me. And the people who disagree with me ought to be able to come back into the space the next Wednesday and find that they agree with me.

I get some wonderful mail from people telling me how confused they are by me, that they'll be enraged by some of the stuff I write and then they'll find themselves agreeing with me. Or the opposite. I had a terrible tempest here this year with Planned Parenthood because of the columns I wrote about John Salvi, who was the man convicted of killing two women in abortion clinics up here.

I believed from the very beginning that John Salvi was a paranoid schizophrenic and the trial only convinced me further. I also thought that the trial wasn't about whether he was mentally incompetent, it was about politics, and that there was no way that John Salvi was not going to be convicted in Massachusetts for these crimes. And I said so and I said that I thought it was a shame.

There was a gag order in this case, so that Salvi's attorneys weren't allowed to talk; neither were the attorneys for the prosecution. But Planned Parenthood was on the steps of the courthouse every day, denouncing him for this evil-intentioned act.

So they were the surrogates for the prosecution. And I suggested in one column that Planned Parenthood should sit down and shut up. It is possible to be pro-choice, which I am, and write pro-choice columns about the issue of abortion and have a very, very different perspective on speech and on someone's right to a fair trial.

This trial became about abortion, when I thought it ought to have been about mental illness and criminal responsibility. But it was very painful to take the heat, in a way, from people who thought I was a friend, but it was very revealing to me and very good for me, and I hope for them, to realize that your opinions about issues are very complicated and that if we don't look at the gradations, then we're all just automatons marching in lock step, and that doesn't serve the purpose of democracy very well.

You don't seem like an armchair columnist at all.

I hope I'm not and I don't ever want to be. Here's an example from yesterday that's a perfect example of why you should never, ever be an armchair columnist.

We had a group of women up here called the Framingham Eight. They were women who were imprisoned for having killed their abusive partners. They were either pardoned or paroled by the governor of Massachusetts because they had never been allowed to introduce evidence of the abuse they suffered at their trials. So they were released from prison.

We had a story in the paper this week in which one of them was identified as a parole violator and having been hauled off to jail. I sat down to write a column about second chances and how sometimes they're not enough and what a shame it was that this woman's life had not turned around.

If I had written that column without doing any reporting, I would not have found out what I did find out and what I wrote in the paper yesterday. They didn't arrest that woman; it was a mistaken identity. They arrested somebody else and they publicly identified her as Shannon Booker, but it wasn't Shannon Booker, it was somebody else. While this woman was being arrested, Shannon Booker was at her job in the inner city, counseling drug addicts.

Her daughter heard on the news that her mother had been arrested for parole violations and was traumatized. Shannon was traumatized, too. She had a hard time convincing her friends this week that it wasn't her.

And the state police had some sort of marginal explanation for how this kind of a mistake could have happened. When I asked them whether they would apologize to her or not, they were very cavalier about the trauma she suffered then. They said, "Well, you know, it's not really our job."

That's a very different column than the one I set out to write. Imagine, had I written the first one and never checked, and no one else checked, either. So the fact that I wrote the column meant that we cleared her name.

Eileen, the other thing in addition to reporting is storytelling. I don't think most people associate columns with storytelling.

Well, that's what the best ones really are. I mean that's what the best journalism is, isn't it, telling stories? We have the best job in the world. You know, strangers invite us into their lives and they share things with us that are very personal and very poignant, sometimes very universal. And they trust us to take their stories and give them to the world or at least to our circulation area. And it's a fairly awesome responsibility, I think. People's stories are like the fabric of life, and columns should tell stories.

You can do a column lots of ways. You can wag your finger at people and you can tsk, tsk, tsk at people. But I suspect that most people get enough of that in their real lives.

I mean they get it from their boss and they get it from their spouse and they get it from their kids. They get it from their schoolteachers. They get it from their parents. They get it from everyplace.

So I don't think they need that from me. And this is said with absolute humility. Who cares what I think, really, about the great issues of the day? You know, my opinion has no more validity than the person sitting next to me on the city bus. So although there are times when I feel a compelling need to comment on the issues of the day, I think those are my weakest columns.

The best columns are when you just tell a story, a story that has a point, a moral, even if it doesn't have a moral, even if it evokes a visceral reaction, something identifiable.

The difference between you and the person on the bus may be your ability to tell that story well.

Right.

Although I know lots of people who aren't journalists who are great storytellers, as I'm sure you do.

Sure. I'm Irish, of course I do.

How did you become a good storyteller?

It's hard-wired. You know, you can't be Irish and not tell stories. Where do you trace your storytelling ways to? To the corner bar where your father held forth, to the parlor where your father and your uncle told stories. I think it's the nature of working class, ethnic people to tell stories. I'm 44 years old, so in my early years, we didn't have a television.

Where did you grow up?

I grew up in North Cambridge, Tip O'Neill's district, in a working class neighborhood of three-family houses, we call them three-deckers here in Boston, where people struggled a little for some joy in life. And I think they found it in each other's company at the corner bar, they found it in each other's living rooms. And I think I've been an observer all my life. I think I watched them and I listened to them and I saw the value in their stories.

Are there columnists whose voices you connect with?

There's a lot of columnists I admire and have long admired. I work at the same newspaper as one of the greatest columnists in America and she's been doing it for 20 years now. And to me, there's still not a better example of a person who brings real human, everyday experience into her interpretation of public policy. That's Ellen Goodman.

The New York Times's John Leonard. He used to write a column for the Living Pages. It was a terrific column. He wrote about his personal experience, he wrote about when the basement flooded and what he did. I remember one particularly touching column about a friend who had died who was 47 and about the feelings that evoked in him, and going to the funeral and how the deceased's wonderful children had dressed him in the tennis clothes he was wearing when he died of a heart attack. It was really a celebration of his friend's life, but also a metaphor for the rest of us. And I found in all of his columns something I could take away that was for me. And he's also just a beautiful writer. In one column, and I don't remember what the column was about, he described the graciousness in the act of women who remove an earring when they talk on the telephone, like how the demise of clip-on earrings has lost that gesture to society. His language was so beautiful that I just remember the pleasure that I had in reading it, still.

None of us invents this. You're grateful to the Meyer Bergers and the Ellen Goodmans and the Frank Clines and the John Leonards who went before you, who showed you how to do it.

Is it true that you started at the *Globe* as a secretary?

I was a secretary with a master's degree from the Columbia University School of Journalism and an undergraduate degree from Barnard College and experienced as a campus correspondent with the *New York Daily News*. But it was 1974, you know, women were...

Underappreciated, undervalued?

Yes. I had some journalistic experience. I wanted to come to Boston, so when I got out of Columbia, I said no to an AP job in Jackson, Mississippi. I've never been sure that that was a good idea, in a way, because Jackson, Mississippi, is the place where I probably could have gained some different experience.

But I also have always had the suspicion, and it's only been reinforced by time, that you are in part a product of place and I'm a product of this place. Boston. And I couldn't have written these columns anywhere else. I could be a journalist in New York, but I wouldn't be as good a journalist as I am here, because this is what I am, this is in my skin. And I've been away enough—I've worked in Washington and I went to school in New York-that I don't feel parochial, but I also feel that there is something to be said for a sense of place.

So when I had an opportunity to work as a secretary here, I took it.

I mean the value of the experience wasn't in the typing because I still type with two fingers. The value in the experience was being exposed to one of the best editors in the business, Bob Phelps. What ethics I didn't learn from the Dominican nuns I learned from Bob Phelps, especially my journalistic ethics. I learned simply from watching him.

The other thing is if you're a secretary, you're invisible, so I would be filing and I would be privy to very interesting conversations about news judgment among editors, about why they were doing something, about why they shouldn't have done something.

And I found myself in the presence of very candid conversations because nobody noticed me because I was a secretary. I learned a lot that year, so it was a valuable year for me.

Can we just talk about Catholicism for a second?

Oh, sure. Even though I'm a Unitarian now. But it isn't Unitarianism that shaped me, it's Catholicism. I mean I had 12 years of parochial school and I was the dissenter in class. I ran afoul of the nuns more often than not because I didn't think you'd go to hell because you had something to say.

I lost my institutional connection to the church as an adolescent, I think. I had way, way too many questions that they couldn't answer, wouldn't answer, and at the time bristled at for being asked.

But I know how much I owe of who I am to that training. I mean, I read a lot of columnists who don't feel when they come to work that they have a mission. This is where you fight against being sanctimonious in a column.

I really think journalism does have a mission and it isn't a political mission, but it is to give a voice to people who don't have a voice. And if we don't, who will?

The Times

Teddy Allen

Finalist, Commentary

Teddy Allen is a columnist for *The Times* in Shreveport, La., where he has been writing three columns a week and general assignment features since 1990. Prior to that he wrote sports for *The Longview* (Texas) *Journal, The Monroe* (La.) *News-Star, The Times, The Shreveport Journal,* and the *New Orleans Times-Picayune.* He was raised in rural South Carolina. Allen twice won the Associated Press Sports Editors national award for feature writing and has published two books, *And There You Have It* and *Blue Plate Special.*

In this suspenseful column about a boy injured in a hunting accident, Allen uses a simple device—counting—to recreate the terror in a father's heart and to keep readers holding their breath. Notice how Allen's structure flaunts the newswriting standard of giving away the ending in the first paragraph; he lets readers experience a story from start to finish.

Learning to count again and seeing it all add up

MAY 5, 1996

The men in the boat had to go slow because if they hit a stump and sheared the motor's pin, they would lose time and maybe everything that mattered. The boy would lose hope and lose more blood.

He was running out of both.

They cut the water quietly. The only sounds that registered were the low purr of the motor and something in unison from the men and the boy. Strange ...they were counting.

"121, 122, 123, 124..."

In the ugly minutes since the sound of the shotgun had exploded in the duck blind and echoed through the Arkansas reservoir, the 8-year-old boy, his father and two other men had become bonded for eternity. An accident plunged the four into a situation as real as life gets. As real as death gets.

Lying on his back in the too-slow boat in the January cold, the boy, bleeding from wounds to his chest and his partially severed hand, looked up, looked into the face of his father.

"Daddy, am I going to die?"

The boat was slow. Stumps everywhere. Cold. The boy feeling hot in his chest. Eighteen miles from a country hospital, much more than that to a medical center.

The son looked to the father for an answer. His head was in his father's lap. His father held the boy's right arm toward heaven to slow the bleeding.

"No, you're not going to die." Half command, half compassion. "Not today. Not anytime soon."

And that's when he told his son to start counting. And to keep counting. And they did.

"One, two, three, four..."

Around the stumps, toward the truck, in the peaceful and painful mid-morning, the men and the boy counted. Kept going.

They'd been planning the trip for a while, the dad and the son and their duck-hunting friends. The guys.

And now it was the last hunt of the trip, the last shots of the morning. It would be over in a few minutes. Time to head in.

Time to go home.

But when the ducks came, the boy reached for the gun and in the cold it slipped. The butt hit hard against the blind's bench.

And then the explosion. Suddenly everything was wrong.

Two feet separated father and son. The scene was unthinkable. It was reflex after that. Into the boat. A tourniquet. Quick whispers and lengthy prayers said in half-seconds.

"83, 84, 85, 86..."

They made it to the truck, to the hospital, and from there the boy was airlifted to Little Rock. The father had to stay behind. Still numb. Still reflex. Still counting.

Before one of the men drove him to Little Rock, the dad went to the hotel to gather their things. It hit him when he opened the door. His son's clothes laid out for the trip home. A book on baseball. A toothbrush.

"1,006, 1,007, 1,008, 1,009..."

Nearly four months have passed. Few knew how remarkable it was last week when a young left-hander took the mound at the Shreveport Little League Complex, a baseball in his left hand, a glove covering his injured right. Nine pellets remain in his hand, 15 in his shoulder. Physical therapy will continue for at least a year.

Maybe he'll be able to make a fist with his right hand again. Maybe he'll be able to spread his fingers apart again.

Maybe, he told his father on the bench between innings last Saturday, the umpire will open his eyes and call a few more strikes.

The joy of little-boy frustration.

The days continue to go by, one by one, and the father and son keep counting. It worked that day when their world turned dark, when the sun went out and time seemed to have run out.

And it's worked since, as the miracles mount. The father and son keep counting. Counting the days. Counting the moments. Counting their blessings.

Lessons Learned

BY TEDDY ALLEN

My sisters gave me Neil Simon's *Rewrites* for Christmas. I added this gesture to the list of Reasons Why I Love My Sisters. That's not to be confused with the other list I keep, the list of People I Might Have To Kill One Of These Days. (Don't worry; you're not on it. Yet.)

In *Rewrites,* Simon says people often ask him where he gets his ideas. And he offers something I can relate to but could never put into words. Ideas, he says, are easy. He has bundles of them. They are out there in his mind like little lights, sparkling, plain to see. But getting one to work for him at a certain time (like right now!), getting it to crystallize, that's the problem. That's the challenge.

And so it was with this story. I knew about it the day it happened, the day Gentry was shot in the duck blind. But I didn't want to write it then. Could have, but it just didn't feel right. So I waited, and, of course, it stayed in my mind.

Then about four months after the accident, I asked Gentry's father, Mark, about him, and he told me Gentry had been griping between innings the night before in a Little League game. Gentry was pitching and was less than thrilled with the home plate umpire.

And that's when I knew it was time. I wrote the story the next day.

Writing isn't rocket science; I've found it's mostly trying, rolling the sentences and words around over and over in your head. Reading and practicing. Besides, most people don't want to hear the labor pains; they just want to see the baby. But since this book's purpose is to amplify the labor pains *and* display the babies, I'll do my best to tell you what I was thinking when I wrote the column. When it comes to trying to write better, I suppose journalistic war stories help. I know they help me.

I felt the story would be more effective without names, without the proper nouns. I felt this would make it easier for all parents to see in the story both themselves and their children. They could more easily plug themselves into the pronouns.

The beginning described what there was to lose: time, hope, blood, the boy.

The counting came to me during those months I was waiting to write the story. It was a way to tie the time together.

Again I felt readers would be able to add their own thoughts in those spots, that the sameness of the counting, the uncertainty of when or where the numbers would end, would both keep the reader active and help me tell in a little space what was a long story.

I often begin writing with the end in mind, but I didn't have it when I started this story. But I had to start, so I did. And it came to me when I was almost finished. The counting again. Often, if you think long enough, that will happen. And while it wasn't perfect, it was what I was trying to say.

A couple of other things. The short sentences helped with the sense of urgency and the way I imagined the men were thinking at the time, moment to moment, bits of information tiny but dramatic. Not knowing what would come next. They were unable, in a crisis like that, to sustain long thoughts.

And finally, I wanted to be true to the faith of both Mark and Gentry. They believed God was with them, and today they feel the incident has given each a testimony he didn't have before. But no one likes to be "preached at." So I tried to make the references subtle: the son looked into the face of his father, the father held the boy's right arm toward heaven, the father told the son he wasn't going to die. And another reference later in the story hinted at the uncertainty we all live with: "It would be over in a few minutes. Time to head in. Time to go home."

The headline, cliché-ridden though it is, was what I wanted the story to say.

I guess that, overall, I don't like many of the stories I write, at least not for long. You know how you look back at them and see that one word or phrase you should have re-re-thought? You see how you never got around to saying what you really wanted to say? How you swung hard but missed by a solid foot? I just hate that.

But this story I liked OK. I wish all my stories could read more like this one, could have the same impact or be this starched and clean. But I'm a writer, or at least I'm trying to be, so I know better. Even though I'll keep trying hard to make them all this way and I'll keep hoping hard they'll all turn out this way...I won't count on it.

Mike Deupree

Finalist, Commentary

Mike Deupree is a columnist for the Cedar Rapids *Gazette,* where his commentaries appear three times a week. A native Iowan, Deupree grew up in the Missouri Valley area. He studied aerospace engineering at Iowa State University, later changed his major to journalism, transferred to the University of Iowa, and received a B.A. in 1969. After four years as sports editor, columnist, and general assignment reporter for the *Blackfoot* (Idaho) *News,* Deupree came to *The Gazette* as city hall reporter. He subsequently served as state editor and editorial writer before becoming a columnist full time in 1987. His work has won numerous awards, including first-place honors in competitions sponsored by the National Society of Newspaper Columnists (1994), the Iowa Associated Press Managing Editors (1995), and the Iowa Newspaper Association (1984, 1987, and 1991).

Deupree recounts the consequences of consuming the fake fat, Olestra, and the cost of brief celebrity in a humorous column that demonstrates how far a columnist on deadline will go to entertain readers.

Trotting onto the world stage

JUNE 9, 1996

Andy Warhol said that in the future, everyone would be famous for 15 minutes.

What he didn't mention was that in order to get our 15 minutes of fame, it might be necessary for some of us to share intimate information about our gastrointestinal processes with the entire free world.

It's true, and it brings a whole new meaning to the phrase, "fame is fleeting." In the past few weeks, my digestion has been a topic, in varying degrees of specificity, in this newspaper, *The New York Times,* radio stations on both coasts and the *London Daily Telegraph.* Commuters in the San Francisco Bay area learned more about my lower G.I. tract on their car radios at 6 a.m. the other day than our family doctor did during my annual physical exam.

The same topic also has put me into indirect contact with such diverse institutions as the Center for Science in the Public Interest and the Excellence In Broadcasting Network.

Why have my innards, unremarkable in most respects, become the object of such worldwide fascination? Because they have at various times contained Olestra, that's why.

* * *

As most Eastern Iowans must know by now, Olestra is the fake fat used in the "Max" line of snacks being test-marketed by Frito-Lay in Cedar Rapids.

The positive aspect of the product is a good-tasting, low-calorie, zero-fat potato chip. The negative aspect is the tendency of these chips, especially when consumed in large quantities, to foment unrest in the southern regions of some alimentary canals.

This potential side effect enabled critics to pressure the Food and Drug Administration into requiring a warning on the label that says the product may lead to "abdominal cramping and loose stools."

This adds excitement to an already interesting topic. When *New York Times* food critic Marian Burros visited Cedar Rapids and went away with a lengthy front-page story on the test marketing, she quoted many people. The only one identified well enough to be contacted by readers for more information, though, was the columnist for the local paper.

Thus the day the story ran in the *Times,* WCBS in New York City called for an interview. A few days later came a similar request from KPIX in San Francisco. Then Thursday the phone rang at home and a voice so British it could hardly be deciphered wanted to know all there is to know about "these controversial new crisps."

Would I eat them? Yes, in moderation.

Should others try them? Sure, as long as they clear their calendars for the following day, just in case they are among the unlucky few.

Would I serve them to guests at a dinner party? Not without telling the guests.

The Olestra products are illegal for sale in Great Britain, confided the reporter, but he and his staff had arranged for a Cedar Rapids supermarket to send some samples.

He wasn't too keen on trying them, he said, but stood "ready to give my all for England."

He also asked who else might comment, which is how I got indirectly involved with the Excellence In Broadcasting Network, a.k.a. Rush Limbaugh. I remembered we carried a story that said WMT had sent Limbaugh some chips, so I suggested him as an interview subject. I'm told Limbaugh mentioned on that day's program that he had, indeed, talked with a British reporter about the crisps.

As for the Center for Science in the Public Interest —which is basically two guys with a fax machine and an attitude—it entered the picture because the CSPI was instrumental in forcing the warning label.

The label has done its job in spades, in the process shedding light on the way people think.

* * *

A number of people flatly said they wouldn't try the chips. I do not understand this. For heaven's sake, the label doesn't say the chips will kill you.

The same results they can produce are produced in some people by any number of foods. Some folks can't tolerate dairy products. Others, if they sat down to a big meal of fresh sweet corn, tomatoes and rhubarb, wouldn't be able to leave the house for a week.

Prune lore produced one of the more famous advertising slogans of our times: "Are three enough? Are six too many?"

Does this mean there should be warning labels over the produce at the City Market?

Or if you go into a restaurant and order onion rings and a super burrito smothered in chili, should your server be required to ship out a little card and, like a police officer reading a miscreant his constitutional rights, warn you of potential difficulties?

The CSPI would probably answer "yes" to those questions, but normal people would not.

As the apparent leading authority on such things, I recommend prudent experimentation. If you have no problems, fine. If you do have problems, kindly keep them to yourselves.

There's only room in this business for one media superstar, and besides, I want to keep the phone lines open in case Oprah calls.

Lessons Learned

BY MIKE DEUPREE

If there's a lesson to be found in the column about Olestra, it has to do with the wisdom of moderation. You have to be careful not to overdo things, whether choosing a diet or following a rule of journalism.

The column shatters one of the more familiar of those rules, the one about avoiding the first person.

Most compendiums of advice for columnists warn us not to write about our dog, our children, or our vacation, because when it comes to boring readers, the "I's" have it. Make your column too personal, says this rule, and readers will regard your work as the printed counterpart of watching the neighbor's home videos.

Well, yes and no. Like Olestra, this advice is excellent in theory and usually harmless in practice, but too much of it isn't necessarily a good thing.

Heck, even your attitude toward watching the neighbor's home videos could vary, depending upon whether you live next door to my family or to Tommy and Pamela Anderson Lee.

The argument for an exception to the rule in the Olestra column was pretty obvious. Readers already knew about the test marketing of Procter & Gamble's fat substitute and the claims, as well as what the opponents had to say about it. What they had *not* had was a first-person account of the Olestra experience. Even a columnist who ordinarily shuns the first person might have made the same exception.

You can justify breaking the I-rule, though, even it you aren't writing about a bizarre bodily function.

A first-person column usually will work even with the most mundane of topics—in fact, sometimes the more mundane, the better—if the writer remembers two points.

First, Rodney Dangerfield didn't get rich and famous by telling audiences how rich and famous he was.

Second, unless the experience you're relating is something on the order of wrestling a crocodile, it had better be an experience the readers have shared.

The point of the first point is that self-deprecatory humor is always in style. You can't go wrong providing readers with evidence they're smarter or luckier than you are, which is why some of the best personal columns are based on painful experiences. Not painful as in losing a loved one. Painful as in driving in Boston.

The second point comes down to boredom. You may be the only person who cares about Old Shep, so don't write about your dog. Write about dogs. Of course, there's no reason you can't use Shep as an example.

If the column comes off as a dog column instead of a Shep column, most readers will stick with you until the end. Then you will have done your job as a writer, and Shep will have done his as a literary device.

Offering general advice on how to write a column is like telling someone what they should pay for a used car without knowing what kind of car it is and how much it's been used.

But—please excuse the first person—if my vacation consisted of mosquitoes, car trouble, and fruitless fishing, I'd ignore the rule and write about it. If, on the other hand, I was on a perfect Caribbean cruise while the readers shivered in the sub-zero cold during an economic depression, I'd save my story for the friends and family.

There would be plenty of time to tell it to them while I was rewinding the home video.

Newsday

Murray Kempton

Finalist, Commentary

Murray Kempton joined *Newsday* in 1981 as a columnist. During his career as a journalist he worked for the *New York Post,* the *New York Review of Books,* the *New York World Telegram,* and was a commentator on the CBS program, *Spectrum.* He graduated from Johns Hopkins University in 1939. Among the journalism awards he won are the Sidney Hillman Award in 1954, the George Polk Award in 1967, the Society of Silurian Award in 1978, and the Pulitzer Prize for Commentary in 1985. In 1990, he was the first recipient of the New York Press Club's Distinguished Service Award and in 1995 he was inducted into the American Academy of Arts and Letters. During his career he was a publicity director, writer, labor reporter, assistant editor, labor editor, columnist, and free-lance writer. He wrote numerous books and columns and was a contributor to periodicals including the *New York Review of Books, Reporter, Commonweal, Life, Harper's, Atlantic Monthly, Esquire,* and *Playboy.*

The column he produced on the eve of Sen. Robert Dole's acceptance speech at the 1996 Republican convention was quintessential Kempton: prescient, acerbic, rich with history and an equally firm grasp of today's political realities, sprinkled with metaphors and insults cocooned in velvet prose. His death in April 1997 ended a distinguished career as a graceful, insightful observer of American political life.

GOP spleen is Dole's Achilles heel

AUGUST 15, 1996

SAN DIEGO—Bob Dole will enter upon his latest and probably final date with destiny tonight; and, as so often for him, it is a destiny painted in darkening colors.

He had stumbled distressingly often enough on the path to the crown; and now his party has tripped him sprawling in the doorway to the coronation.

He must deliver his acceptance speech three days after Colin Powell set a standard at once irreproachable and unapproachable for just how this sort of thing ought to be done and then took his aristocratic distance while the Republican proles worked the miracle of transforming the possibilities of an honorable defeat into the probabilities of a shameful disaster.

Bob Dole's triumphant welcome has turned to the dust of grudging acceptance by a party so little in his style that even Jack Kemp must turn rightward to feel assured of giving it satisfaction.

The chords of Henry Mencken's overture to the 1932 Democratic Convention began, approximately, "The Democrats have gathered to consummate their quadrennial suicide pact."

Mencken's vision was as flawed as his cadences were perfect, because he was looking at the convention that would nominate Franklin D. Roosevelt. He cannot be blamed for not seeing the future; he could do no more than describe the loss-habituated Democratic Party of the 1920s and in the process wonderfully describe the Republican Party that nominated Bob Dole last night.

Seventy years ago the Democrats were an incongruous conglomeration of Reconstruction-resenting Southerners and wage-enslaved Northerners of Irish and Italo identity and Catholic faith. Take Al Smith out of the mixture; there could hardly be an unlikelier apparition on this scene than a Happy Warrior. Multiply the dosage of spleen, bile, and defiance of the actualities of existence. And there you have this week's Republican Party.

The hegemony of white Southerners is even more sovereign than it used to be with the Democrats in the '20s. The most powerful delegation on the floor is Mississippi, birthplace of the national chairman and the majority leader of the United States Senate. The Mississippi Republican Party is indistinguishable from the Mississippi Democratic Party, circa 1936, which is only proper because all its leaders used to be Democrats and are to be commended for expressing themselves about the aspirations of persons of color with distinctly improved propriety.

The days are long gone when Theodore Roosevelt could speak of the Episcopal Church as the Republican Party at prayer. Protestant corpuscles still flood in the party's arteries but they have been richly infused by new blood in strains unfamiliarly ethnic.

Names like Voinovich, Kasich, Molinari and Fong all flourish as symbols of their new power on the program and the surges of newer and healthier trees around her make Gov. Christine Todd Whitman look most touchingly like a last leaf on the blighted oak that is all that remains of the majestic Eastern Republican enlightened Tory estate.

And yet this sight that ought to exhilarate instead casts down the heart, because all these divergent strains from noble old civilizations have united with this not ignoble new one to croak in common chorus an unremitting litany of love for America and hatred for its president.

I cannot say how this is playing across the land. But I have my suspicions. Mine is a hand that would wither with palsy if I brought it within one foot of a lever next to Bill Clinton. Distaste for another human being is unappetizing; hatred is unspeakable. It is the one vice that ought to dare not speak and yet these people have insisted upon shouting it without surcease.

Slanders have been piled upon invectives and defamations upon slanders for three days now and will doubtless mount higher through one more; and my mind is already so hammered upon by the heavy hand of spleen that it feels like a tired piano.

If these are the sensations of someone as fixedly disinclined to like Bill Clinton as myself, what must be those of the majority of persons still possessed of the decency that keeps an open mind? Dole's only hope is that they have already switched channels and may return for another look at him when the delegates depart and take their fit away with them. He still has my vote, but he needs more than that and he certainly deserves a better plate than these chefs have cooked for him.

A new shape for the news

BY ROY PETER CLARK

In 1983 I wrote an article that changed the shape of newswriting in America.
I wish.
Truth to tell, all I did was to offer a new name for a new shape—from pyramid to hourglass. In christening this form, I hoped to give writers a new tool for organizing stories. Here's what I wrote back then:

For more than a century, a single story form has been the workhorse of American newspaper writing. Born with the telegraph and the Civil War, adopted and perfected by the wire services, the inverted pyramid has served the needs of readers in a hurry, reporters on deadline, and editors who love to hack from the bottom.

In the pyramid, reporters organize information in descending levels of importance. The readers absorb the most important news first and continue down the page until their interest flags:

A 43-year-old Seffner man was killed Thursday evening when his car collided head-on with a semitrailer truck, according to a Florida Highway patrol spokesman.

James Johnson of 143 Oak St. was headed west on State Road 574 when his 1986 Buick inexplicably crossed the median line and hit the truck, the spokesman said.

The driver of the truck, Stan Simmons, 26, of 435 High St., was not hurt, the spokesman said.

Such writing is as straightforward and undecorated as a fullback running over left tackle. Some journalists learn no other style.

Despite its pre-eminence, the inverted pyramid has important weaknesses as a form of communication. Some reporters think it is an unnatural way to tell a story. "The inverted pyramid is at war with the narrative tradition," says columnist Charles McDowell of the *Richmond Times-Dispatch.* "We write upside-down and tell stories backwards."

Famed journalism teacher Melvin Mencher also dislikes the image: "The term is somewhat misleading. An inverted pyramid story is an unbalanced monolith, a huge top teetering on a pin-point base. It is a monstrous image for journalists, for the top of a story should be deft and pointed."

When badly written, the inverted pyramid peters out into insignificance. "No reader reads more than three paragraphs into a story," a reporter once told me. For him it was a self-fulfilling prophecy.

Some reporters let the pyramid control the content so that the news comes out homogenized. Traffic fatalities, three-alarm fires, and new city ordinances begin to look alike. In extreme cases, reporters have been known to keep files of story forms in their computers. Fill in the blanks. Stick it in the paper.

Reporters have always tested the conventions of newswriting. In the last 25 years, we've seen many narrative experiments. These daring approaches can be exciting, but, when overwrought, can leave the reader hanging. The news is buried in the 11th paragraph, after the jump, the prose is thick with needless detail, and the writer's unchained melody goes on forever.

There is a third alternative for the news writer, a story form that respects traditional news values, considers the needs of the reader, takes advantage of narrative, and spurs the writer to new levels of reporting. [This form had no name until I gave it one in 1983.] I call it "the hourglass."

The hourglass has three parts:

1) The *top,* which tells the news quickly to the reader, usually in three or four paragraphs.

2) The *turn,* a nimble transition.

3) The *narrative,* a chronological retelling of events.

Examples of this story form go back many years, but it has grown more popular, especially for dramatic stories that beg to be told in chronological order:

> Bleeding from bullet wounds, a St. Petersburg man held a 5-year-old boy hostage in the child's own home for three hours Thursday evening before surrendering to police.

Glenn Smith, 24, of 1750 Flamingo Drive, was taken to Bayfront Medical Center and admitted with bullet wounds in both thighs. He was listed in fair condition early this morning. Police said he has been charged with attempted murder.

Donny Rogers, a dark-haired moppet wearing a red-and-yellow Amazing Spiderman T-shirt, seemed calm after the ordeal. Answering a few reporters' questions from the safety of his father's arms, he said his captor told him, "I had to have a place to hide."

Smith allegedly shot St. Petersburg police officer Edward Johnson at the start of the incident. Johnson was hit in the arm and the chest. He was listed in fair condition in the intensive-care unit of Bayfront this morning. The officer reportedly had a collapsed lung.

For some readers, this *top* would have been enough. But the writer makes a *turn:* "Police and neighbors gave this account of what happened." What follows is the bottom of the hourglass, 30 short paragraphs written in chronological order and filled with dramatic details:

The intruder startled Mrs. Rogers, who was at the dinner table with Donny and her 3-year-old daughter, Vanessa. Mrs. Rogers grabbed Vanessa and ran screaming out the back door, thinking Donny would follow. Instead, it was the armed man who followed.

Such a structure works beautifully for certain police stories, courtroom dramas, and other incidents that lend themselves to chronological narration. I have seen it used in stories about a high-speed chase, the rescue of a man pinned under a car, the murder of an infant by two other children, the rescue of a manatee caught in a fishing net.

The key to the structure of the hourglass is the turn, which moves the story from news to narration. This transition can be subtle or obvious. Here are some examples:

1) "The incident occurred after Mrs. Veer left her job as a clerk at the shopping center and headed home."

2) "This account of what happened is provided by the mother of the victim."

3) "Graham was walking home after working in his grandmother's yard when he heard the yells of 55-year-old Robert Gomez."

4) "But Davis Olden said Monday night that Trevillian gave him the following account of what happened."

For the right kind of story, the hourglass offers these advantages:

- Readers get the important news high in the story.
- The writer can take advantage of narrative.
- The story repeats the most important information in the top and bottom, so readers have a better chance to absorb it.
- Unlike the top-heavy pyramid, the hourglass has a balanced structure.
- It invites readers to keep reading, rather than bail out.
- It encourages editors to stop slashing from the bottom.

Stories written in the hourglass form are richer in detail than conventional versions. The form inspires reporters to work a little harder to gather those details that bring the narrative to life for the reader: "Through it all, a lawn sprinkler ticking from side to side on the Rogers' front yard kept time like an annoying metronome."

My affection for the hourglass leaves me open to criticism that I favor "formula writing." Truth be told, the sonnet is a formula, and a quite demanding one. "There's a formula for a triple backflip off the high board," says Steve Lovelady, "but that doesn't mean it's easy to perform."

Poets learn that a formula can be a liberating device, a lens through which they can discover what they want to say. They do not cram reality into a formula, or square words into round forms. Instead, writers discover the best story form during the process of writing. That is why journalists should master many story forms: the inverted pyramid, the hourglass, and a hundred others.

N. Don Wycliff
Editorial Writing

N. Don Wycliff is editorial page editor of the *Chicago Tribune*. He has been a journalist since 1971 when he left graduate studies at the University of Chicago to become a general assignment reporter for the *Houston Post*. He has worked as a reporter for the *Dayton Daily News, Chicago Daily News, Seattle Post-Intelligencer,* and as education reporter for the *Dallas Times Herald*. He was a regional editor at *The New York Times*'s Week in Review and worked as an editorial writer and higher education reporter for the *Times* before joining the *Tribune* in 1990 as deputy editorial page editor. He is a graduate of the University of Notre Dame. He was a finalist for the Pulitzer Prize in 1996.

Writing about racism, the importance of education, and a drug treatment program that helps women break free of addiction, Wycliff is a thoughtful and informed observer of society who encourages others to reflect on their own attitudes and opinions. Acknowledging his desire to influence readers' attitudes, his editorials are passionate and thoughtful reflections about issues and events that make the news and shape society.

—Christopher Scanlan

Plessy's plea,
a dissenter's vision

MAY 18, 1996

Friday was the 42nd anniversary of the Supreme Court's historic decision in *Brown v. Board of Education of Topeka.* Today marks the 100th anniversary of the decision that Brown reversed, *Plessy v. Ferguson.*

One wonders whether 100 years from now Americans will be wrestling with the implications of these two landmarks of constitutional jurisprudence, and with the issue at the core of both: race.

Regrettably—and largely because of the Plessy decision—we still must wrestle with them today. Because for all the progress that has been made, race remains the great unhealed sore on the American body social.

The Plessy decision did not create racial segregation and second-class citizenship for black Americans. That was done de facto by Ku Klux Klan terrorism, Black Codes, and other actions of white-dominated southern state legislatures intent on repealing Reconstruction and the post-Civil War constitutional amendments that were supposed to ensure the rights of blacks as citizens.

But Plessy ratified those actions and put the seal of judicial approval on the nefarious doctrine of "separate but equal."

It is ironic that the most enduring element of Plessy was not anything said by the seven-member Supreme Court majority. Rather, it was the opinion of the lone dissenter, Justice John Marshall Harlan, and in particular his eloquent statement of constitutional principle:

"In the view of the Constitution, in the eye of the law, there is in this country no superior or dominant ruling class of citizens. There is no caste here. Our Constitution is color blind, and neither knows nor tolerates classes among citizens. In respect of civil rights, all citizens are equal before the law."

Had Harlan prevailed then, before the American system of apartheid had been locked into place, we might not now be wracked with disagreements over affirmative action and quotas and set-asides and reverse discrimination. But he didn't prevail, and while it is often said that the Brown decision vindicated him, it did not.

The principle of the colorblind Constitution—of rights that belong to an individual solely because he or she is a citizen—remains our challenge today.

It is not just a legal challenge. Indeed, it is not even primarily legal. The fact is that only when we become more nearly equal cross the racial divide—equal economically, educationally and otherwise—will "colorblind" jurisprudence become intellectually and politically sustainable. Until we become more equal, colorblind jurisprudence will look like nothing so much as an effort by the white majority to lock in advantages grabbed under the old Plessy regime.

The challenge is to keep the Harlan principle inviolate, while we struggle toward equality. The principle must never be lost, for without it, America would cease to be.

Writers' Workshop

Talking Points

1) Discuss what vestiges of racism exist in your community. Look in the spheres that Wycliff focuses on in the penultimate paragraph: economic and educational inequality.

2) Editorial writers must be students of history, the law, and society. Ask yourself if you could write an editorial that reflects the depth of scholarship and understanding of this one.

3) In this editorial, Wycliff explores the ramifications of events and decisions probably made before you were born. One of the most important roles the editorial writer plays is to help society deal with its current problems by reminding readers of the lessons of the past. Discuss how editorial writers can meet this responsibility.

Assignment Desk

1) Read the Supreme Court decisions cited in this editorial: *Brown v. Board of Education of Topeka* and *Plessy v. Ferguson.*

2) Write a series of editorials on the subject of racism, what Wycliff calls "the great unhealed sore."

3) Research and write an "anniversary" editorial that, like "Plessy's Plea, a Dissenter's Vision," takes a close look at a little-noticed aspect of a long-ago event.

To an athlete failing young

JULY 24, 1996

Ronnie Fields, Illinois' reigning Mr. Basketball, has an uncanny ability to leap high and always land on his feet. So it's unlikely he'll be undone by the latest setback in his young life: denial of admission, on academic grounds, to DePaul University, where he had hoped to stop off briefly before embarking on a career in the National Basketball Association.

Nevertheless, Fields' experience may prove instructive to the many young athletes who have less talent than he and don't always land on their feet. The lesson is simple, but it can't be overemphasized: It's not enough to put up the numbers on the scoreboard; you've also got to put them up on the blackboard. Grades count!

Fields went to Farragut High School, which, not incidentally, sent Kevin Garnett straight from its halls to the NBA a year ago. Fields has never made any secret of his NBA ambitions and, in fact, was considering following Garnett's fast route until Feb. 26.

That's when he suffered serious back injuries in a car accident. His senior basketball season ended prematurely and any hopes he had of jumping directly to the pros were dashed.

In May he went to Plan B, signing a letter of intent to play for DePaul. But it's one thing to make the grade as an athlete, another to do so as a student. DePaul's admissions committee concluded that Fields' high school grades and college admission test scores met neither the university's nor the NCAA's qualifying standards. Suddenly, Fields must find a Plan C.

He has options: He could attend an open-admissions junior college or he could try out for the new Teenage Professional Basketball League.

He has talent: Even though only 6 feet 3, he has extraordinary leaping ability, and some say he's the best player ever to come out of the Chicago public school system.

What he doesn't have, unfortunately, is grades, and that's too bad. Because just as an accident took away his option to leap straight to the NBA, some other freak occurrence could take away his ability to play basketball altogether. With good grades, he could be on his way to college and a degree. And that's a credential that's good for life.

Writers' Workshop

Talking Points

1) Notice how this editorial employs the device of repetition, in paragraphs six through eight, to make its point. "He has options." "He has talent." "What he doesn't have, unfortunately, is grades, and that's too bad."

2) Newspaper editors and publishers continue to bemoan the loss of young readers. Whom do you think Wycliff is trying to reach with this editorial? Do you think young people will read this editorial? Would it persuade them that grades count?

3) Diction, the choice of words the writer makes, is especially important in editorial writing, where space is at a premium. Notice how many times and when Wycliff uses the word "leap" in this piece. What is the effect of that word selection?

Assignment Desk

1) Study the way Wycliff and Michael Gartner, a finalist in this category, use repetition in their writing. Model your writing after them by looking for ways to employ repetition to achieve rhythm and power.

2) Effective writers pay close attention to the words they choose. Re-read your editorials to see if you could improve diction in your writing. Take extra time to pick just the right word.

3) Write an editorial extolling the virtues of academic achievement.

Faith, religion and help for pain

JULY 31, 1996

In his recent book *Integrity,* Yale University law professor Stephen Carter observed that "in an earlier age, when religious devotion was more common, no laws against perjury existed because everybody assumed that God would take His own measures against false swearing."

How different things are now.

"In the cynicism of our age," Carter writes, "nobody assumes that simply because an individual swears by God to tell the truth that the person thereby *is* telling the truth. Indeed, hardly anybody seems to think that an individual who swears by God to tell the truth is *probably* telling the truth."

And the reason for that is that, deep down, few of us believe in a God of that old sort.

Carter's astute observation about the effect of this loss of faith on the legal system is but one evidence that while Americans may be among the most religious peoples in the world, they are not necessarily the most *faith-filled.*

"The Sea of Faith," evoked a century ago by the English poet Matthew Arnold, has retreated under the relentless advance of modernity and rationalism, leaving us with the forms of religion, but not, it often seems, with the faith that is its substance.

Another recent example of this loss of faith has emerged in the aftermath of the dreadful, tragic crash two weeks ago of TWA Flight 800 off the coast of Long Island.

To the dismay of many observers, some family members of victims have routinely conducted news conferences at which they take to task the authorities for not giving appropriate priority to the recovery of the bodies of their loved ones.

This has not been remarked about much publicly, because no one wants to seem unsympathetic to people who have experienced losses that for most of us would be grievous beyond the power of words to express.

What's more, there is legitimate reason to question the actions of some of those involved in handling this disaster—New York Gov. George Pataki comes most readily to mind.

But people have dealt with such losses throughout human history, and generally not by excoriating blameless third parties. Remember Job? He had to contend with the loss of his entire family. He complained to and argued with his God, but ultimately found solace in Him.

Why is it, apparently, impossible for so many of us—the TWA families are hardly unique in their behavior—to find such solace? It is a vexing question for a disconsolate age in which religion abounds but faith, alas, is elusive.

Writers' Workshop

Talking Points

1) The news peg for this editorial is the criticism family members of victims of TWA Flight 800 raised over the recovery of their loved ones' bodies. Wycliff waits until the seventh paragraph to make this connection. Why do you think he waited so long? Should the reason for the editorial have been made clear sooner? If so, why? If not, why not?

2) Wycliff says he felt great sympathy for the families of TWA Flight 800's victims and worried about writing an editorial criticizing their behavior. Discuss the responsibility of the editorial writer to take the unpopular stand.

3) The observations by Yale Law School professor Stephen Carter in his book *Integrity* is "but one evidence," Wycliff writes, that Americans have lost their faith. Discuss other examples in the news that you think support this contention.

Assignment Desk

1) Rewrite this editorial by moving the TWA Flight 800 connection into the lead. How does that change it?

2) In this editorial, Wycliff alludes to "the sea of faith," from the poem "Dover Beach" by Matthew Arnold. It is a poem that Wycliff remembers from his high school days. Is there a poem in your past that has stayed with you? Use it in an editorial.

3) Read *Integrity* by Stephen Carter and draw on your reading in an editorial.

4) The history of editorial writing is replete with examples of courageous editors taking unpopular stands. One celebrated writer is Eugene Patterson who won the Pulitzer Prize for his civil rights editorials in the *Atlanta Journal and Constitution*. Do a research paper on Patterson or another editor who risked community censure in the service of responsible opinion.

Reclaiming those lost to addiction

SEPTEMBER 30, 1996

There is a cross atop the roof and the words "St. Nicholas Convent" are etched into the stained glass above the front entrance of the pale red brick building at 114th and State streets. Both are relics of a time long past, when this building was part of a Catholic parish serving a largely white, working-class community on the Far South Side.

The neighborhood is now mainly African-American, and the building no longer serves its original purpose. But it still houses a sisterhood, and the work in which they are engaged is very much a spiritual endeavor: rescuing women from the ravages of drug abuse; retrieving lost sheep, as it were, and returning them to the fold of sober, productive humanity.

What once was St. Nicholas Convent is now the 16-bed Harriet Tubman residential drug-abuse treatment center. Operated by Human Resources Development Institute Inc., it is unusual in that it allows women in treatment to keep with them their children up to age 4.

That, as the experts explain, can be crucial, since it often is for love of their children—and out of fear that they may lose them—that women seek treatment.

September, now expiring, was "Treatment Works!" month in Illinois, by proclamation of Gov. Jim Edgar. Like most such observances, this one passed largely unnoticed except by those involved in the business, whether as suppliers of treatment or recipients of it.

But it's useful to visit from time to time a place like the Harriet Tubman center, to understand both why some people turn to drugs and why treatment is worth the investment.

On one recent morning, the women in treatment, some holding babes in arms, were gathered in a first-floor meeting room with their own mothers. Led by Anjil Muhammad, a staff member, daughters and mothers tried to open up to each other, to understand what motivated their resort to drugs and begin developing the strength to keep them from relapsing.

There were commonplace stories—missing fathers and the emotional void that they left was a common theme. And there were harrowing stories: One young woman told of being raped, of losing her bearings afterward and seeking solace in drugs. That elicited a mildly impatient response from an elderly woman, mother of one of the clients: She had been raped twice, she said, and she kept her bearings by seeking God's help.

Obviously, getting treated for drug abuse isn't like going to the doctor and getting an injection of antibiotics. There is no magic potion, no quick fix. Treatment involves the mind and the spirit as much as the body. And not everyone who goes through treatment succeeds in staying off permanently.

But that treatment works and is cost-effective for society is beyond question. Studies indicate that savings —on crime and punishment, health care, social and family services—amount to $7 for every $1 invested in drug treatment.

Illinois currently spends about $200 million a year on treatment. Even so, an estimated 81,000 persons in need of treatment are unable to get it; the budget would need to just about double to cover them all.

There are any number of worthy claims on the state's fiscal resources. Few of them, however, could be more worthy than drug treatment.

Writers' Workshop

Talking Points

1) Editorials operate under certain restrictions such as space and the need for an institutional voice. What other conventions of editorial writing influence the way an editorial is written and how it differs from other journalistic writing? Consider, for example, how a feature writer might have handled this story. What elements, such as dialogue and names of specific people, are missing? Discuss the reasons for their absence.

2) Editorials, like news stories, are often inspired by events that serve as "pegs" to justify their appearance. What is the news peg for this story? What is the value of the news peg and is one always necessary?

3) Wycliff combined interviews, research, and on-scene reporting to write this editorial. Try to distinguish the source for the information he uses. Defend your choices.

Assignment Desk

1) Wycliff visited the drug treatment center described in this editorial and says he wishes he and other editorial writers spent more time on the street. Write the first draft of an editorial on a subject without doing any outside reporting. Then hit the streets and interview someone involved in the issue. Rewrite the editorial. What are the major differences?

2) As you read editorials in your local newspaper, try to determine which, if any, are the result of street reporting. If you don't think any has been done, identify specific places you could go to get first-hand exposure to the people and issues being written about.

A conversation with
N. Don Wycliff

CHRISTOPHER SCANLAN: How long have you been an editorial writer?

DON WYCLIFF: Since 1985. I started writing editorials full time at *The New York Times.* I've been at the *Tribune* since September 1990.

Can you trace your career path in journalism?

I started out in journalism in April of 1970, at the *Houston Post.* I was hired as an intern there. This was after I dropped out of graduate school at the University of Chicago. I was pursuing a Ph.D. in political science and became much enamored of journalism, and particularly newspaper journalism, after the shootout here in Chicago between the police and the Black Panthers. Actually, it was not a shootout; it was the police shooting up the Black Panther headquarters here, back on Dec. 3, 1969.

That story, for some reason, gripped me, and in the succeeding days and weeks I picked up every one of the four Chicago newspapers every day and read all I could about it. That was the first time I had ever really thought about journalism as a career. A few months later I decided I was going to drop out of graduate school and do journalism, and was fortunate enough to get a job at the *Houston Post.* There've been a lot of stops between then and now.

In May 1979, I ended up at *The New York Times* as one of the regional editors at the Week in Review section. I worked there until August 1981, when I came back to Chicago to the *Sun-Times* and was here until February 1985, when Max Frankel and Jack Rosenthal hired me to write editorials at the *Times.* And I did that until Jack Fuller, at the *Tribune,* lured me away in 1990.

Kind of a vagabond's history. I was just feeling my way along most of the time. I guess from the very beginning I knew I wanted to write opinion. I've always been a very opinionated person. But it was only in 1985, at the *Times,* that I got the chance to do it and that was kind of miraculous.

What are you trying to do with your editorials?

Mainly I want to influence the way people think about things. I want people to consider points of view they may not have before. I guess I don't really expect people to, in a blinding flash, change their whole way of behavior. I do hope to influence the way they think and maybe, over time, cause them to consider a point of view that they hadn't before.

Do you have a reader in mind? Who are you writing for?

I just assume that I'm talking to somebody who's reasonably intelligent and who, if we were in the same room, would make a smart response. I think pretty highly of readers' intelligence.

Do you think that you are teaching?

Yeah. In fact, I've always thought of this as another way of teaching.

Tell me about your parents.

My mother was a homemaker; she raised nine kids. My father was an educator. He ran education programs in federal prisons. When he retired, he was running a halfway house pre-release center in Dallas. He's always told me he most liked working in youth institutions because he felt like he could make a change in some child's life. Today, he's retired but he's also a deacon in the Catholic Church.

Are you the first journalist in your family?

I'm the only journalist.

Did you ever aspire to the ministry? There is, at times, a preacherly voice in your work.

I think there's some wisdom in religion that we can all benefit from, and so I like to use the opportunity, whenever I can, to put some of it out there for public consumption.

Do you have role models for you as editorial writers?

Not as an editorial writer. As somebody who runs an editorial page, I guess I pattern myself after Jack Rosenthal, for whom I worked at the *Times*. Just in the way I try to deal with people.

What was it about him that you admire and try to emulate?

He was always low key and personal. I try not to be a guy who's distant. I just like to have regular and frequent interchange with my people, and make them feel comfortable and talk a lot and try to get things out of people that way. As opposed to being some kind of order giver.

Describe your job.

I preside over the daily editorial board meeting and make the assignments to the extent anybody needs to be told. We all have our beats and so people pretty much know what they're responsible for. But I determine the lineup each day and take care of what bureaucratic stuff is involved in running this page. When there's an issue on which we can't reach consensus, it's my call. I try not to do it very often, but if I feel one way and everybody else feels another, what I say goes. And I guess that's nice in a certain way, but it's not the sort of thing one makes promiscuous use of.

How many editorial writers are there?

There are 11 of us who write regularly for the page. Some of us write columns also.

Do you do any hands-on editing of other editorial writers' work?

That's another major aspect of my job. Everything that goes in, either I or Bruce Dold, my deputy, reads. I read most of them, edit them, recommend changes when I think I can get them by recommending and sometimes, if necessary, I rewrite to a considerable degree.

How often do you write?

I write two, three editorials a week.

What is your beat?

The waterfront, actually. I have to know a little bit about everything. What I like to write about most is welfare/social policy type things. Religion and its role in society are very important to me. And I don't do a lot of it any more, but I also like to write about education because I think it's essential.

Is writing an enjoyable, painless process for you?

It's an enjoyable process. It isn't always painless. Because I try to fill whatever gaps may occur, somebody's on vacation, whatever else, I end up writing stuff I may not know a lot about, but I know as much about it as anybody else who happens to be here. I too often have to write without having done enough research. We're encouraged to go out and give speeches and be involved in community activities, so I don't get to spend as much time reporting as I'd like.

Do you come in knowing what you're going to write?

Some days I do. Some nights I guess I am awake most of the night, framing pieces in my mind, when I know it's a really heavy-duty piece.

What are you worrying about?

Bringing the end and the beginning together. I'll have discovered what my lead is going to be but I can't figure out how I'm going to make it work. These generally are political-type editorials that give me a lot of trouble, where there's a lot of reporting involved. We're making harsh judgments about the president or somebody else.

Are you concerned about getting it right?

Very concerned. That's basic. But also about checking my judgments. I don't like to draw a faulty, unwarranted conclusion. And frankly, sometimes, we will have had editorial board debates and somebody will have said something that really makes me question myself, and that's healthy.

One of the things that struck me was the depth of your knowledge. In "Faith, Religion and Help for Pain," you cite Stephen Carter's book *Integrity* and Matthew Arnold's concept of the "sea of faith" to support a discussion of a timeless topic as it relates to a newsworthy issue, namely the reaction of family members to the recovery efforts after the TWA Flight 800 crash. Could you describe the process of writing that editorial?

That one was incubating for about a week or so. I forget the actual sequence, but I recall the day when I watched a news conference where some of the survivors of the ones who died were on TV, talking about their frustration with the delay in recovering their relatives' remains. We talked about it in our editorial board meeting, and it's a difficult thing to write about because, gosh, these people have experienced a pain beyond imagining. And yet, you know, they're not the first. *Dover Beach,* from which Arnold's "sea of faith" comes, has been a favorite poem of mine since I was in college, and it goes to exactly that issue; what role faith plays and the consolation faith brings to us.

I happened to recall the Carter book because I had reviewed it a few months earlier, and so over about a week, I wanted to write about that issue, of these people taking people to task for not finding their relatives' bodies fast enough. It seemed such an irrational thing and so many other people on the editorial board I know felt the same way, but we were all looking for words to express what we wanted to say.

Finally, one day it just came together for me and I sat down and started writing. It didn't take very long to do, because I pretty much had it written in my head before I started to put it into the machine. Maybe a couple of hours to get it into final shape. When it came, it came easily.

What brought to mind the "sea of faith"?

Dover Beach speaks to the issue of consolation for people in this modern life. The last lines of it, in fact, were on the opening plate of my senior year college yearbook, and it's just been a presence. Whenever I think of things like this, I think of those lines.

What's the subject matter?

It's done in the manner of a reflection, Arnold speaking of being on Dover Beach in England at night, and he describes the sound of the waves crashing in, and then launches into a reflection, "Sophocles heard it long ago on the Aegean." He says, "The sea of faith was once too at the full," and he was lamenting that even in his day, a century ago, faith was weak. It wasn't strong enough to overcome some of the disconsolate feelings that people were having then.

Is that part of the job of an editorial writer, to offer consolation?

I think so. I was just talking about this with one of my people at lunch. Policy analysis is something we do a lot of, offering policy prescriptions and excoriating public officials for one thing or another. But I like to think that one of the services we can do is to offer some balm for the soul, a little reflection, some understanding, some empathy for what people may be feeling in life. And that's what I try to do from time to time.

In the editorial about Ronnie Fields, yours is the voice of a parent. In "Faith, Religion and Help for Pain," you almost sound like a minister. At a time when editorial writers do spend a lot of time focus-

ing on policies, you're talking about fairly timeless issues and values. Is that an accurate assessment?

That's accurate and, to be very frank, I try consciously to do that. Because heaven and earth will pass away and so will most of what we write, but if you can write about some eternal themes once in a while maybe they'll last a little longer.

Why did you write "To an Athlete Failing Young"?

When I was a sophomore in high school some lady asked me what I was going to do when I grew up, and I said I was going to be a pro basketball player. I know how easy it is to think that. And particularly when you're as good a player as Ronnie Fields is. The kid's a stupendous player, but he's also a kid. It was as if somebody had scripted his life so that he could be an object lesson to all other kids out there.

Here's this guy, he's on top of the world one day and the next day he's riding home in a car he shouldn't have had, and he cracks up and his basketball season is over, his high school career is over. He gets over that problem and he finds out he's been led along, given his grades, and he really can't play college ball because he just can't cut it in the classroom. It would have been a terrible dereliction on my part if I hadn't written that piece, frankly. It just demanded to be written by somebody.

The language that you use is often of timeless, almost Biblical, quality.

I think one of the greatest losses we've suffered in this country in recent years has been that we no longer read the King James version of the Bible. Remember Ken Burns's *Civil War,* and the letters that those people wrote? You could hear that King James English in there, throughout, and it was beautiful. And these weren't, in every case, the highly literate upper crust. These were ordinary folks, and that's what they read and that's how they learned to read and write. And it's kind of sad that we don't do that routinely any more.

How does the writing of an editorial begin?

I search for a lead. I guess I've always been a believer that if I've got two hours in which to do something, the best investment I can make is to spend the first hour and 45 minutes of it getting a good lead, because after that everything else will come easily.

What is the lead?

It varies from piece to piece, but usually it's those first two or three paragraphs, before you kind of take your breath and then start backgrounding folks and giving them the stuff they need to understand your point at the end.

Do you write to length or do you write long and cut back?

I can only write to length. I find it hard to cut. So I try to avoid writing beyond my assigned length.

Why do you find it hard to cut?

Usually because I try to construct my pieces so that it's not like the old inverted pyramid, where you can just cut from the bottom. One thing leads to another and, in particular, one phrase leads to another. Also I guess I'm just a fairly jealous writer. I don't like to leave my best phrases on the cutting room floor.

Your editorials often come full circle in a really nice way. Every word counts. Do you outline this structure? Do you plan this? Or, again, does this go on in your head?

It's all in the head. I never outline. I just can't do that.

Why?

If I'm outlining, I might as well be writing. And that's also part of the reason that I invest so much effort in a lead, because I know the lead has to, or ought to, in some way, also be the end. You're supposed to bring it full circle, with pieces like these, anyway.

Why?

I guess it goes back to something one of my college teachers or high school teachers said: "You tell them what you're going to tell them, then you tell them, and then you tell them what you told them." It just seems like it ought to be part of the structure of things.

How important is thinking to what you do?

Oh, it's *the* most important thing. Because you can't write clearly unless you think clearly. In fact, back when I used to teach, that's what I'd always tell kids: "Clear thinking begets clear writing." And it's a simple equation.

In "Reclaiming Those Lost to Addiction," you hit the streets. How frequently do you do that?

Not often enough. I do it maybe two, three times a year. And in this case, I did it because a guy from this organization came in with the head of the state Department of Substance Abuse Services to visit us, and I just thought, "I'd like to see what a drug treatment program really is about." And so I arranged to do it, and I was glad I did.

Why were you glad you did?

It feels like being a journalist again, to get out and be in touch with people again, and see things at first hand and be a reporter again.

Do you think editorial pages need more of that reporting?

Without doubt.

Why don't they?

Because it's so easy to get under the gun and it's also easy to get very comfortable in an office and say, well, "There's tomorrow, tomorrow, tomorrow." Living in an office and in an ivory tower is very seductive.

Why should editorial writers get out of the office?

Because the beginning of all journalism is getting out into the world and seeing live people dealing with real life. It's the beginning of all philosophy and it's the beginning of all journalism. It's the starting point for everything.

You have two potent images in this piece from your visit. One is the cross and the name of the convent, and the other is the scene with the mothers, all the babes in arms. And the elderly woman who said she had been raped twice and she kept her bearings by seeking God's help. Why was the cross your lead?

In drug treatment, like AA or like any of those 12-step programs, there's a spiritual element, and I was really struck by what I saw going on in that place that day. In fact, it wasn't until I was leaving that I noticed the St. Nicholas Convent thing and I thought, "Wow, that's really powerful." But what I saw going on that day was a kind of a spiritual thing, and I knew I had to represent that in some way in the piece. And when I realized this had been a convent, I went outside before I left and looked the building over and saw the cross at the top.

What are the most important lessons you've learned about writing?

Think long; think hard. Beyond that, as a writer said, "Don't let the perfect be the enemy of the good."

I try to do other writing, aside from the writing I do here as an editorial writer, and I am always allowing the perfect to be the enemy of the good.

As editorial page editor, what do you look for in an editorial writer?

Good intelligence, to begin with, and good skills as a reporter. Because you never stop being a reporter. That's basic. And an analytical ability. I just assume that anybody who's been a reporter is going to have to teach himself to express opinion, because you spend so much time training yourself not to. When I first started writing editorials, it was really hard for me to stick the opinion in there. Then you've got to unlearn that and start putting it in. Basic writing skill. But the intelligence, the ability to analyze, is critical, and the disposition to continue being a good reporter. Those are the most important things.

How do you stay informed?

I read a lot of periodicals: *The Economist, Time, Newsweek, Daedalus, Wilson Quarterly Review, New Republic,* in addition to the newspapers, four or five of them, *The New York Times* and all that. But the one great regret I have is that I never, any more, get to read novels. Well, I do read novels. I'm reading *The Star Wars–Young Jedi Knight* series to my son at night.

How old is your son?

This particular one is 10, and he's really hooked on these. And the other one likes to have the Bible read to him. He's 8. He loves those stories.

In the editorial "Plessy's Plea" you call racism America's "great unhealed sore." How deeply does that issue penetrate your life?

Race is a factor in my life, always has been, always will be. I guess that was part of the reason that the Black Panther story gripped me so much. And I desperately want to see the country deal with it successfully and intelligently. And that's harder than just picking one side or the other in these polarized debates. But I think that thinking the issue through is a service, and I try to do that kind of thinking out loud in my pieces.

What was it about the Black Panther shootings that led you to this work?

Two men were killed in it, Fred Hampton, the leader
of the Illinois Black Panthers, and Mark Clark, one of
the members of that group. I didn't know either of
them. That was the time of a lot of ferment and, to be
absolutely frank, I was feeling, in graduate school,
kind of like a fifth wheel. The world was exploding,
there was all kinds of activity, and I felt kind of useless
spending my days in libraries and classrooms, especially at an institution like the University of Chicago,
which is so steeped in the life of the mind and so removed from the factitious cares of daily life.

When I woke up the morning of Dec. 4 and turned
on the radio and heard that those guys had been killed,
I felt like something terrible had been done. I had seen
Hampton on TV just once, a few weeks before that,
and it struck me that—I don't mean to be naive about
this, I mean, he was no great hero or anything—but he
was about my age at the time, and he seemed like a
guy who was struggling to find his way and do something useful in the world. I just had the sense that it
was senseless that this man had been killed like that.
And I was particularly impressed with the work of the
Chicago Sun-Times over the weeks that followed as
they ferreted out the truth of this thing and exposed
what really was an ambush by the police.

And the sense that something terrible had been
done was what really moved me, but along with that
was the sense that, "Wow, this journalism thing looks
like a really useful thing to do in life."

Has it proven to be that? A useful thing to do?

Yeah, it has been. There's a lot more indirection involved than I ever supposed. I thought I was going to
mount the pulpit and preach to the world and everybody would say, "Ah! He's right. We'll change our
ways." It doesn't work that way, but it has been a useful thing to do. I've never really done the great thing in
journalism that I'd really wanted to do. I've never
saved anybody from some terrible injustice or anything like that. And that disappoints me, but you know,
there's tomorrow. So I'll keep working.

THE RECORD

Ian Darling

Finalist, Editorial Writing

Ian Darling started as an editorial writer at the Kitchener-Waterloo *Record* in 1981. In 1989 he left the editorial board to work in the newsroom in various capacities, including assistant news editor and business editor before returning to the editorial board in 1996. Prior to that he worked at various smaller papers, including the now-defunct *Oshawa Times* in Oshawa, Ontario, the *Vancouver Province,* and the *Globe and Mail* in Toronto. Darling received a B.A. from the University of Guelph and an M.A. from the University of Toronto, both in political studies. In addition to writing editorials, he works as a part-time instructor in the English department at Wilfrid Laurier University in Waterloo, Ontario. He is the winner of several awards for editorial writing from organizations such as the Western Ontario Newspaper Awards, the Canadian Farm Writers Federation, and the Ontario Safety League.

Editorial writing is easy. Humor is hard. But in just seven paragraphs, Darling manages to gently mock two national characters, the American and his own country's, with observations that produce a sight rarely seen around the editorial page: a smile.

Keep Ottawa beautiful; stop the U.S. embassy

JUNE 14, 1996

The Americans must be stopped. They are about to erect the biggest, ugliest embassy ever built in our national capital. It is time for Canadians to rally around the nation's capital; O Ottawa, we stand on guard for thee.

Judging by a photo of a model of the building, the embassy will resemble a long, low, cheap apartment building. Ottawa city councillor Richard Cannings called the model banal and mundane. "It's too American-looking," he added.

Yes, the model is banal and mundane, but we should assure our American friends, before they want to renew the War of 1812 over this vituperative comment, that there is no truth to the accusation that it "looks American."

An embassy that "looks American" would be dazzling and ostentatious. Its windows would glitter with gold; its bricks would come from every one of the 50 states and its murals would depict Hollywood stars singing "The Star-Spangled Banner." Come to think of it, perhaps we should be thankful that the Yanks do not want to put up a building that reflects their nation's true character.

There is still another way of looking at this Ottawa spat: No matter what the Americans build, we won't be stuck with it for long. Since they are the ones who mastered the concept of planned obsolescence, any building that goes up today will be quickly torn down when new and improved sketches are ready.

But if the Americans do decide not to go ahead with this building, Ottawa should be prepared to buy the plans. This surely would keep the Americans happy.

Moreover, since the plans are banal and mundane, they seem more than suitable for the next embassy that Canada builds abroad.

Lessons Learned

BY IAN DARLING

Humor is a much more serious business than it might first appear. It can easily get you into trouble. I remember writing one editorial a few years ago that compared a Canadian politician who had an image of being a loser with the Toronto Maple Leafs hockey team, which has a reputation for having one-game winning streaks once a month. I thought the editorial was funny and clever, but the publisher at the time didn't think it deserved either of these descriptions, so he removed the editorial between editions. He said it was frivolous. The difference between frivolity and brilliant wit is always in the eye of someone else.

More recently, I wrote an editorial poking fun at a local council for deciding the council chamber could be rented for wedding ceremonies. We suggested that the ministers conducting the ceremonies should stick around so they could say a few blissful words for the benefit of the quarrelsome council. One member of the council didn't think this was funny at all, and he publicly lambasted *The Record* at the next council meeting. Oh, well.

In general, I think the risks of offending a few people with humor are worth taking. People tire of reading heavy, ponderous editorials—or, at least, I suspect they do. Humor provides a break, and might even make a point with readers that would otherwise not be made.

Our ideas for humorous editorials come from both news stories and from daily life. I, and the other members of the editorial department, just keep our eyes open for off-beat ideas. We've treated countless subjects with humor—everything from Bill Gates to baby boomers. You have to know the limits, however. I've seen one writer try to use humor about death, and it was appalling.

The editorial "Keep Ottawa Beautiful; Stop the U.S. Embassy" came out of a news story. I just thought there was something odd about the U.S. government putting up a bland building. At the time I started to write the editorial, I didn't know exactly what I was going to say. I hoped that something would come. If it didn't, I would have killed the editorial and moved on to something else.

Perhaps this reflects the best suggestion I can offer someone who wants to write humor: Don't force it. If the writing process is strained, the end result will probably appear strained. I never write humor with a deadline in front of me. Readers may be prepared to accept a straight editorial that is competent but isn't super, but they're less tolerant of something that is supposed to be funny but isn't.

The humorous editorials that I think work best are those that have a political point or that try to offer insight. In this piece, I was really dealing with the theme that the American culture is more ostentatious than the Canadian culture. I also think self-deprecating humor is invaluable because it maintains balance. This is why I turned the editorial near the end to comment on Canadians being bland.

I see myself as a skeptical observer of both American and Canadian societies. It's possible one day we might do an editorial recommending the creation of a new country between the U.S. and Canada. We'll just take chunks of Michigan and Ontario and put them together. No citizen will be allowed to be either ostentatious or bland. Some reader will probably take the editorial seriously. Oh, well.

THE LAURINBURG
EXCHANGE

Mike Foley

Finalist, Editorial Writing

Mike Foley began his journalism career as sports editor of his high school paper in Farmington Hills, Mich. He graduated from Michigan State University in 1983 with a bachelor's degree in journalism and is working toward a master's degree in mass communications at the University of West Florida. His jobs have ranged from one-man news staff at *The Elsie* (Mich.) *Advertiser* to city editor at *The Northwest Florida Daily News* in Fort Walton Beach. He also covered city hall for the *Gaston* (N.C.) *Gazette,* was a staff writer for the *News & Record* in Greensboro, N.C., and edited the *Lancaster* (S.C.) *Daily News.* At *The Laurinburg* (N.C.) *Exchange,* he was editor and sole editorial writer.

While humor may be the best weapon against bureaucratic stupidity, it's too rarely wielded on editorial pages. In this comment about a half-baked proposal to ban sagging pants favored by kids in his town, Foley manages to skewer the idea and redirect the community's attention to the younger generation's real needs.

'Sagging' ban is a misguided effort

SEPTEMBER 26, 1996

It appears there's a move afoot in Maxton to ban some fashions that have inflamed the passions of some residents.

Seeing that, we have to wonder whether the town's fathers—in years past—sought to ban other fashions, fads and particular manners of dress.

If so, we ought to be able to dredge up old town ordinances banning greasy ducktail haircuts, Beatles-type mop-top hairdos, love beads and bell bottom jeans and more recent fads such as mohawk haircuts and pierced noses.

Those looks came and went—some of them—and apparently were never such a threat the town felt the need to try and ban them. Good taste, prevailing attitudes and time took care of any problems the town fathers most likely saw with those trends.

But now comes sagging.

It has apparently erupted a minor furor in Maxton as youngsters sport baggy trousers that hang low enough so a strip of underwear is exposed above the top of their pants.

Good golly, Miss Molly, someone call the cops!

Does Maxton really need to invent a problem? Because that's what the town will do if it tries to write and then enforce a law banning sagging.

And where would it lead?

A prohibition on wearing ball caps backward?

A ban on shorts or dresses showing any leg above the knee?

Or how about a law requiring males to wear shirts, ties and slacks in public. And for women, a requirement to wear dresses covering their arms to their wrists and down to their ankles?

Where does this madness stop?

Surely, that's what this could become. How else can we explain the effort by some in town to legislate good taste.

We're not suggesting here that we have any desire to see anyone's underwear in public. This fashion trend will come and go in the weeks or months—or God help us—years to come. Surely, though, it will pass.

Meanwhile, everyone in town's efforts would be better served by turning the other cheek, so to speak, and allowing youths a little personal freedom to wear clothes as they see fit.

Instead of concentrating on droopy drawers, why not direct efforts toward helping Maxton's youth?

Why doesn't the town worry about providing summer educational opportunities or after-school recreational facilities for town youth?

How about career counseling, job training or a mentoring program for our adults of tomorrow?

Maxton needs to forget an ordinance to legislate taste.

Any attempt to pass such a law will only further open the mawing generation gap that's obviously present in town.

Lessons Learned

BY MIKE FOLEY

History repeats, I learned, when one of my reporters trooped into our newsroom with the news that the town council in one of our small locales was discussing the possibility of banning "sagging," the hip-hop gangsta style whereby youth wear their baggy trousers so low a strip of their underwear is evident above their belt line.

In this small town, the style was horrifying to some civic leaders.

I first learned just how horrifying the style can be almost a year earlier when I was editor of a three-times-a-week newspaper in South Carolina. There, a town council also sought to ban sagging from the town. This is the same town that a few years earlier had decreed that no one could go shirtless on public property within the town limits.

The first time I encountered the issue I wrote a straightforward editorial denouncing the ban, saying it was government delving into an issue that would likely take care of itself. I also pointed out that since the fashion was largely popular with black youth, the council could set itself up for a lawsuit challenging its ruling by the ACLU or a likeminded organization.

The council never brought the issue to a vote, although the topic was hot for several months.

Having already been through the issue once, I brought a little bit of history with me and, I guess, a bit of outrage the second time I was confronted with the issue.

Generally, ideas for our newspaper's editorials come through weekly meetings of our editorial board. A group of senior managers of the newspaper gets together and discusses ideas that can be generated into stances for the newspaper to take on the editorial page. We take informal votes if an obvious consensus is not forthcoming, but usually I just take notes on what is said and then repair to my office to try to create a serviceable editorial at a later date.

The sagging editorial, however, came through a different route. When the reporter covering the town council meeting returned to the office saying, "You're not going to believe what they want to do..." I knew that was likely the same thing many readers would say the next day after they read her story. After talking to the reporter, I sat down and quickly wrote the first draft of the editorial.

I let the piece sit for a day and then reread it with the added benefit of having read her story. Then I called the mayor of the town to get his take on the issue before sitting down and revising. After letting it sit for several more hours, I went back and removed most of all I had added since the first writing.

I think you have to understand the small town where the issue was taking place. The town, with a population of about 2,400, has little industry. It has few recreational opportunities for youth. It is served by a tiny public library. High school students attend class at a consolidated school about 15 miles away. The youth have few prospects for meaningful employment locally and few reasons to stick around after their high school years are over, that is, if they ever graduate.

They are not bad kids, although it appears that more and more of them are becoming that way. While the sagging trend first appeared in the nation's big cities years ago, it has only recently surfaced here. It is by far the least of the problems afflicting the town as a whole, and town youth, in particular.

My first take on the issue was to make light of the council's heavy-handed approach to solving this problem. Later, I rethought that approach. I rewrote it to make it a straight-laced editorial decrying the town council's inability to tackle tough problems and its willingness to take on an issue ripe with racial overtones. Finally, I recapitulated and decided to go with my first instinct.

The editorial created a minor stir. Town councilmen must have gotten the newspaper's message, somehow, because a formal resolution to ban sagging was never introduced, and no mention of the issue was ever broached in a town council meeting again. I finally asked the mayor one day, several months later, what had become of the issue, and he paused.

For dramatic effect he assured me with a wink that the matter was being studied—intently—and would continue to be studied indefinitely.

As for our readers, many didn't seem to grasp the main intent of the editorial, that town leaders have more important issues to deal with concerning the fate of the town's youth than their choices in how to wear their clothes.

We received and published more than a dozen letters on the issue. Most of those letters seemed to stick to a central theme: Why is the staff of the newspaper interested in seeing the underwear of town youth?

THE DAILY TRIBUNE

Michael Gartner

Finalist, Editorial Writing

Michael Gartner makes his fourth consecutive appearance in *Best Newspaper Writing*. In 1994, he became the first past president of the American Society of Newspaper Editors to receive its Distinguished Writing Award for editorials. He was a finalist in the category in 1995 and again in 1996. Gartner is co-owner and one-person editorial page of *The Daily Tribune,* a 10,000-circulation newspaper 38 miles from his hometown of Des Moines. The son and grandson of Iowa newspapermen, Gartner has been in the news business for four decades. He is a former Page One editor of *The Wall Street Journal,* former editor and president of *The Des Moines Register,* former editor of the *Courier-Journal* of Louisville, former general news executive of Gannett Co. and *USA Today,* and, most recently, former president of NBC News. Gartner began his newspaper career at age 15 when he took a job answering phones and taking dictation in the sports department of *The Des Moines Register.*

Gartner's readership benefits from his relentless editorial focus on community issues. Two days before Christmas, he addressed a more personal, yet universal, topic in this touching tribute to his teenage son Christopher, who died in 1994. Gartner's work was also awarded the 1997 Pulitzer Prize for editorial writing.

Holiday message tucked away in park

DECEMBER 23, 1996

We have more than a passing interest, of course, in Christopher Gartner Memorial Park in west Ames. We stopped by, throughout the fall, and watched the children playing on the little playground or romping on the two acres of lawn. We smiled when we saw a mother or father with a youngster—pushing a swing, perhaps, or tossing a ball, or just sitting and watching. We grinned, especially, the day we saw a little boy with a big dog, each watching out for the other. We laughed out loud when we saw two little boys getting into harmless mischief.

The park, just a few months old, is already serving its purpose, we thought.

That purpose is to provide joy unbounded—joy for little kids, joy for their parents, joy for their dogs.

For Christopher Carl Gartner was the most joyous boy that ever lived.

He was born grinning, and the grin only got bigger as he grew—and grew and grew and grew. He laughed at everything—when he was little, at his grandpa's wild stories; when he was bigger, at his pals' wild escapades. By the time he was 15, he was an exuberant storyteller, regaling his pals with the latest funny thing his friend Andrew said, the latest crazy thing his friend Joey did. His grin and his laughter were infectious. Life for him was fun, and he wanted his friends and his mom and his dad and his grandparents to have fun, too. (He was genuinely kind, as well as cheerful, and early on he figured out that was an advantage. "You know," he once clued in his little brother, "if you're nice to your teachers you don't have to study nearly as hard," something he liked because being nice was a lot easier for him than studying.)

Life for him was love, too. By his early teens, he was a bear of a boy, probably six-feet-three-inches or so, and he would almost have to bend over double to kiss his tiny grandma, whom he stopped by to see almost every day. But he never had that reticence or shyness that boys sometimes develop. He was an unabashed hugger from the day he was born in 1976 till the day he died in 1994. His last words to his father, as he lay in the hospital early in the morning of the summer day he died so suddenly and unexpectedly, were, "I love you, too, dad."

We tell you this today, with more joy than sadness, for a couple of reasons. The first is just a technical one. The deed to the park was turned over to the city the other evening, so Christopher Gartner Memorial Park is now an official city park, and we just thought we'd tell you a bit about the boy the park is named after. (We could tell you much more—about how he goofily learned to walk with the help of a big unruly dog, who cushioned every fall; about how he drove his mother's new convertible into a tree the very day he got his driver's license—it was the tree's fault, he laughingly argued; about how he'd wake his parents at midnight to report in—and then tell them funny stories of what happened at the game or the party or wherever he'd been. All those or the million other happy memories that vie for space against the grieving a hundred times a day.)

The second reason we tell all this is because this is the Christmas season, the time of joy and of families and of fun and of love. We thought there was no better way to wish you a merry Christmas than to tell you the story of a boy who embodied laughter and love and giving, a boy who brought so much joy to so many people in just 17 years.

Our purpose surely is evident: to urge you to have fun this holiday season with your kids or your parents—or both. To urge you to sit around and tell family stories as two or three or sometimes four generations gather at the table—to share in the laughter. And to urge you to tell one another, the young and the old and the very old, that your family is a pretty nice family—to share in the love.

Finally, if it's a nice day tomorrow, you might want to wander over to Christopher Gartner Park—it's tucked away at the dead end of Abraham Drive—and toss a ball around or romp with a dog or push a swing. And think nice thoughts about the cheerful boy who has lent it his name.

It's too bad you never knew him.
You'd have loved his laugh.
You'd have loved him.

Lessons Learned

BY MICHAEL GARTNER

I have a friend who, 40 years ago, was an intern on the *Baltimore News-American,* a newspaper that no longer exists.

Early on, a wise and wizened editor called him over. "Young man," he said, "there are 2 million people in this city, and every one of them has a story to tell." My friend, a worldly Princeton student, began to roll his eyes, but the old editor continued. "And the thing for you to remember," the editor said, "is this: Most of those stories are crappy."

That's the way I feel about first-person columns and editorials. Most of them are awful. Boring. Or sophomoric. Or tasteless. Or maudlin.

They're written by columnists or editorial writers or feature reporters on slow days. These columnists or editorial writers or feature reporters think the readers care about the cute things their children said, care about the long line they had to stand in to go to the movies, care about their personal crises with drink or divorce, care about what the writer thought about as he drove across Kansas with his mother-in-law. It is egotism run amuck.

So the admonition here is this: When you're tempted to write a personal column, resist that temptation. Go look for another idea. Go report a good column. Go walk the dog. (Walking the dog is what most readers will choose to do when they see you've written yet another column about the trivialities of your life and times. Difficult as it might be for you to accept, they don't care about your life or thoughts. They want facts or stories or vignettes about things that interest them or are important to them.)

In 40 years as a reporter and editor and columnist, I've written maybe a half-dozen personal pieces. That's probably a half-dozen too many. Yet Chip Scanlan chose one to be in this book—it isn't what I would have chosen—and so personal writing is what this essay has to be about. A personal essay about personal essays seems doubly perilous.

Let me reiterate:

My first piece of advice is this: Don't write it.

The second is this: If you do write it, have something worthwhile to say. Write it so that your story is almost incidental to the point you want to make. Use your own story just as you would use an anecdotal lead on a feature piece or an example in a news story. Use it as evidence, as argument, as background to the point of view, the moral you want to get across. Even then, the story must be so compelling, or interesting, or unusual that it will keep the reader's attention.

I can remember—without going through anthologies—only three great pieces of first-person journalism. One was William Allen White's essay on the death of his daughter Mary. It was so matter-of-fact that it broke my heart, yet the message of youthful exuberance and family love—always implied, never preached—became etched in my mind. The second was an editorial, or maybe a column, that Vermont Royster wrote in *The Wall Street Journal* after his pocket was picked on the subway. He always carried a spare $100 bill, just for emergencies, he noted, but he had never used it. Now the pickpocket had it, and he would put it into circulation. Royster then went on to use this as an amusing, but informative, lesson on economics and the money supply. It was wonderful. The third was by James Reston of *The New York Times*. He was one of the first American reporters to visit China after it was reopened to the West, and while he was there he developed appendicitis. The Chinese doctors took out his appendix—using acupuncture on him. His lead was something like this: "Let me tell you about *my* operation."

The first of those three was so compelling—terrible and lovely—that you could not put it down. The second was simply an amusing way of making a point. The third was a fascinating experience that also went on to talk about a practice we knew little about.

My own piece, reprinted here, was easy to write. Though the death of my son Christopher is a tragedy of unimaginable and continuing sadness and despair, it has reinforced some beliefs and heightened some memories. Those beliefs and memories kept striking me throughout the fall of 1996 as I stopped by a park that was named for him in Ames, Iowa, where I work. As Christmas approached, the montage of images—of Christopher growing up, of the children in the park, of families together, of Christmas mornings—just assembled themselves in my head.

I wanted to write a gentle piece about families and love and Christmas.

So I wrote about Christopher.

I read it again after I wrote it. Then I read it to myself out loud. I wondered if it was awful. Or boring. Or sophomoric. Or tasteless. Or maudlin.

I hoped I had written it for the reader, not for myself.

I hoped I had made my point.

I wondered—it actually occurred to me—what the old editor in Baltimore would have said.

David A. Waters
Religion/Spirituality Writing

David Waters is a die-hard Cleveland Indians fan, and he says that's one word: "diehardIndiansfan." He was born in Cleveland, the oldest of four children in what he called "a wonderful, suburban two-parent household." His mother stayed home with the four and was, for a while, a part-time reporter for a suburban newspaper. She was also the family spiritual force, leading the children to the Congregational Church, but letting them decide whether they wanted to continue there. Waters left around age 15.

He discovered journalism at Miami University of Ohio when he took a class and decided to interview the mayor. The story turned a failing grade into a passing "C," and kept Waters interested in writing. When his parents moved to Tennessee, Waters joined them and earned a degree in journalism and political science from Memphis State University.

In 1984 he began working for the Memphis *Commercial Appeal* as a bureau reporter based in Jackson,

Tenn. Over the years, he was a copy editor, wire editor, politics editor, special projects reporter, education reporter, national political reporter, then religion reporter.

He has won a number of awards, including regional awards from the Society of Professional Journalists and national awards from the Scripps-Howard newspaper company.

—Karen F. Brown

Big man's big voice beats life in the bad lane

MAY 26, 1996

Big Teddy Carr was big enough to have his way and bad enough to lose it.

Kids made fun of his size until he found out his size could put a stop to that. Teddy's bearlike stature was a source of shame. Then it became a source of income, mostly illegal.

Criminals hired him for protection. Then they had to find protection from him. Teddy the bodyguard turned into Teddy the drug dealer, armed robber and finally jailbird.

Teddy's 6-foot-7, 325-pound size got him into a lot of trouble. His voice carried him out.

No one ever made fun of his voice. It's a deep voice risen from a howl, strong as the black bars of a jail cell, plush as red velvet cushions on church pews.

Big Teddy sang in church, on the streets, in prison. He sang for cops and killers and bishops. For years, he sang for everyone else.

But Teddy's big bad life didn't change until he decided to sing for himself—and for God.

Let Teddy explain his redemption:

"God is so good, man. Look here. To be cold. To be out there so far, so hard until you don't care what happens to you. I didn't believe in God. There was no God. But God took me and changed me. *Me.* A guy who could be your worst nightmare. A guy with bullets in him."

Theodore Roosevelt Carr Jr. was born 36 years ago. He was named for a man who was named for a president. It was a big name, but not big enough to hide behind.

Teddy stood over 6 feet tall in junior high. He wore size 18 shoes. He weighed nearly 300 pounds. The clothes his mother and father could afford just didn't fit. There's no clothing allowance on welfare.

Teddy remembers: "I can laugh about it now, but I was so big it was embarrassing. I'd walk to school and walk home and smell like a horse. Kids in school were always asking me if I had failed. All the young boys were looking good. I just wanted to look good. I just couldn't look good."

Not without money, he couldn't.

When Teddy was 13 he went into a convenience store and grabbed some watches. But he was too big to hide. Someone saw him. Police found him. Teddy's father whupped him. The watches were returned.

He still wanted money. Now all he had to sell was his size.

One day in high school, a kid asked Teddy to hang around for protection. The kid was selling drugs. Teddy was his bodyguard. Easy money. Favors turned into jobs. After high school, those jobs became Teddy's career.

Teddy made more money in a week than his father made in a year. He guarded men and money—shoeboxes full of money, car trunks full of money. Teddy figured if he could guard the money, he could take it just as easily. So, Teddy was stealing from drug dealers and guarding his own life.

They called him nothing nice.

That's not just a description. That was his nickname. "Nothing Nice" Teddy Carr. Didn't bother him. It was a title he relished. Put it on the front of his Mercedes, a criminal's self-promotion. He was a criminal and he was livin' large.

Teddy got his money the old-fashioned way. He stole it. Stole from rich drug dealers and gave to the poor in spirit—himself. Robin in the 'Hood. Teddy was no hero, though. He stole from stores. He sold drugs. He hurt people.

When he was on the run, he hid in graveyards. Sometimes his only moments of peace were nights spent among the dead.

"I just turned bad and then I lived it up," he said.

"But I was scared to do anything. Go anywhere. I'd be peeping out the windows all the time. Bought myself a house. Buried myself in that house. Had tinted windows in my car. Built a fence around my house. I was a prisoner in my own home."

'GOD TALKS TO YOU'

There are gaps in Teddy's life. Gaps in his own memory. Gaps he won't talk about. Gaps that can't be filled by public documents.

This much is known for sure.   —> *Chron.*

Teddy Carr was born Feb. 29, 1960. He was arrested for theft on April 26, 1973. He graduated from Treadwell High School in 1979. From 1984 to 1989, he worked for wages with legitimate companies making from $5 to $7 an hour.

"I tried to straighten out my life," Teddy said. "I just wanted too much too fast."

From June 1988 to October 1989, Teddy was arrested six times on charges such as criminal trespass, assault and battery, grand larceny and possession of controlled substances with intent to sell. He made bail or slept in jail.

On Oct. 26, 1989, a Shelby County court convicted Teddy for stealing and drug dealing. In a pre-sentencing report filed the following month, Teddy made this promise:

"I can assure the court that I have learned my lesson and I will not be back again. If I come back, the judge can throw away the key. There is so much involved that I can't make an adequate statement. All of these things have happened for a reason and have served to make me better."

Teddy was sentenced to two years' probation.

"Mr. Carr does not appear to be a violent threat to the community," the court concluded.

Thirty-three days later, Teddy was arrested again.

"He was observed by police with a pistol, which he shot several times," the police report stated.

Teddy and another man were charged with aggravated robbery, aggravated kidnapping and aggravated attempted murder in the first degree.

Teddy claimed the men who were chasing him and shooting really were chasing the man he was with. Teddy said he was shooting back in self-defense. No one was hurt.

Teddy spent the next 18 months in the Shelby County Jail waiting for the judicial system to sort it all out.

In jail, Teddy found his way again—and his voice.

"I had been to church as a kid and served the Lord and ran off from it. I couldn't feel the fire. Everybody else was dancing and praying and feeling good and I was wondering if this fire was ever gonna hit me. Is a lightning bolt gonna come down? Was God gonna say something to me? I didn't hear nothing. But God does talk to you. You have to listen for it. I wasn't a good listener."

'FORGIVEN MUCH'

Teddy remembers sitting in his cell looking at a Bible someone had given him. Some church lady. He opened it and found Hosea 10:12. When he listened, this is what he heard:

"Sow for yourselves righteousness; reap the fruit of steadfast love; break up your fallow ground, for it is time to seek the Lord."

The verse seemed to begin, Dear Teddy. Teddy was tired of the life. Tired of running and dealing and ducking. Tired of jail. He decided to give it up. He had met two women from the prison ministry at Calvary Episcopal Church. Teddy became their bodyguard.

"I was a little nervous the first time we went into the men's jail," Carol Gardner said. "Teddy looked down and said, 'Little Carol, you don't have a thing to worry about. Big Teddy is here.'"

Teddy was made the chaplain's trusty. He helped lead worship services. That's when he started to sing for God.

"What a fabulous voice," said Novella Smith Arnold, leader of Calvary's prison outreach. "When he sang, grown men cried."

Teddy spent 18 months in the Shelby County Jail. Prosecutors found the charges against Teddy didn't add up. On July 15, 1991, Judge Joseph B. McCartie ordered Teddy released and placed him on five years' probation.

"It appeared to the satisfaction of this court that the defendant is not likely again to engage in a criminal course of conduct," McCartie wrote.

Smith Arnold helped Teddy get a job at Calvary. Gardner hired Teddy's wife, Estella, as a housekeeper. Then they hooked him up with Father Colenzo Hubbard, executive director of the Emmanuel Episcopal Center.

Emmanuel Center sits in Cleaborn Homes public housing development. It's a safe haven for the children in the projects. Teddy began working with the children. He visited their parents. He spoke their language. They loved to hear him sing.

"I knew that God could change anyone's life," Hubbard said. "What I saw in Teddy was God at work. He is a witness. The Bible talks about those who have been forgiven little will love little, but those who have been forgiven much will love much.

"I think Teddy's love for the Lord has a direct relationship to the fact that he has been forgiven much."

'I THANK GOD'

By all accounts, Teddy hasn't returned to his past life. There have been no more arrests. Even bishops vouch for him. Not long ago, Teddy sang at a church event. Episcopal Bishop Edmond Browning jumped up and kissed him on the cheek.

"The Lord keeps putting these people on my path," Teddy said.

People like Michael "Busta" Jones and Lona Mc Callister.

Jones, a local music producer who died late last year, heard the soul music of his day in Teddy's voice. He asked Teddy to sing on "Forbidden Love," a compact disc released last year.

That encouraged Teddy to work on his own songs and maybe make his own record. Once again, Teddy found himself needing money. This time, he didn't use his size to get it.

Teddy works for St. Peter Villa nursing home. Residents stop him in the hall and ask him to sing. Resident Linda Greer was his biggest fan. When she died in 1994, the family asked Teddy to sing at her funeral. He sang "Amazing Grace."

Lona McCallister, Greer's sister-in-law, was there.

"He had such a beautiful voice," Lona said. "The Lord just said, 'Lona, this is what I want you to do.'"

After the funeral, Lona asked Teddy if he sang professionally. He told her of his dream to cut a record. She asked him if he needed any money. She gave him $10,000.

Jones and McCallister helped Teddy produce *In His Hands,* a gospel CD that is getting some local airplay.

Last Sunday, Teddy performed in a talent showcase sponsored by WLOK-AM 1340. General manager Art

Gilliam Jr. said the station is looking at Teddy for its record label.

Teddy hopes his music brings financial success. That's not why he sings.

His voice was a gift from God. His voice is his gift to others. It's all he had to give his mother and father. Turns out, that's all they wanted.

"When I had money I couldn't never give my father nothing," Teddy said. "He wouldn't take it. He said he knew where it came from. He even stopped calling me his son."

Theodore Roosevelt Sr. died Nov. 7, 1994. He was 91. Teddy's mother died three months later. Ida Mae Carr was 66.

The night before Teddy's father died, he asked Teddy to sing. "He looked at me and said, 'Teddy, son, sing me my favorite song. Sing "Swing Low Sweet Chariot." ' He called me son again. I thank God for that.

"Whatever else happens to me, I thank God for that."

Writers' Workshop

Talking Points

1) Writers usually keep control of the storytelling micro-phone in stories, yielding it briefly for quotes. Early in this story David Waters passes the mike to Teddy Carr with the phrase, "Let Teddy explain his redemption." What is the effect of the extended quote that follows? At what other points does Carr tell his story? When should writers let sources tell their stories in their own words?

2) News writers regularly use a person's full name in first reference, and the last name in subsequent references. Notice Waters's practices on references in this story and others. He calls Carr "Big Teddy," "Teddy Carr," and usually "Teddy." List reasons for and against references other than the last name. Is the use of "Teddy" patronizing?

3) Waters said, "One thing I try to do when I write a story is to capture with my choice of words and my syntax the mood and mind of that subject, the mood, the mind, and the environment of that subject." What are some of the words or phrases that create the voice in this story?

Assignment Desk

1) Consider the imagery in this story. In the fifth paragraph, Waters writes, "It's a deep voice...strong as the black bars of a jail cell, plush as red velvet cushions on church pews." Ask several people about the memories and images stirred by this sentence. What must a writer consider about the various images created in readers' minds? Find ways to use more colorful imagery in your articles.

2) Waters tells about Carr's life from the lead, but includes two retellings of Carr's life. The first begins, "Theodore Roosevelt Carr Jr. was born 36 years ago." The second begins, "There are gaps in Teddy's life.... This much is known for sure." What is achieved with the retellings? Diagram the structure of the story.

God's telegram boy has messages to deliver at 77

SEPTEMBER 29, 1996

CHARLOTTE, N.C.—The old evangelist held out a Bible in a trembling hand and told them to come just as they are, just as he did here so many years ago when this was a small town and he was a farm boy.

"This is the most important night of your life," the grandfatherly man said from the stage, and as he said it they began to believe it. "I want you to get out of your seat and come here. We will wait for you."

He waited. And they came—first one, then several, then dozens from all levels and corners of the giant football stadium. Five, 10, 15 minutes passed and they were still coming. Elderly couples stepping gently arm in arm. Parents tugging children. Teenagers, some smiling, others crying their eyes out.

The choir, 7,000 volunteers draped in blood-red robes, softly sang "Just As I Am." Over the north end scoreboard, the Earth's shadow crept across the moon. For a moment, the old evangelist felt his own presence eclipsing the true light.

"You're coming tonight not to Billy Graham," he reminded them. "I know my name has been used too many times. Far too much. And it's embarrassing. No, you are coming tonight to the Lord Jesus Christ."

They came, thousands of them during the Carolinas Billy Graham Crusade, because of the hope of the gospel and its promise of new life. They came to meet Jesus, to give their lives to Him for once or once again. But they also came because the invitation was issued by the Rev. Dr. Billy Graham, their hometown hero and the world's most famous preacher.

Graham's voice has lost some of its vigor but none of its authority.

He's not the same fire-breathing devil-slayer he was when he left his home here 50 years ago, his voice all fight and fury. He called himself God's Western Union boy then. "I have a death message," he would shout. "I must tell you plainly—you are going to hell."

Graham talks more about heaven than hell now. And he doesn't shout anymore. His voice has weakened with age and illness and the change is noticeable. But the elegant tone and graceful accent are unmistakable.

It is a voice that will fill the soundtrack of the 20th century. It is the authentic, unapologetic voice of modern evangelism.

The Carolinas Billy Graham Crusade, which ends today, may or may not be Graham's last crusade. It certainly will be his final crusade in his Carolina home.

The 77-year-old evangelist suffers from Parkinson's, a progressive disease that cripples the body's ability to control muscles. He can't write. He doesn't move well. His hands shake and his voice fades.

His faith is steadfast.

"I think God has sent (Parkinson's) at this age to show me that I am totally dependent on Him," Graham told reporters here last week.

"And when I go into the pulpit to preach, I may have to have a little bit of help getting to the pulpit. But when I get there, I can sense the presence and power of the Lord..."

This town is in a tizzy. Charlotte's new professional football team, the Carolina Panthers, is in first place. The team's new $80 million home, Ericsson Stadium, opened last month. And now, Billy Frank has come home.

That's what people called him back then—Billy Frank, the lanky dairy farmer's son who loved baseball and girls and sold Fuller brushes until he found his true calling.

Graham was 16 when he asked Christ to run his life. It was during the Depression. People were hungry for hope. Traveling evangelists always drew a crowd. One night in 1934, Mordecai Ham's revival drew Billy Frank Graham. When Ham issued the invitation to meet Jesus, young Billy went forward.

Now, generations later, Graham is standing a few miles from the place he was born and the place he was born again. He is asking 65,000 others to make the same commitment he made that night.

"It was a fall, moonlit night much like this one," Graham told the crusade crowd Thursday evening.

"I came down front and I thought to myself, 'Now what in the world am I doing?' A lady next to me was crying and I didn't feel like crying. I started to go back. But I stayed. It's simple to give your life to Christ. So simple people stumble over it. You receive Christ by simple childlike faith."

Billy Graham has the faith of a child. It's his life-sustaining secret, one he has shared personally with the entire world.

Read the Bible and believe what it says, he tells people. Trust God. No one is more powerful. Follow Jesus. No one is more worthy. We're all sinners but we're all forgiven. We'll all die but we all can have eternal life. Repent and believe.

Graham left home to evangelize the world in 1945. He has delivered the same clear, simple gospel message personally to more than 200 million people in more than 185 countries.

By pulling the old-time tent revival out of the hills and plugging it into the 20th century, he revolutionized the evangelical element in world Christianity, said Dr. Martin Marty, senior editor of *The Christian Century*.

Had he not, Marty added, "I fear that North American Protestantism might have gone the way of tired, late-establishment Anglo-European Protestantism, with its empty monumental cathedrals and its often listless parish churches."

There's nothing empty and listless about a Billy Graham crusade. He takes the guts of the old camp meeting—a soulful engine finely tuned to run on a combustible mixture of sin and salvation—and puts them in the biggest, most modern state-of-the-art arenas the world has to offer.

Each meeting is a Super Revival, a special blend of celebrity, tradition and emotion aimed at producing a climactic victory for Jesus.

The order of worship changes as often as the order of the New Testament.

Homegrown choirs sing old and new standards, "Amazing Grace" and "Majesty."

Celebrities perform and testify. The four-night lineup here featured contemporary Christian stars Michael W. Smith and dc TALK along with regional heroes Johnny Cash and Charlie Daniels.

Local dignitaries bring greetings. An offering is collected to cover broadcast costs.

Then the Graham Team takes over. Cliff Barrows, the ever-present master of ceremonies, prays. George Beverly Shea, Graham's personal soloist, sings. Graham preaches and issues the invitation. The choir sings "Just As I Am."

And then, the "inquirers" begin to come forward. They always come.

Graham knows that most of the people who come forward already go to church. More than 900 churches across North and South Carolina have been working for months to plan and prepare for this crusade. The parking lots are lined with hundreds of church buses.

But Graham also knows that even churchgoers are hungry, hurting, searching for something to fill the God-sized holes in their lives. He wants them to take that first simple, genuine step toward Jesus.

"His genius for satisfying a hungry soul is unmatched," Marty said. "He can talk about heaven and hell without inspiring terror. I like to look at the faces of the people who come forward. There is no terror."

A crusade is a massive undertaking—18 months of planning involving hundreds of local churches and thousands of volunteers. The Graham Team doesn't miss a detail.

Speak a different language? No problem. Interpreters translate the crusade in 11 languages through radio headsets available at the door.

Worried about the new grass at Ericsson Stadium? Don't. The field was covered with sheets of ribbed plastic that protect each blade and still let sunlight and water pass through. But just in case, two lots of rye grass sod are being grown in Florida.

Wonder what happens to all those souls saved each night? Trained counselors meet them on the spot. Their names and church preferences are passed on to local clergy.

Crusade coordinators also started an outreach for needy kids that will continue after Graham is gone.

"It's kind of like the circus come to town," said Rev. Bill Wood, pastor of First Presbyterian Church here.

"Except when they leave, they leave something good behind."

But preparation is not what brought 300,000 people here to see Billy Graham. The crusade still works because Graham has changed and adapted.

When he started, he was a brash, judgmental, self-appointed rescuer of filthy, sinful mankind. He also wore white-buck shoes. Times change, so do people.

Graham still believes there is a hell for those who reject Christ. But heaven is the promise he delivers now.

"The overwhelming message is the grace and the love and the mercy of God," he told reporters last week. "That's what I emphasize now a lot more than I did in the earlier years."

The crusade also works because Graham has been tested and can be trusted. He has avoided scandal by avoiding the temptations of sex, money and power.

He never allowed himself to be alone in a room with a woman he wasn't related to. A board in Minnesota runs his entire operation. Local committees run and audit each crusade.

Graham gets no speaking fees, special offerings or book royalties. Each year, he is paid a salary of about $100,000 and a housing allowance of $35,000. That's it.

Graham still keeps company with presidents but he stays out of politics. He didn't join the Moral Majority and won't join the Christian Coalition.

Thursday evening, North Carolina native Elizabeth Dole was at the crusade. Graham welcomed her but also told the crowd President Clinton also has attended his crusades.

Graham is an ordained Southern Baptist minister, but doesn't let himself bog down in denominational struggles or theological debates.

The crusade still works for all those reasons. But mostly, it works because Billy Graham speaks to thousands, millions of people as if he knows each one.

He talks to them about their fears and doubts. He talks plainly about guilt and temptation and death. He offers them the gospel pure and clear with its promise of peace, hope and unconditional love.

"He doesn't pretend to speak to God, he doesn't come off holier-than-thou," said Jenny Ryan of Atlanta, who answered Graham's invitation Friday evening. "But when he speaks I feel the presence of God. He makes it so clear, so simple. And it really is."

Writers' Workshop

Talking Points

1) What can you say about Billy Graham that hasn't already been said during his half-century of ministry? What can you say that is fresh and engaging about his farewell tour when much of the nation's media are covering it? David Waters chose this challenge. What makes his story different? What did you learn from it? How should reporters approach stories that follow well-worn paths?

2) Consider the reporting in the story. It included personal interviews, attending the crusade, and information from the crusade's media relations group. What other sources are evident? What other sources could have been used? What kind of information could online services provide?

3) Of Waters's collection of winning stories, this is the primary one that might be considered traditional religion writing. It is about a well-known religious figure engaged in a religious event. Compare this story to the others. What is the domain of the religion writer today?

Assignment Desk

1) Waters's story notes that the Billy Graham Crusade is much more complex than old-style tent meetings. Among the entities in the crusade is the media relations operations. How should reporters interact with public relations efforts? Engage a conversation between editors and reporters and PR representatives for new ideas about the role of public relations in journalism.

2) The kicker in this story, the ending, is a statement from a believer. She speaks of the "presence of God." What does this mean to an unbeliever? Discuss the understanding and needs of broad audiences. How do writers cover matters of faith without leaving out unbelievers? Examine your stories for instances in which a broader audience might be confused by any insider jargon.

A tree grows in Bellevue

DECEMBER 15, 1996

The Singing Christmas Tree towers nearly five stories over mortals who stand at its base, rising like some great piney pyramid above a make-believe tinsel town inside a church that seems perfectly designed to host it, as if the architect started with the tree and drew Bellevue Baptist Church around it.

Inside the tree, though, all that space is swallowed by steel ribs, catwalks, air-conditioning ducts, wires and bodies, allowing the 165 singing high school students, who crawl through like spelunkers on their hands and knees in the dark to find their places for show time, just enough room to stand still and move their mouths.

The Singing Christmas Tree doesn't sing, of course. The tree is a glorified prop—a gigantic, inanimate, man-made conglomeration, almost 4 tons of steel, plastic, wire, glass, fake pine and finery that doesn't have a thing to say.

Sure, this spectacular prop is mainly what the multitudes come to see (and hear, in a way). It attracts carloads and busloads of people, now more than 50,000 a year, three-quarters of a million people since 1976 when Bellevue was just a really big church downtown and its Singing Christmas Tree was simply a creative way to wrap a choir stand for the holidays.

The tree really is the object of the story, not the subject. Bellevue's annual musical extravaganza isn't about a tree any more than Jesus's parable of the fig tree in the Gospel of Mark. Like the needleless tree in *A Charlie Brown Christmas,* this tree is a device, a mechanical contrivance, a construction, not a creation.

The real story of Bellevue's Singing Christmas Tree is what happens inside the tree and, even more, inside the hundreds of people who assemble it, wire it, decorate it, program it, write and arrange music for it, sing in and around it and come to it—all of them looking for fun, joy and meaning.

"I've seen people come to see a play and leave with a new heart. I've seen broken homes brought back to life. I've seen broken people brought back to life," said Rev. Jim Whitmire, Bellevue's minister of music, who saw a singing Christmas tree in California in the late 1960s and brought the idea back home.

"It's not the tree, of course. It's the Gospel message that goes with it. But the tree is always there."

* * *

Sure it's big.

This is Bellevue's annual Christmas gift to the community. Big is who they are. This is a church with 27,000 members, enough people to populate Bartlett. This is a church with 350 Sunday School classes and a Newborn Suite. This is a church with its own loading dock.

"The first time I saw the tree I was in awe," said Martha Witcher.

"I was in awe that a church existed in Memphis with the ability to do something like this. I was raised in a small church. We had little programs, little Nativities. We didn't even have a spotlight."

This electronic explosion doesn't need a spotlight.

The steel infrastructure is wrapped with green plastic chicken wire and loaded with enough decorations to dress dozens of regular Christmas trees: 1,800 feet of garland, 1,050 ornaments, 69 wreaths and a fiber optic star.

And 5,500 bulbs—about 120 per foot.

A computer runs the lights, which alternately blaze, flicker, twinkle and strobe red, green, blue, white and rainbow, depending on the song, the mood and the message.

A separate series of white lights on the tree forms the outline of a cross. After all, this is a program about a cross, not a tree. And the spirit doesn't confine itself to show time.

Jesse Griggs is a training specialist for the State of Tennessee. In his spare time, he assembles Singing Christmas Trees.

The tree is stored in sections in a warehouse on site, moved to the sanctuary by truck, then carried inside and reassembled by a dozen volunteers in the course of several long evenings.

Griggs joins the late-night reconstruction crew year after year. He never knows how he will be blessed, but he knows he will. Take the first year, for instance.

One night while he was working on the tree, his wife called from home. She called to tell him that his father had professed his faith in Christ publicly that very night at a church in Arkansas.

"It's hard to describe the feeling here," said Griggs, a Bellevue usher.

"The fellowship here among 40 or 50 men you won't find anywhere else. No one brings his ego. We all have a common purpose. We all work together.

"I can't sing. I'm not a performer. But the Lord blessed me with a strong back and a willingness to work. This is my way of serving the Lord."

Robert Wagner is another volunteer tree-builder. He dates his salvation to Bellevue's Easter Passion Play in March 1991. At that performance, he accepted Jesus Christ as his savior and joined Bellevue.

"I was your typical guy who wore a Budweiser T-shirt," said Wagner, a diesel truck mechanic.

"The Clydesdales were my team. I thought a new car and a home in Cordova was what made you happy. But I wasn't happy.

"I gambled. I drank. I spent money. I tried everything but God. If it hadn't been for that tree and the Passion Play, I'd probably be divorced today. Instead I have a hunger to know Jesus Christ. God is the head of my life."

Now Wagner is an usher, Sunday School teacher, volunteer evangelist and tree hugger. He's part of the annual tree-assembly fellowship.

The Passion Play saved him, but the Singing Christmas Tree sustains him.

Of course, the tree itself is not what leads Wagner and hundreds of volunteers and church staffers to devote significant portions of their lives each year to the tree.

It's the message, the hope, the promise of the Gospel that brings these people together into what becomes a community within the congregation.

"Every time I work on the tree, nobody's grumbling, everybody's as happy as can be," Wagner said.

"God's presence is all around."

* * *

In the beginning in 1976, Bellevue's Singing Christmas Tree was just a show, a traditional church Christmas program filled mostly with familiar carols and hymns.

Now the tree is merely the main attraction of a 90-minute musical production. This year's tree is cast as a turn-of-the-century town's community Christmas tree. The tree is lit and comes to life in the second half of the production, just after the play's main character accepts Christ in his life.

Whitmire got the singing tree idea from First Baptist Church in Van Nuys, Calif., by most accounts home of the original singing tree.

"I saw their tree, and it grew on me," Whitmire said.

"The first year I just wanted to give the church a taste of what could be. I didn't know how long it would last."

Twenty-one years, so far. The tree has been rewired a couple of times, but this year's cascading centerpiece is the same structure architect Gene Strong designed 21 years ago.

The decorated tree weighs about 7,500 pounds— and about 30,000 pounds (15 tons) fully loaded with teenagers. Eleven tiers offer standing room for 165 members of Bellevue's Senior High Choir.

"It's like a big erector set, a well-labeled erector set," said Pat Musgrave, another of the dozens of Bellevue men who donate the services of their arms, legs and backs to the tree each year.

"We just want the Lord to use what we're doing, whether it's hauling the tree, running a screw through a flat or putting gaffer tape over mistakes. It's the Lord's work."

Other production members have the same sense of divine teamwork.

Witcher is the program's volunteer prop master. This is her fifth tree. If a cast member is carrying it, using it or looking at it, chances are Witcher found it. A sled. A wagon. The toys in the toy store window.

But she doesn't work alone.

"I talk to the Lord every day about my props," she said.

"Before I go hunting, I pray. I say, 'Lord, I know what I need is out there.' I don't know where. But I find it. He helps me find it. He knows what I need, and He leads me to it."

Carolyn "Miss Higgy" Higginbotham is in charge of costumes. She and her staff of a dozen volunteer seamstresses fit hundreds of cast members as well as members of the tree choir.

They have learned to appreciate little tricks of the costuming trade.

"When I get to heaven I want to meet two people," she said.

"The persons who invented the safety pin and Velcro. I'm sure they'll be there."

For nearly 20 years, Miss Higgy has bought every piece of cloth and cut every costume. There are more than 300 in this year's performance, including more than 200 turn-of-the-century dresses and women's hats. No two are alike.

With no formal training in costuming, Miss Higgy puts her trust in the Lord. She calls it the miracle of costuming.

"I ask the Lord for two things," she said.

"The first is selection of patterns. And I ask the Lord to guide me to the fabrics that are the best for the cheapest price. I don't go asking for something special just because we're Bellevue.

"And it's awesome what just turns up at the sales table."

This year's program, basically the same as last year's, was written and directed by John Lewis, a Hollywood screenwriter and director whose credits include *Pistol Pete* about basketball great Pete Maravich. Lewis is one of only a handful of production staffers who are paid for their work.

Lewis began his assignment with some parameters. The script had to incorporate the tree and the Nativity. It had to have a moral. And it had to have a point at which someone accepts Christ.

"Even if it's an original script, we have to Bellevue-ize it," Whitmire said.

Lewis focused the story on a young father who hates Christmas. The man turned his back on God when his sister was killed in a sledding accident.

When his daughter gets hurt in a similar accident, he confronts God with his anger and his need.

Lewis drew on his own experiences. His father and brother are preachers, but he rejected God until he went to Vietnam as a medic.

"I held people and watched them die," Lewis said.

"I saw tough guys during the day go get drunk and come back crying. They were searching for something, for meaning. When you're scared and face to face with death, that's the moment you want to believe."

* * *

Tree positions are awarded, not taken. Members of Bellevue's Senior High Choir compete for the best spots near the middle and at the top.

Attendance at choir practice is one factor. School grades are another. Those numbers are fed into a computer, along with logistics such as height, voice and class.

The most prized position is the single post at the top of the tree. Soloists audition for that slot. The member with the best attendance and grades gets the second-most sought-after spot: dead center, where lights that form the cross intersect.

Last year, Stacey Tranum stood in that spot. Stacey, 17, is a senior at Evangelical Christian School. This year will be her fourth, and final, performance perched in the tree. Only senior high students sing in the tree.

"Some of my friends think it's kind of weird, but it's not strange to me," said Stacey.

"I've grown up always seeing people singing in a tree."

The tree is unlit and lifeless until the second half of the program. That's when Stacey and the other teen tree-trimmers file quietly out of the choir room behind the stage and into the tree.

The kids have six minutes to reach their places. They climb on hands and knees in the dark in silence.

Two adults are positioned inside each tier. They count feet to see if someone is sick or late. Other adults eye the tree from a sanctuary skybox.

"We've got maneuvers the military would be proud of," said Lewis.

The adults stand by with water, juice, aspirin and flexible air-conditioning ducts. A kid who needs a drink or quick burst of cool air taps a leg or snaps a finger.

Volunteer firefighters, nurses and emergency medical technicians—all Bellevue members—stand backstage just in case. In 20 years of performances, they have been needed only once.

Last year, a girl fainted and fell one level into a safety net. She had a cut and some bruises but was OK.

With the choir in position, a cast member onstage flips a switch or pushes a button and the tree explodes with light and sound. The choir sings four or five songs accompanied by the tree's dazzling light show.

Most of the songs used to be old standards. Now the show relies on original compositions, many by Scott Sturtevant.

"What we do is so us, it's hard to find prepackaged music that fits," said Sturtevant, Bellevue's associate music minister.

Sturtevant first saw the tree in 1985 as a high school student. "I was blown away," he said.

For this year's production, he wrote several songs for the main character, the young man whose sister was killed and daughter badly hurt in similar accidents.

"I don't have a daughter; my sister is OK," Sturtevant said.

"To be able to portray a father's agony in an authentic way, well, I was inspired by the Lord. It's Him. I have no experiences like that to draw on. I know the lyrics are coming from Him."

* * *

At the end of each performance, Dr. Adrian Rogers asks members of the audience if they believe.

"You can be saved tonight, right where you are, instantaneously and forever," Rogers, senior pastor, said last year.

"Salvation is a gift."

Cards are passed out during each performance. Audience members are asked to check a box, if they have prayed during the show to receive Christ. Whitmire keeps a running count.

Last year, 2,341 people made professions of faith, bringing the 20-year total to 30,743.

But Whitmire and others who nourish the tree each year don't dwell on big numbers.

In fact, compared to Bellevue's normal enormous-
ness, the tree offers church members a regular and perhaps rare opportunity to become part of something
much smaller.

Each year, Miss Higgy gets together with her seamstresses, Whitmire and Sturtevant with their singers
and musicians, Griggs and Wagner with their fellow
setbuilders, Tranum with her fellow cast members.

They talk about work and family and God. They
pray and laugh and sweat together.

For a few glorious weeks, each joins a small community of Christians working without pay on a common project they believe can help and heal others just
as it has helped and healed them.

"There's something in each of us that was put there
especially to help the body of Christ," said production
designer Mark Alexander.

"The tree gives us each a way to apply those gifts
and, in the process, we become a family."

Writers' Workshop

Talking Points

1) You could say this story is three stories in one: (1) the story of the tree; (2) a look at the faith of people behind the scenes; (3) a story on the production including the choir. What is another way of describing the story's structure? Outline the divisions, including where they begin and end.

2) Early in the story Waters writes, "Bellevue's annual musical extravaganza isn't about a tree any more than Jesus's parable of the fig tree in the Gospel of Mark." How much does a religion writer need to know about the scriptures and other aspects of various faiths?

3) Reporters are taught to be skeptical, to ask tough questions, to test every statement given. How should a reporter respond when a source says, "Before I go hunting, I pray. I say, 'Lord, I know what I need is out there.' I don't know where. But I find it. He helps me find it. He knows what I need, and He leads me to it."?

Assignment Desk

1) A number of characters populate this story. Box the name of each. What is the function of each? Could any have been omitted? How does the writer keep from confusing readers when there are so many characters? Try different ways to keep the identities of characters clear in your articles.

2) Part of the writer's challenge in this story is describing a massive, unusual structure in ways that are clear. Waters begins by using a human base of comparison rather than numbers. His lead says, "The Singing Christmas Tree towers nearly five stories over mortals who stand at its base..." Can you picture the tree throughout? Make mental notes or actual drawings at various places in the story. How does the writer help readers see the story? Describe a complicated building or structure on your beat or in your city using comparisons, not just raw numbers.

Grace supplied strength to heal and renew

DECEMBER 25, 1996

The bishop's phone rang. It was the Christmas call he was dreading.

A church he helped found a few years earlier was between priests. Would he lead the Christmas Eve service?

The altar was the last place Rev. Alex Dickson wanted to be last Christmas Eve.

Dickson had retired as bishop of the Episcopal Diocese of West Tennessee in 1994, but that wasn't why he resisted the invitation.

His wife, Charnelle, and eldest son, Alex III, both had died of cancer in 1995.

His spiritual foundation had cracked and crumbled beneath him. His faith in God, which began six decades earlier in his grandmother's lap, had all but died with them.

"God is good" was the only prayer he could utter. And that was partly a praise and partly a question.

The Christmas Eve service was to be at Church of the Annunciation. The annunciation was the angel Gabriel's announcement to Mary that she was to be the mother of Jesus, the Christ child.

"Hail, full of grace, the Lord is with Thee," the angel told Mary in Luke's Gospel.

Dickson knew the words by heart, but they had lost their power. How could a bishop in Christ's church stand at the altar on Christmas Eve not believing?

"My heart felt like it had been torn out," Dickson said one recent afternoon as he sat in his quiet East Memphis home and told the story.

"I told God, 'My heart's in paradise and all I've got left is the hole. I need some sort of physical contact with Charnelle and Alex.'

"And then the Lord spoke to me."

* * *

I cried out to God for help
I cried out to God to hear me
When I was in distress, I sought the Lord

326

at night I stretched out untiring hands
and my soul refused to be comforted

—Psalm 77: 1-2

Dickson's story begins 70 years ago in the soil-rich and dirt-poor Mississippi Delta.

He was born on his grandfather's cotton plantation near Alligator, Miss., just down Highway 61 from Clarksdale. His grandfather and father were farmers. Dickson figured he'd be one, too. Years later he found out being a parish priest and a bishop wasn't all that different. Seeds were sown and nourished. Have faith and God would provide.

Dickson never lacked faith. He was evangelized in the arms of his grandmother, Maud Wicks. Jesus was real to her, so Jesus was real to him.

As a child, he'd awaken each morning to see his grandmother sitting by a window reading the Bible and praying.

"What you doin'?" he'd ask.

"I'm readin' about Jesus," she'd say.

"Tell me about Jesus," he'd say.

"Come over and get in my lap."

* * *

Alex Dickson and Charnelle Perkins were married in 1948. They had met three months earlier on a blind date. "I knew I didn't want to let her get away," he said.

After he graduated from Ole Miss, Dickson began farming with his father. Alex III was born in 1949; a second son, Charles, in 1951; a third, John, in 1953.

Dickson figured to spend the rest of his days as a Delta planter. Then the flood came. It was not a flood of biblical proportion, but it rained enough to wash away a year's income. Dickson left the farm and signed on with a cotton oil company that sent him and his family to Charlotte, N.C.

Faith needs less nourishment and attention when life is warm and sunny. But when clouds form and winds rise, faith begins to bow and struggle. That's when the roots and sinews of faith are tested.

One day in Charlotte the wind picked up and blew his little boy's balloon up a tree. Little Alex was 4. He backed up to take a look and backed into the highway. A truck knocked him into a coma.

Dickson stayed with his son and prayed. His faith roots were deep and sturdy. Even when he wasn't a regular in church, he was talking to Jesus just like he did in his grandmother's lap.

One night in the hospital, Dickson felt a need to talk privately to God. He got inside a phone booth and got on his knees.

"I said, 'Lord, I would do anything to save this little boy.' Then I said words that astounded me when they came out. I didn't think them up. They were given to me.

"I said, 'Lord, I would do anything to save this little boy, but if you're ready for him, I give him back to you.'

"I died on my knees."

Years later, Dickson realized that was his first lesson in stewardship. That everything comes from God and belongs to him and is to be returned with thanksgiving.

He would have to learn the lesson again.

* * *

You kept my eyes from closing;
I was too troubled to speak.
I thought about the former days,
the years of long ago;
I remembered my songs in the night.

—Psalm 77: 4-6

Little Alex came out of his coma a few days later. His father and mother took him home and he learned to walk again. The Dicksons were overcome with gratitude to God.

"How do you respond?" Dickson asked.

"You can't pay God back. Everything is His. All you can do is say, 'Thank you.' So we began to try to live a Thank You life."

The couple began to volunteer at St. Mark's Episcopal Church in Charlotte. They swept the inside, mowed the outside. They led a youth group. Dickson was a lay reader at Sunday services.

When the priest moved to another parish, Dickson and another layman continued to lead services. Friends began to ask—some were kidding, some weren't—when he was going to seminary.

Most preachers say the call to preach sends them running at first, hard and fast away from the call.

Dickson ran, too. But eventually, he found he wasn't running away from it but toward it.

In 1955, he entered seminary. Three years later, he was assigned to Chapel of the Cross in Rolling Fork, Miss., Charnelle's home parish.

From there, Dickson's new vocation took him from Rolling Fork to another parish in Jackson, Miss., then to All Saints' Episcopal School in Vicksburg. Dickson was rector and headmaster for 15 years.

"Alex is a genuine product of Alligator, Miss.," said Bishop John Allin, the former Presiding Bishop of the Episcopal Church and Dickson's mentor and close friend.

"He's a man's man. There's no wimp about Alex Dickson. When he's with you, he's with you. There's no fluff in the man."

In 1983, Dickson was elected first bishop of the newly formed Episcopal Diocese of West Tennessee. When he retired in 1994, Dickson told a reporter he wasn't quitting, merely bringing another part of his ministry to a close.

"I'm waiting to see what the Lord wants me to do next," he said then.

Now he knows, of course. He has a story to tell.

As he sat in his home recently, the retired bishop smoothed his clerical collar and glanced over at a photograph on the mantel. He asked if he could preface the story with a prayer.

"Almighty and most gracious father," he said, leaning forward and bowing slightly in his chair, eyes closed, hands clasped.

"You have given me a story to tell. And in obedience, I do so."

* * *

My heart mused and my spirit inquired:
Will the Lord reject forever?
Will he never show favor again?
Has his unfailing love vanished forever?
Has his promise failed for all time?
Has God forgotten to be merciful?
—Psalm 77: 6-9

At first, they thought Alex III had pneumonia. He'd had it before. The symptoms were familiar. But on July 13, 1994, the son called the father and told him he had been diagnosed with lung cancer. It was more than a shock. Their eldest son was a healthy 45-year-old man who had never smoked.

Dickson flew to his son's home in Slidell, La., and took him to a specialist in Houston. Too late for surgery, but not for chemotherapy and radiation treatment.

Dickson's son got better for a while, long enough to return to home and work as a special education teacher, long enough to complete a program that helped his students find jobs.

But by March 1995, his son had run out of options. He was back in a Houston hospital. He almost died on a Monday evening. Dickson asked if his son could be kept alive long enough to be flown home to see his wife and two young sons. They said he could. On Tuesday evening, Alex talked to his father.

"He said, 'Daddy, God pulled back the curtain and I saw the glory last night and I'm ready to go. It's wonderful. I just want to get home and see my boys and then I'm ready.'"

They flew Alex home Wednesday morning. He saw his boys. He died Thursday evening. He was 45.

Three months later, Charnelle Dickson was diagnosed with advanced brain cancer.

Back to Houston they went. Surgeons operated. Radiation treatments began. Charnelle already was too weak. Over the next few weeks, she lost the use of her right arm and leg, her sight and speech.

Dickson was a priest, a bishop. He knew dying was part of living. But he couldn't bring himself to give up. He was by her side day and night. He thought maybe if he tried hard enough, prayed long enough, maybe they'd win and Charnelle would live.

Near the end, all Charnelle could do to express her love was to squeeze her husband's hand. All Dickson could pray was "Lord have mercy. Christ have mercy."

On Sunday morning, Oct. 15, Dickson gave his wife communion. Early the next morning she died. She was 65.

The roots of his faith were dying. His faith was withering. There was nothing left to hold it up, hold him up. He felt he had run out of grace.

He began to question God. Imagine that. A bishop of the church questioning God:

"I was asking, 'Jesus, are you alive? Are Charnelle and Alex with you? Is it all true?'"

For weeks Dickson struggled. He kept returning to John's Gospel. Slowly, he saw he had been trying to make Jesus prove Himself.

"I've been saying that if You had healed Alex, if You had healed Charnelle, I'd believe," Dickson said.

"I'm not going to do that anymore. Father, I give Charnelle and Alex back to You."

* * *

Then I thought, 'To this I will appeal;
the year of the right hand of the Most High.'
I will remember the deeds of the Lord;
yes, I will remember your miracles of long ago.
I will meditate on all your works
and consider all your mighty deeds.
Your ways, O God, are holy.

—Psalm 77: 10-13

That wasn't the end of it. Grace returned but the pain remained. As Christmas drew near, Dickson would wander around his empty house, praying and crying, looking.

"I would look for something that Charnelle had made, some needlepoint or something, just to rub my hand over it because I wanted to have some physical contact," he said.

"I'd go inside her closet and stand inside and put my face against a dress, hoping I would get some aroma, some contact with her.

"I cried out, 'Lord, I didn't know it was going to hurt so much after I gave them back to You.'"

Dickson prayed to God and God told Dickson to meet him at the altar. As another Christmas drew near, Dickson sat in his home and finished the story. It's a story he will tell often and for the rest of his life. It's his Christmas story:

"The Lord said, 'I told my disciples the night before I died that if they would take bread and give thanks and take wine and give thanks for the recalling of Me, I would be present with them.'

"He said, 'Alex, you know that. You've met me at the altar for years. When you come to the altar to touch Me and be touched by Me, you will also touch

Charnelle and Alex and be touched by them, because
they are with Me.'

"I don't need to tell you, I ran to the altar.

"Christmas Eve was wonderful at Annunciation. I
was able to preach again. My son John and his family
were in the pew, and Jesus and Charnelle and Alex and
I were up at the altar.

"It was a real Christmas."

Friends of Dickson now see Christmas in his face.

"He was as devastated and lost as any of us ever
was," said Rev. L. Noland Pipes, rector of St. John's
Episcopal Church.

"He was touched by grace in a way that trans-
formed. He's more at peace now, more joyful, more
playful. There's more of a sparkle in his eye.

"You can see it in him when he comes to the altar
rail. There's an inner glow."

Writers' Workshop

Talking Points

1) Three voices appear in this story. The first voice is the journalistic voice of narrative, quotations, and paraphrases. The second is the writer's voice in sections such as this: "Faith needs less nourishment and attention when life is warm and sunny. But when clouds form and winds rise, faith begins to bow and struggle. That's when the roots and sinews of faith are tested." The third voice is the voice of the scriptures in Psalm 77. What dimensions do the voices bring to the story?

2) Waters uses short and long sentences to control the pacing of the story. Consider two passages: "Back to Houston they went. Surgeons operated. Radiation treatments began. Charnelle already was too weak. Over the next few weeks, she lost the use of her right arm and leg, her sight and speech." The second reads: "The roots of his faith were dying. His faith was withering. There was nothing left to hold it up, hold him up. He felt he had run out of grace." How does sentence length affect the pacing?

Assignment Desk

1) The headline in this story personifies "grace." Where does "grace" appear in this story? What does grace mean? How does the reader know the meaning of grace? Write a story about a matter of faith. What do you need to define the belief? How do personal examples from the lives of other people help you describe it?

2) What is the news in this story? Make an argument for including this story, and others without story news pegs, in newspapers.

A conversation with
David A. Waters

KAREN BROWN: How would you describe your job?

DAVID WATERS: Well, it took me a few years to understand this job, or at least attempt to understand it. Everything I'd covered before—education, government, politics—all of those beats had a center. There was a person or a group, a committee, an institution, a building, someplace where you could be at the center of that beat and the stories. Religion was completely different.

There was no center. Denominations were all over the place. There are 2,000 churches in Memphis, and there's no center of those churches. There are 500,000 people in Memphis who go to church, so there's no center there. It took me awhile to realize what the center was; then it started to click. To me, the center was God. Once I figured that out, then I felt like looking for God.

How did you determine that God is the center?

Well, no matter what faith, they all generally have a common belief in a god. At least in this part of the world, a single god. And everything they do when it relates to faith relates to their belief about that god. So I just started looking for God in everything I wrote about.

Is it *a* God or is it *the* gods? In other words, to what degree do you cover the range of faiths?

Well, I try to cover everybody equally, but in this part of the buckle of the Bible Belt one out of every five citizens is a Baptist. Most everyone here is Protestant or Catholic. There are some Jews and there are a handful of Muslims. Very few Buddhists, very few Hindus. So when you're talking about probably 95 to 98 percent of the people in this area, whatever the variations on their doctrines or beliefs, they all believe in one god. Whether it's God of the Old Testament, God of the New Testament, or God of the Koran.

How did you become the religion reporter?

I asked for the job. In 1992, I was covering the presidential elections and we had a couple of local boys in the race, Bill Clinton and Al Gore, and I did a lot of national reporting that year. When the year ended, I was looking for something else that was interesting to cover. Like I said, this is "the" buckle of the Bible Belt, and I don't think there's anything more interesting to write about than religion and its impact on people.

When I grew up in Nashville and we talked about Memphis, we talked about the Beale Street Blues and Elvis, but somehow I didn't think of it as a highly religious place. Why do you call it the "buckle of the Bible Belt"?

Well, I guess everybody in every town in the South figures their town is the buckle of the Bible Belt. Religion is so important to the South. Memphis is the home of three Protestant denominations, and everybody here goes to church, or at least claims to. The black church is very influential here, very powerful, and so is the white church. They are two very distinct groups. And those two probably have more impact on what goes on in this town than any other aspect of the community. Including politics.

How do you define your beat?

That was another difficulty I had. I tried initially to sit down and prioritize what it was that I covered. There were so many options, but I've tried to focus on God. I look for stories that are interesting, that have some impact either on the community at large or just on some individual or some group, and then I write about where God is in that story.

Do you invade other beats?

I don't see it as invasion. I think that's another mis-perception that a lot of newspapers have about cover-ing religion. I saw no borders, no boundaries of what I could cover. I've gotten into politics, I've gotten into education, I've gotten into individual features. I just feel like everything is open. If I happen to cross into somebody else's beat, I talk to them first, let them know I'm there, and see if it's OK with them. But I don't try to limit myself.

One of the things that I told the editors on the front end was that I didn't want my stuff running on the re-ligion page on Saturday. To me, that's just an adver-tiser's gimmick, and it really doesn't serve a great purpose. If I write a story that doesn't end up on the front page or on the front of the local section, I feel like I've failed because I think that God and faith are such a huge aspect of everyone's life that it ought to be a part of the daily run of the newspaper.

Is there a stigma about religion writing?

Yeah, I think so. I think religion has always been a very difficult thing for reporters to cover, especially reporters who claim to be objective. Religion is such a personal, subjective, and somewhat abstract notion that a lot of reporters who are trained in inverted pyra-mids and the five W's find it very hard to maintain ob-jectivity. A lot of people stay away from it for that reason. Other people don't see a whole lot of front-page news in it. They see it as kind of an odd, featurey, soft news beat that's not going to get you on the front page or get you noticed. But I feel just the opposite.

Now you're saying that many people are not com-fortable trying to be objective in matters of reli-gion. How do you handle that?

Well, one of the things I did when I started was I told myself that I was going to take everybody's faith se-riously. I have my own beliefs, but I don't claim to have any answers about God. I can't judge anyone else's beliefs.

Really, now, what if you're covering a religion that seems very strange or dangerous? Snake-handlers, for instance. Is there a point at which you determine that your role is to report something in a way that says it's not the norm?

If I found a bunch of crazy cult people down the street who were sacrificing babies, sure, I'd report that immediately.

I've covered all the groups that you could possibly say are just a little out of the norm. And I disagreed with them and I felt uncomfortable at times when I was with them, and in their services, but I just tried to ignore that and tried to write about who they were and what they thought, and present that as accurately as I could to the community.

Tell me about your faith.

I think my asking for the beat had something to do with my "faith journey." I've had a strange, kind of winding faith journey through the years, going from close to atheism to agnosticism and to real deep Christian belief. I think I took the beat not only because I thought it was interesting and challenging and page one-worthy, but because I thought I'd learn a lot about God. In a strange way while I've been looking for God in other people I've been trying to find God for myself. It's been an amazing adventure. I have learned more about faith than I could possibly have learned in any other way. It has changed me.

I'm sure as you work on many stories people ask you what is your faith. What's your answer?

Well, it depends on the situation. If I'm talking to somebody at length and I'm trying to get them to open up, and I need them to trust me with some very deep personal ideas and feelings, then I ought to be able to trust them with my own thoughts. I try not to open up the subject, but if they ask and I think the situation is warranted, then I'll discuss it with them, as briefly as possible.

I don't really think my own beliefs are relevant to

what I write.

Do you believe they're relevant to this interview?

I don't know. I don't think so. I've always wondered if
a religion reporter ought to believe in God. Can an
atheist be a good religion reporter? And I'd have to
say I don't think so. I think you have to come at it
from a certain understanding of what God means to
people and why, and I'm not sure atheists have that
sort of level of understanding.

**Let me ask my question the way people asked it
when I grew up. Where do you go to church?**

I go to every church. I go to more churches than most
pastors. One of the things I did when I started this job
was tell the editor, as hard as he found it to understand, "I want to work on Sunday." I just think it's
crazy for a religion reporter to be off on Sunday. It's
like the NFL reporter being off on Sunday. If you're
going to cover religion, you ought to work Sunday.

**OK, I'll go to another subject. How do you sharpen
your craft? Do you have favorite writers or newspapers that you turn to?**

I have favorite writers, but I don't look for people who
just write about religion. Several of the old ASNE
winners are my favorites. I go to them for inspiration,
motivation. I go to Rick Bragg; whatever he writes I
try to read. Walt Harrington, guys like that. Richard
Ben Cramer is a great writer. I don't look for the area
so much as the style of writing, the kinds of things
they write about.

How did you develop as a writer?

I've always liked to write. I've always loved words.
I've always loved to read, and I try to read as much as
I can. I try to find people who write things that I enjoy
reading and that I wish I could write. For a while it
was non-fiction, and then it was fiction, and now I'm
going back to non-fiction. But I guess I look for story-

tellers. I think that's the common thread. I try to find people who tell stories, whether that's Walt Harrington or John Steinbeck, they all tell great stories. There's no doubt, *Grapes of Wrath* is the greatest book ever written. John Steinbeck is a wonder.

What's your career goal?

Well, I think my goal is to write stories, write great stories. It doesn't matter about what. Just to have the freedom and the license to write great stories.

That's a segue to some great stories. Let's talk about your winning pieces. Do you have a favorite of the group?

I guess if I have a favorite, it's Teddy. Big Teddy Carr.

Where did you find Teddy?

I met him at an Easter service a year before I wrote the story. He was singing, and I was amazed by his voice. Really moved by it. And he gave a little testimony after he sang, just a glimpse of what his life was like. I thought, "This guy would make a great story," but I didn't have the time that day and I never got back to him until a year later.

I knew there was enough material there for a really good story. But you never know how much someone has thought about their own life, thought about their own story, and how well someone can articulate that. To me he made the story because he could talk about his own story.

My colleague here at Poynter, Chip Scanlan, often approaches stories by saying writers ought to consider two questions: what's the news and what's the story. The story is clear here, but what's the news?

Well, I would say that probably most journalism professors wouldn't find any news at all in this story under the traditional definition of news. I guess there really isn't any news. He didn't win an award. He didn't get a recording contract. He didn't just get out of jail or just join a church. There's no hook to hang this story on. But I think there are other definitions of news, especially when you're covering religion, and I think how God affects people's lives is as much a part of the news of a community as anything.

You write in a very clear and folksy style. You say "Teddy's father whupped him." Do editors express concerns when you decide to use expressions like "whup"?

Yeah, they get a little nervous if something like that is not in quotes. One thing I try to do when I write a story is to capture with my choice of words and my syntax the mood, the mind, and the environment of that subject. Teddy is not the most educated guy in the world. He grew up on the streets, and he never went to college. He's a very simple-spoken person, although I think what he says is very poignant and deep, he still talks the way most people talk in the streets, and I try to capture that.

When Tom Wolfe writes about the chic people in New York or the good old boys driving race cars down in South Carolina, he captures their mood and their tone, their atmosphere and their cadence, and that's what I try to do. I try to bring that person to the reader, not only through his own quotes but through my writing, as well.

I try to see where they live, feel where they live, and listen to them, how they talk, what they talk about, how they phrase things, the tone of their voice.

You also surprise your readers. One section says, "Teddy got his money the old-fashioned way. He stole it." Another says, "Stole from rich drug dealers and gave to the poor in spirit—himself." So on two occasions you give a familiar phrase a different twist. Are you using gold coins at these points to bring the reader along?

Yeah, I'm very conscious of them when I write, and I use them intentionally. The best writers, I think, surprise people. Not just at the beginning of stories but throughout the stories, with foreshadowing and flash-back and word choice and word juxtaposition. There ought to be little nuggets all the way through stories. The middle of a story is the most difficult part of writing for me. If you keep people going through the middle, then you've got something.

How do you keep from going too far in word choices, imagery, or other techniques?

I hope my editors will keep me from going too far.

How do you keep the story flowing clearly? How do you decide what to leave out?

That's probably the most difficult thing. If I have a tendency, it's probably to want to put too much in. So I just kind of go back and use the old cleaning-out-the-closet allusion. I try to throw out as much extraneous, superfluous stuff as I can find. I don't really have a rule of thumb. I go with my instinct.

It does take a certain discipline. Are there any other lessons for writers you'd like to mention?

I think it's important for writers to pay attention to other sources of writing than just themselves. Ask people if they have diaries, ask people if they have written letters about what they're talking about, ask people to record them, let them talk, and see how they phrase things.

Let me go on to the Billy Graham story. Many would have covered this story by simply going to the crusade and writing about what happened. Several elements in your story suggest that you did some research: the number of people who have been involved over the years, facts about the stadium, the news that Graham was formerly known as Billy Frank. What kind of background work do you do on a story like this?

If I have the time, I read as much as I possibly can about the person or subject I'm writing about. I read books, I read magazine articles, I read things they have written. I'm a trivia buff, and I'm intrigued by little fact nuggets. So I guess I'm just naturally inclined to look for those things. I think if you throw little fact nuggets and details in the stories, it adds little touches to help people understand. I don't know who said it, but it's true in writing, "God is in the details."

Good writing also comes from observation. You wrote, "The choir, 7,000 volunteers draped in blood-red robes, softly sang "Just As I Am." Over the north end scoreboard, the Earth's shadow crept across the moon. For a moment, the old evangelist felt his own presence eclipsing the true light." Did you just see the eclipse and decide to work it into the story?

Yeah, I was just standing out there on the field and I looked up and the eclipse was starting. I'd known there was going to be an eclipse but I had forgotten, and I just looked up and there it was. And that's about the time Graham started talking about himself. When he started saying that the audience was coming for Jesus, not for him, I thought that was a critical element of who Billy Graham is, and why he has been so successful and so influential. In his mind, at least, and in his life, the ministry was not about him.

The challenge in the Billy Graham story was that so much has been written about Graham over the years. It seems that the challenge in writing "A Tree Grows in Bellevue" was telling about such a large, popular project. Why did you decide to do this story, and how did you decide to focus on the people rather than on the tree?

Everybody in Memphis knows Bellevue Church and probably everybody in Christendom knows Adrian Rogers. I think when you have institutions like that in town that are so big and so well-known, you tend to overlook them because everybody's written about them.

I assumed that most people knew about it, whether they'd been to see it or not. I thought the challenge was, first, to find God in this tree and, two, to write about it in a way that gave people information they didn't have. Now, even if you'd been to see the tree every year for 20 years, you're not going to go behind the scenes, you're not going to talk to the people who work on it.

What stands out about the people is the casual way in which they talk about faith. One person says, "I talk to the Lord every day." What does it take to get people to talk that openly?

I think they have to trust you, and I think they have to believe that you are going to be careful with their beliefs. A lot of reporters might have taken that first quote, about the person talking to God every day, and said, "Aw, this person's nuts. You know, I can't put that in a story. Who's going to believe that?" Well, that's not the point. The point is, you're writing about this person and what she's doing and why. She's sitting there telling you she talks to God every day and that's the reason she's involved in the project. That's the story.

Have you ever gone to a place of worship and found that God wasn't there?

Yeah. There have been a few occasions when I've gone to a service or an event and it was so obvious that it was a scam or just people wanting money. But most of that was at the level of the church official, it was the pastor or the board of deacons. It wasn't the people in the pews. So when that happens I try to totally divorce my own thoughts and feelings about the veracity of those people.

Tell me about "Keeping the Faith."

A friend of mine heard the bishop talk about his problems in the past when his wife and son died in the same year. I thought it would make a great story as soon as I heard it, but I doubted whether he'd be willing to go public with it. Many years ago I had written something and he had called to complain that there was an error in it. So our relationship was not very trusting. I had doubts that he would even want to talk to me, let alone give me the story.

But I called and talked to him, and I did one thing that I've never done before. I sent him a couple of articles that I'd written and told him to first read the articles and see what kind of work I do.

Well, he read the articles and then he invited me over to his home and we talked, and he was so gracious. But before we began the interview, he prayed for us. He prayed for me to hear his story and he asked God to give me the sense to treat it kindly. I was pretty impressed by that. I mean, it's not very often that somebody wants to pray with you at the beginning of an interview.

The organization of the story is of interest to me. What were your thoughts in putting this story together?

Well, I thought it ought to be chronological, and I look for moments. I try to find moments in people's lives that affect them. The moment with his grandmother in the bedroom and watching her pray and her reading the Bible to him was wonderful.

Then the next moment was when his son got sick when he was a little boy, and Dickson was in the phone booth praying. Now, that was not only a great moment but that was a foreshadowing. So I just looked for moments and then I tried to string them together. I tried to take the reader from one to the next, to the climax of the story.

How did Psalms become part of the story?

As I sat down to write I was looking for some inspiration, and I thought that this story struck me as a Psalm. So I opened up the Bible and looked at the Psalms, and the first thing I saw was Psalm 77, and I read it and it was his story. I was amazed. I mean, these kind of things happen to the people I write about, not to me.

What was the response to this story?

I got more calls about that story than anything I've ever done.

Everyone who told me they read it, told me they cried. And I think that's critical. I don't think it's a matter of manipulating people, I think it's just a matter of getting them to get inside the story. And there's no way you can get inside his story and not cry. If you write it and they don't cry, then you did something wrong.

The main thing I try to do is to evoke some kind of feeling from people who read my stuff. Whether it's sorrow or sadness or happiness or curiosity. It may be as simple as outrage at something that's happened with the president, but that's a feeling, it's not just a thought process. If I'm writing about something and I don't feel it as I'm writing it, if I don't feel what I'm trying to convey, what I'm trying to evoke, then it's not working and I go back.

Why is it important for people to feel, not just think?

Well, I think it's what people do best. They feel. We're in the information business, but I think people are looking for more than information. They're looking for hope, for inspiration, and I think they're looking for positive aspects of their community as well as negative.

Would those thoughts about writing apply outside of a religion beat?

Oh, absolutely. You can cover an incredibly boring government committee meeting, and if you're falling asleep, you're bored to tears, you can't write anything worthwhile. If you're bored by it, readers are going to be bored by it. Writers have to ask: Why is this meeting boring? What makes it so boring? Is it irrelevant? Is this government body irrelevant? Are they going about it the wrong way? Are they getting anything accomplished? There's a story there. And it's based on a feeling. It's based on a feeling of boredom.

Too often reporters are content just to recite the information.

Absolutely, and then you bore people to death. Readers have a feeling then. It is, "Put the paper down."

What's the most important thing you learned about writing as an editor?

I think what I learned as an editor was, number one, how important it is to maintain a reader's interest. It's too easy to stop reading a story and turn the page. Especially at the jumps. Second, any story can be cut. My training in writing headlines helped me. You only have a few words to work with, and you've got to get the most out of them.

I was an editor for five or six years, and I think editing stories helps you tremendously in writing. I think writers ought to be editors at some point, and vice versa.

You have described how you redefined your religion beat. Are others moving in the same direction? Is there a shift in religion writing?

Well, I think if there's a shift it's a shift toward viewing religion as important and as something worth spending some resources and some time covering. Not as something you just shove into the Saturday newspaper so you can fill up the space between the ads for the different churches.

One thing strikes me as strange. With so many people in this country who claim they believe in God, who claim they go to church, and with at least 25 percent who really do, it's strange that most newspapers have no more than one reporter covering all this.

I think there are papers around the country—Dallas and Atlanta come to mind—that have created entire sections for coverage of faith and spiritual issues. And I think that shows that reporters and editors are finding what I found, that there's no more interesting, fascinating, relevant beat in this country than religion.

The Washington Post

Laurie Goodstein

Finalist, Religion/Spirituality Writing

Laurie Goodstein is the national religion correspondent for *The Washington Post.* For her coverage in both
1995 and 1996, she won the top two awards given by
the Religion Newswriters Association: the John
Templeton Religion Reporter of the Year, and the
Supple Award for Religion Writer of the Year. Goodstein began working for the *Post* in 1989 as news aide
in the paper's New York bureau. Goodstein received
her B.A. from the University of California at Berkeley
and her master's degree from the Columbia University
Graduate School of Journalism. She taught school in
rural Kenya and was director of an inner-city youth
program in East Oakland, Calif., before deciding to
pursue a career in journalism. She also worked briefly
for *Newsday.*

Goodstein's editor says her religion stories introduce
readers to the "voice of people who are too often dismissed or ignored by mainstream journalism." In the
profile of Ganga Stone (excerpted here), an AIDS volunteer who teaches a course in dying, Goodstein tells
the story of one woman's quixotic search for understanding and the impact she has on those she teaches.

Good grief: Death is no laughing matter. Or is it?

JUNE 9, 1996

Outside, the sunlight is fading across a field of uneven rooftops; inside, lounging on tasteful beige couches, are 25 people, each with AIDS, cancer or an equally deadly illness, or intimately involved with someone who is. Ganga Stone is passing newspaper clippings around her class, and soon the room is filled with laughter.

Here's a clipping about a California woman swept to her death by a giant wave while scattering her mother's ashes in the ocean. The class cackles. There's another about the tenor who had a fatal heart attack onstage atop a ladder after singing an aria bemoaning the brevity of life.

"And here's one of my favorites," the 54-year-old Stone says merrily, waving a creased clipping on the untimely end of two evangelists squashed in a parking lot by a crashing plane. "Get this—the husband was in the *extermination business!*"

The class bursts into raucous laughter.

Grief should be shadowing the walls of this SoHo loft where the dying and their loved ones come for solace, but Stone had banished it at the door. For the most part the class complies, succumbing to the notion that this casually dressed woman in chinos and a green oxford shirt, someone who could easily be standing behind you in the supermarket line, is an authority on a matter most consider unknowable. Ganga Stone is convinced that she knows what happens when you die.

"If you come to me and say, 'Ganga, I'm dying,' and I say, 'I'm sorry,' there's two lies there," she tells her class. "One is that you have a condition we don't all have. The other is that it's a drag to be dying."

She has been leading these classes for seven years now, soon after founding an organization to deliver hot meals to people with AIDS. God's Love We Deliver, something of a modern urban miracle, now has a $5.3 million budget, 63 full-time staffers and more than 2,000 volunteers to deliver about a thousand meals a day.

Stone has known hundreds of people—too many to keep count—now dead from AIDS. Each death only deepened her certainty that dying is nothing to fear. Death is "the mere fork in the road" at which the spirit parts company with the body and continues on, she says. She has laid out what she calls "the facts" like a mathematical proof in a book released this month called *Start the Conversation: The Book About Death You Were Hoping to Find.*

Yet this woman who so confidently preaches serenity in the face of death was devastated for more than a decade by her own mother's tortured end. This feminist married a husband who hit her and worshipped a guru who slapped her. This saint who built a charity that feeds thousands of suffering souls abandoned her own son to an alcoholic father. But Stone seems to have taken all these paradoxes of her life and forged them into a rocklike faith that is consoling to some, infuriating to others and confounding to many.

"If you can know that death is not annihilation, like I know that, then you have no reason to fear death," she says, her words coming out in a torrent as if her thoughts were on fast forward. She might appear severe except for her habit of smiling at the ends of her sentences. A hand shoots up from a student who has been shaking his head from time to time.

"How *do* you know that?" says the student, a slim young man, slowly chewing gum.

"That's a good question," she responds, and begins to describe what led to her epiphany about death. It was 1965, she was 23 and her mother, Winifred Stone —"the only person who could stand me in the family"—was dying of Lou Gehrig's disease, diagnosed less than a year earlier. She had held her mother's hand in the hospital as her breathing slowed and her body slowly turned blue.

For the next 11 years, Stone said, she was nearly paralyzed by grief. She married, had a son, divorced, found a guru—but found no joy in anything. Until one day when she was leaving a summer stint in an ashram in upstate New York and was trading addresses with a new friend. The friend went to write her name on a piece of paper but put down "Winifred Stone" in a handwriting not at all hers.

Stone stared at the paper, perplexed. Her friend hadn't even known her mother's name. "My mom's hand was a big, bold hand, and there it was," Stone said. That slip of paper she saw as proof that her mother, wherever she was, in whatever form, still existed.

As Stone concludes, the man is raising his eyebrows. Later, he says in an interview that his name is Victor and he spent two years nursing his lover, who died of AIDS in January. "I would love to believe in a higher being, and in life after death," Victor says, "but you got more people who die and don't tell us there's life after death...That to me is proof that you don't come back."

He keeps coming to class, drawn to Stone. Yet he resents her for trying to rob him of his grief. From the very first class she made dying seem so trivial, Victor says. "Honestly, I felt like punching her out."

Lessons Learned

BY LAURIE GOODSTEIN

A friend introduced me to Ganga Stone, and immediately my life became more complicated. I had just returned to work from maternity leave and was hoping to bang out some quick stories just to get back in the swing of it. I found Ganga appealing because she was someone who had put her eclectic theology into action. She was well known in New York City for creating a successful charity that delivered hot meals to people with AIDS. She had been profiled in other publications under headlines such as "Certifiable Saint." Now that she had written a book on death—a central theme for any religion reporter—I thought it gave *The Washington Post* a good peg for us to do our own profile.

I followed her to church. I sat in on her class. I interviewed her for three hours. I read sermons she'd delivered, talks by her guru, journals on near-death studies. I interviewed her students, co-workers, friends, and her detractors, because she definitely had some of those. I thought I was ready to write.

But Ganga's life was a tangle of contradictions that emerged as I tried to put her story on paper. She still reveres the guru who repeatedly slugged her. She is devoted to her daughter but had abandoned her son. In short, she was no saint, which was OK. The problem was that I was finding parts of her tale unbelievable.

I pursued her by telephone as she moved from city to city on her book tour. She called me from hotel rooms in Chicago, Pittsburgh, and Los Angeles—each time filling in blanks, trying to articulate what motivated her. When my editor, Patty Cohen, finally got a look at the first draft, she had more questions, and very good ones. I phoned Ganga again, at a radio station in Seattle. Each call made Ganga increasingly nervous about how deeply I was probing, but the calls also indicated I was taking her seriously and striving for an honest portrait.

Ultimately there was no "banging out" a quick story about Ganga Stone. In my writing I usually struggle for simplicity, to find the narrative through line. But Ganga's story reminded me that people are often motivated by multiple and conflicting factors: religious belief, emotional desire, economic necessity, political conviction. People are complicated. Our stories should be, too.

The Philadelphia Inquirer

David O'Reilly

Finalist, Religion/Spirituality Writing

David O'Reilly is city religion writer for *The Philadelphia Inquirer*, with responsibility for some national and foreign religion stories. Before becoming religion writer in 1995, he worked for the *Inquirer* as a New Jersey reporter and editor. He came to the *Inquirer* in late 1982 after a short stint as an enterprise writer at the late *Philadelphia Evening Bulletin* and has also worked at a small weekly in Brookfield, Conn., and the *News-Times* of Danbury, Conn. At the *Inquirer*, he has won awards from the Pennsylvania Press Association, the New Jersey Associated Press, and the Education Writers Association. In 1996 he was a fellow at the Knight Center for Specialized Journalism for a program on reporting about religion.

O'Reilly's writing about spiritual matters is grounded in meticulous reporting that elevates the mundane to the mystical. His descriptions of the life and work of a cabinetmaker who devoted his life to restoring religious statuary after an angel came to him in a dream is an unforgettable portrait of unfathomable faith.

A calling to restore statuary

SEPTEMBER 2, 1996

Perhaps only angels know if the mysterious, shining being Jim Appleman saw 14 years ago was an angel —or just a dream.

And maybe only God knows if Jim Appleman is a holy man.

But it's plain that Appleman, who lives in a world of cracked virgins, footless saints, chipped angels and broken Jesuses, is a healer of sorts.

Since 1982, when a radiant figure appeared in a dream, he has been restoring religious statuary for churches in and around Philadelphia.

"Oh, I'm nobody special," insists Appleman, a lay Franciscan monk.

So it seems from the outside. Thin, soft-spoken, with glasses, he seems as ordinary as the red brick rowhouse in working-class Fishtown where he has lived most of his 53 years.

Step inside, however, and the religious statuary crowding Appleman's modest living room staggers the senses.

The Virgin Mary gazes down on the room from the television cabinet. St. John Neumann, the 19th-century Philadelphia bishop, reclines on the sofa. St. Therese, the French mystic, stands by a window, clutching flowers and gazing heavenward.

A life-size, smiling Mary, her hands clasped, lies on a work table, indifferent to scorch marks in her gown. A crowned infant Jesus, chipped at its base, sits on a lamp table. A small plaster cherub dangles from the mantelpiece.

Atop the mantel sits yet another Mary, grieving as she holds the wounded body of Christ in her arms. Alongside her, a standing Jesus gazes lovingly on this roomful of saints and angels, blessing it with broken fingers.

But of all the chipped and cracked religious statuary awaiting repair in Appleman's living room, the most powerful is the agonized Jesus, nearly lifesize, lying on a settee near the kitchen door.

Blood pours down his outstretched arms and sunken rib cage. His half-closed eyes ache with pain, suggesting he is near death. Deep nail holes pierce his palms and feet, and thorns ring his matted hair.

Viewed in a church, this old German crucifix would be powerful enough. Encountered here, the sight of this painfully human Jesus dying on Appleman's daybed is staggering.

"This is one of the best pieces I've ever worked on," he says, allowing a rare smile and pointing out some of his restorations since the statue arrived three months ago.

"It had all these cracks in it," he explains, leaning over the recumbent body of Christ. "I had to put 57 pins in it to keep it from cracking more."

He has reattached an arm and a toe on Jesus, but it will take three months more before this plaster-over-wood crucifix returns to St. Joseph's Roman Catholic Church in Limeville, Pa.

Appleman will next fill and paint the chips in the plaster skin, clean it, touch up the paint, and re-coat the waistcloth with 22-karat gold leaf.

"A box of this stuff costs about $500," he says, lifting a gossamer-thin square of gold foil from a small box and laying it on the carved folds of Christ's garment. "But it will be spectacular when it's done."

His journey toward this craft began in childhood, when this very room was a place of torment. His parents were acute (sometimes abusive) alcoholics, and young Jim was so troubled by the domestic chaos that he could not concentrate in school.

His failing grades and difficulty with reading convinced his parents, teachers—and himself—that he was "dumb." Ashamed, he quit school in the fifth grade to work for a local cabinetmaker.

Raised an observant, no-meat-on-Fridays, Mass-on-Sundays Catholic, he became even more devout at age 14 after watching the movie *The Story of Fatima* on television. Compared to the chaos of his home, the film's loving message was so consoling that he "bawled like a baby" as he watched.

Still, he had no sense of religious vocation. At 18, he married to "get away from the situation at home" and relocated to Gettysburg, where he and his wife had two children. There he worked as a furniture refinisher.

After his marriage broke up in 1974—"we were too young," he says—he moved back to his childhood home in Fishtown to care for his dying father. Despite an annulment from the Catholic Church, he never remarried.

Then, in that same house, on a night in 1982, "I had a vision."

Perhaps he was dreaming or "half asleep" when "I saw myself standing before the marble altar rail of a church."

As the dream continued, he said, "I saw a shining man in a white robe, but I could only see his hands. The light around his face was so bright it blotted it out. And his hands had art brushed in them.

"Then I saw bright light on *my* hands, and the brushes appeared in my hands. And even though no words were spoken, I understood the message: 'Go, restore my church.'

"It was so real, I knew it was a message from heaven," Appleman said, shaking his head in awe.

At first, he told no one about his dream.

Then, two weeks later, as Appleman was leaving Mass, the Rev. John Harkins, pastor of St. Michael's Church at Second and Jefferson streets, got to talking about some damaged statues. And he asked if Appleman cared to restore the parish's 19th-century Christmas stable.

"It felt like it was all following a pattern from the dream," Appleman recalled last week. "I said yes. I felt it was a heavenly cause, a chance to do service."

He has been saying yes ever since.

The creche at St. Michael's Church contained 24 large plaster figures and took Appleman a year-and-a-half to restore. Then the pastor of nearby St. Boniface parish asked him to restore a large, plaster *pieta,* given the church in 1876.

"It was a mess," Appleman recalled. But he filled its cracks, made a new, epoxy thumb for Jesus, cleaned it and painted it.

About this same time, he had another vivid dream. This time, a luminous wind-swept figure appeared to him outside his door. In the dream, light and beautiful colors surrounded Appleman, leading him to believe that God, or the angels, approved of his undertaking.

Since then, he guesses, he has restored some 200 statues and other religious objects. He charges "enough to get by" and sometimes refuses payment altogether.

Among the pieces of which he is proudest is the tabernacle of the Spanish altar where Sister Lucia— the sole surviving child who reported visions of Mary at Fatima, Portugal—saw her last vision in 1922, and a Haitian statue of Mary said by some to shed tears.

He has visited the shrine at Fatima seven times and the shrine of Our Lady of Lourdes in France three times.

In 1984, he visited Medjugorje, Yugoslavia, where peasants have reported seeing visions of Mary, to pray for a Philadelphia woman apparently dying of cancer "all over her."

"I walked up the hill in my bare feet. I even got a 2-inch thorn in my foot." Shortly after he returned to Philadelphia, he said, the woman's doctor called to say her cancer was "showing signs of going away." She made a complete recovery, according to Appleman, who shrugs when asked if he feels he played a role.

"I'm just trying to do God's work," he insists.

Today that work includes regular visits to children in hospitals, where he prays for the seriously ill. He also volunteers time with the children of alcoholics, "so they don't hurt as much as I did as a kid."

In 1995, he joined the Franciscans as a lay brother. His vows are not permanent, and he is free to marry. "Who knows?" he says with a soft laugh. "Maybe it will happen." His brown monk's robe and knotted waistcord sit on the back of the sofa, but he wears it only on special occasions.

Indeed, when he helps out at the Franciscan Brothers' soup kitchen at Front and Kensington streets, or visits the sick, he looks just like a working-class guy from Fishtown.

He is, after all, "nobody special."

Lessons Learned

BY DAVID O'REILLY

Religion can be crazy, pompous, or mean sometimes, but spend an hour at a choir practice or a soup kitchen or a Seder and you may get back to the newsroom with a story about joy or hope or truth or eternity. I love this beat.

Because it deals with ultimate questions, religion possesses a *gravitas* hard to match on other beats, but its infinite possibilities overwhelm me sometimes. I get a dozen calls, a dozen faxes, a dozen press releases a day inviting me to write about a retiring pastor, a youth rally, a Holocaust symposium, a Bible translation, a fund drive, an Easter vigil. Talk about infinity! Where do I say no? When do I say yes? Some days I just want to let the phone ring and bury myself in a 12-part series on the meaning of life. But no.

"I want religion stories that are close to the ground," the city editor said when I took over the beat in May 1995. "What does *that* mean?" I wondered, but nodded sagely. This was the beat I'd wanted for years; how the divine appears in the self-understanding of individuals, cultures, and civilizations had long been a private interest of mine, and after a decade as a poky, perfectionist feature writer I had resolved to write at least two religion stories a week. Some weeks it's a breeze, some weeks it's a scramble.

Early in September 1996, I got a note from a man in a working-class neighborhood saying he repaired religious statuary. Would I be interested in writing about him, he wondered? I decided it had "close to the ground" possibilities.

His note and photo hardly prepared me, however, for what I found. When Jim Appleman opened the door of his row house, I stepped into a zone somewhere between heaven and Earth. That may sound like metaphor; I'm not so sure.

I was staggered by the sight of all his chipped, broken, and cracked religious statues crowding every desk, table, chair, and sofa in that little room. My first impression was that Appleman was disturbed, but as he walked me around the major statues, explaining who each was and what repairs he planned for them, I sensed a layer of genuine spirituality beneath his impassive affect. I was moved, too, by the sight of a nearly life-size bleeding Christ—taken literally from a cross—lying on a sheet with arms outstretched. I could be in a modern hospital, I thought, or Gethsemane. Whole planes of reality seemed to be shifting within this space.

We sat down to talk biography, and he got around to his late parents' alcoholism and the shame and suffering of his childhood. I detected much sorrow in his center but sensed his extraordinary religiosity couldn't be dismissed as merely "psychological." His otherness seemed to have roots, and so I asked him if his "calling" as a restorer of church art had been compelled by a religious experience.

I think the question surprised him; I *know* his answer surprised me. A shining angel, he explained, had appeared to him in a vivid dream, shown him paintbrushes, and instructed him to restore churches. He couldn't tell for sure if the angel had been "real" or "just a dream."

Well, neither could I. We journalists are by nature a skeptical positivist bunch; we operate most comfortably within that bandwidth of epistemology known as the tangible, the provable, the evidentiary. Yet here I was, like Alice through the looking glass, not sure of anything.

Appleman and I talked about two hours. He proved to be a good and simple man, and when I got back to the office (bearing prayer cards, a St. Jude medal, and a rosary despite my protestations) I sensed I had a good story.

But what exactly was it about?

It was, I decided, about the uncertainty of reality. The dream-angel, the multitude of statues, and that remarkably lifelike Christ were powerful elements I could manipulate like stage sets to create scenes of surreality. Yup. That would work. And so, when I began to write, I purposely sought to disorient the reader at the outset, just as I had been disoriented when I stepped through Appleman's door. My lead left it uncertain if Appleman's angel was real or imaginary, and the ambiguous paragraph about a roomful of "cracked virgins, footless saints, chipped angels and broken Jesuses" purposefully failed to explain these were statues.

But after I wrote the "cracked virgins" paragraph I realized something was missing. The writing was clever but failed to convey Appleman's goodness, so I inserted a line about his being perhaps a holy man, and added that he was a "healer of sorts."

That lent more mystery, too, and so I proceeded to tell the story of how Jim Appleman, unhappy son of abusive alcoholics, had returned home to care for them in their final illnesses. One night he had an angelic vision, and look: now his home, his mind, and his life brim with saints and angels. The approach worked beautifully, and the image of the agonized Christ, lying on Appleman's daybed and awaiting his touch, added real weight to this notion of surreal religiosity.

My sense of what this story was "about" began to change, however, when I got to my notes about those thin, brown ruts in his broadloom carpet. These were the remnants of those many unhappy days when his parents would nod off, their cigarettes dropping to the floor. As a boy he would watch for them and pick them up to keep the house from catching fire. What emotional scars had all that left on him, I wondered? And what kind of person comes home to care for such parents in their old age?

Hmmm. My earlier line about Appleman being a "healer of sorts" had referred to statuary, but it was dawning on me how far beyond plaster and wood his caring extended. The more I reviewed my notes—especially some portions I first thought subordinate or irrelevant—the more I realized his living room was not just a surrealistic playground. Neither could my story be.

Here was a man who prayed constantly, who made regular pilgrimages abroad to Catholic shrines, and who had told how a Philadelphia woman dying of cancer had been cured after he prayed for her. He worked with children of alcoholics, too, and helped out at a Franciscan soup kitchen. I winced when I realized I had even ignored the fact that he was a lay Franciscan brother.

So. What did I have here? What *was* this story about?

Crouching with paintbrushes over those cracked virgins and broken Jesuses and chipped angels was a man wounded in childhood and whose wounds had never fully healed. Yet passing through those wounds, like sunlight beaming through cracks in a wall, shone a compassion that some might dare to call divine.

My clever story had to change. So did I. Cool, rational, and wry doesn't cut it in the face of goodness and kindness and, er, um, God. I could still use the strangeness of Jim Appleman's living room as a narrative device, but truth required I make it plain that this surreality was not an absurdity; rather, it was home to a simple man living on a plane of reality above most of us.

To paint this more complex (and faithful) portrait of Appleman, I had to discard my initial premise—one that might have made me look clever but Appleman look foolish—and search my notes and myself for who this man really is: a fissured saint binding wounds and healing injuries with plaster and rare kindness. Discovering and communicating this man's holiness demanded vulnerability and self-exposure from me, but doing so served Jim Appleman, our readers, and truth.

Me, too.

THE KANSAS CITY STAR

Bill Tammeus

Finalist, Religion/Spirituality Writing

Bill Tammeus is an editorial page columnist for *The Kansas City Star.* His work is syndicated by *The New York Times* News Service. He's been at the *Star* since 1970, first as a reporter and, since 1977, as a columnist. Before that, he was a reporter for the *Rochester* (N.Y.) *Times-Union.* He's a 1967 graduate of the University of Missouri School of Journalism. He writes a daily humor column as well as a column that runs every other Sunday. Some of the Sunday columns are serious and discuss many theological and spiritual aspects of life—and death. Tammeus is past president of the National Society of Newspaper columnists and has received many writing awards. He was a member of the *Star* staff that won a Pulitzer Prize for reporting on the 1981 Hyatt Hotel disaster in Kansas City. He's also an active Presbyterian and occasionally teaches a course he calls "Theology Even the Clergy Can Understand."

In this column, written after his 83-year-old mother died, Tammeus reminds us how the truth of life's painful realities can hurt and begin to heal.

Pain inevitably
comes into our lives

JUNE 9, 1996

WOODSTOCK, Ill.—The morning we prayed over my mother and buried her the air was the kind of noticeable clean it gets only after a serious rain scrubbing.

In fact, it had been raining for days. The countless nearby fields, freshly planted with corn and soybeans —rich, black Illinois earth like that my parents grew up on and loved—had done their best to sponge up wave after chilly wave of spring storms. But, finally, it was all too much. Brackish, turgid water filled the hollows of fields, an unwelcome, untidy guest.

My mother liked guests, but not the kind that make a mess. Not the kind you have to waste precious time cleaning up after. Time, to her, was too valuable for that. She preferred dainty guests who would nibble on hors d'oeuvres, praise her pot roast and leave at a decent hour.

Mom has passed along to me her preference for decency and order, which may explain why it is taking me so long in this piece to get past the weather and to ponder the brusque reality of having just become, at age 51, an orphan.

My three sisters and I joked a little about being orphans as we gathered with our families to wish Mom Godspeed and to lower her into the muddy earth of Oakland Cemetery here next to my father, who had died in 1992. But, in the end, it is no joke at all, this orphan business. It is, rather, the harsh and inevitable way of a world infected with sin and evil, disease and death.

I do not want you to think for a minute that I believe the world is nothing but pain and gloom. No, no, no. We are given almost unspeakable gifts of grace and beauty, joy and insight, kindness and love. And a life well lived, like my mother's, will be weighted toward those reasons to celebrate.

But we are Pollyanna fools if we don't recognize the part pain plays in our lives, the part evil does, and heartache and disappointment.

So I say it plainly. I am an orphan now and I don't like it. And I wish there were some other way.

Still, as these things go, I've done better than I had any right to expect. My father lived until age 82 and —save for his last two years or so, when senile dementia veiled his active mind with bewilderment—his life was full, productive and fat with purpose.

And Mom, Bertha Amanda Sofia Helander Tammeus, had turned 83 in March. She, too, lived a remarkably productive life until Parkinson's disease and other ailments put her in a wheelchair and in a nursing home a year and a half ago. And as often as not in this frustrating time she was confused about things.

So I have very little room to complain about being left parentless at my age. And yet this is a bad business at any age. It is a pure squealing shout about our own mortality. It's a stern reminder that some day my own daughters will be orphans.

The natural way of things is to be born roughly into this world, shocked—after the comfort of the womb —by the relentless, inhospitable air that grabs us. But after our initial reaction to this rudeness we are soothed to cooing by the loving touch and embrace of the one who gave us birth.

At the other end of life, however, the natural pattern is to go out an orphan and, as we go, to create yet more orphans. Even for those of us deeply convinced that a loving God welcomes us home at our death, this seems like bad planning, a bad design. The Psalmist (in the New Revised Standard Version of Psalm 90) was right: "Our years come to an end like a sigh."

So there we were, four orphans saying farewell to their old mother under a spring-blue dome of sky. Fresh flowers did their important work of beauty on her casket. But flowers, too, soon fade and blow away. And the truest thing I can think to say about all this now is that the world simply works this way. And no one—not even an orphan with three orphan sisters— can change that.

Lessons Learned

BY BILL TAMMEUS

It took too long, but finally I learned that the more open, personal, and vulnerable I can be in my columns, the more readers like them and learn from them.

There is authenticity to words written by someone who is sharing some personal moment that is, at the same time, universal.

When my mother died in 1996, I did not, of course, immediately think this would make a great column. But participating in her funeral and being surrounded by my sisters and other family members helped me see that I was experiencing something that is a common human drama and that perhaps, as a writer, I could draw common meaning out of it.

That caused me, even in the midst of a difficult personal time, to continue paying attention to details that might help me tell this story in a professional way. So, as you will notice when you read the column, I made note of the rain that week and of the extraordinarily clean air that arrived in the rain's wake. And I noticed the fecund Illinois earth again and the land's unevenness in which water had collected.

I'm convinced that a keen eye for detail is necessary even when writing about the most abstract concepts of religion and spirituality—in fact, maybe even more so there than with other subjects.

All that said, however, I think it is possible to be open and honest with readers without giving away everything, the most private of wounds. I did not, for instance, mention in this column the somewhat difficult and occasionally strained relationship my mother and I had had for some decades. That omission did not seem to me to change the truth of what I had to say in the column about becoming an orphan in my 50s, and it did not seem to me to be any of the readers' business. I mention it here simply to say that to write openly and honestly does not mean titillating the reader with deeply personal information that is best left private. How to know what to include and what to omit without compromising the integrity of the piece? Only experience will help one discern that.

Top 10 tools for today's journalists

BY CHRISTOPHER SCANLAN

In the time of Shakespeare, actors carried bags that contained tools of their art—scraps of costume, props, jars of paint—that they used to change into a new role. Here are the tools I think writers need.

A TIGHTROPE

If you're going to be a writer, you need to take a risk. You can always tell safe stories, and there are safe stories all over the paper and all over the broadcasts. The best advice I ever got as a journalism student was a throwaway line from a teacher who said, "You know, you have to be counter-phobic." Meaning, do what you're afraid to do.

Think of the tightrope, and every day walk across it. Walk across it as a reporter. Who's the one person you're afraid to call? Where is the one place in town you've never been because you're afraid to go there? Force yourself to take risks as a reporter. And ask yourself every day, "Have I taken a risk?"

A NET

The best writers cast trawler's nets on stories. And they cast them wide and deep. They'll interview 10 people to get the one quote that sums up the theme. They'll spend half a day mining interviews for the anecdote that reveals the story. They'll hunt through records and reports, looking for the one specific that explains the universal, the detail that captures the person. Anne Hull of the *St. Petersburg Times* described a female police officer in Tampa this way: "In uniform she was petite and muscular, like a beautiful action-figure doll, with piercing green eyes and size 4 steel-toe boots." A telling detail "can help explain the sum of a person," Hull says. In this case, it was "the Terminator meets a ballerina."

A PAIR OF SHOES

Every journalist is equipped with this tool already, but it's surprising how few use them on a daily basis. I'm not talking just about shoe leather reporting, but also about empathy. Empathy is the writer's greatest gift, and perhaps the most important tool. The ability to feel what another person feels. Richard Ben Cramer, talking about the reporting he did in the Middle East in the late '70s, says he tried to give readers a sense of what it is like to be living in a situation of terror, of life on the edge: "It's very hard to know what someone would feel in a situation unless you at least feel something of it yourself."

A LOOM

What do journalists do? We make the connections for people. We connect the police report to the red bungalow in Rocky Point. We connect city hall to the sewage project. Raymond Carver, the writer, said, "Writing is just a process of connections. Things begin to connect up. A line here, a word here." Are you weaving the connections in your stories? In your reading? In your life? Are you asking yourself what line goes to what line, and what makes a whole? Turn your computer into a loom that weaves stories.

A BIBLE

Lower-case b. The sacred writing texts you read for guidance or inspiration.

Joan Beck of the *Chicago Tribune* actually was talking about Bible with a capital B. "I always read a couple of chapters in the Bible every morning, whether I am working or not.... Those cadences get imprinted in your brain; when you write you tend to write in those kinds of patterns and rhythms. The cadences—only in the King James Version—are so effective.... You use them as sort of a touchstone."

Make a list of your sacred texts, books, or stories that you keep nearby when you're getting ready to write a piece and you really want it to be great. When stumped, take inspiration from them.

A ZOOM LENS

David Finkel, staff writer for *The Washington Post Magazine,* says he tries "to look at any site that will be the focus of a narrative passage as if I were a photographer. I not only stand near something, I move away for the long view. I crouch down, I move left and right. I try to view it from every angle possible to see what might be revealed."

Writers need to go in very close. There's a famous passage in a column by Jimmy Breslin about the light coming in and glinting off a mobster's pinkie ring.

But, at the same time, we need to back up, see the whole scene, and understand the context. We need to see the universal as well as the specific.

Think about jewelers. Jewelers use the loupe to distinguish the true diamond from the cubic zirconium. We need to be like a jeweler, looking for the quality and the flaws in our stories.

SIX WORDS

"Tell your story in six words," is the advice former AP feature writer Tad Bartimus gives. By reducing it to the single phrase, reducing it almost to a line of poetry, you can capture the tension of the story. You can capture the entire story. And make it six words, not four or nine, for no other reason than in discipline there is freedom. One classic example, perhaps the shortest short story ever written, "For Sale: Baby shoes, never used." Six words.

AN ACCELERATOR PEDAL

"There are some kinds of writing," William Faulkner said, "that you have to do very fast. Like riding a bicycle on a tightrope." Race past your internal censor. Gail Godwin called it "The watcher at the gates." This is the voice that says, "You're an incompetent. You can't write. That thing you did yesterday? You've lost it. You didn't do the reporting. You're an idiot." So you have to trick the watcher at the gates. And the way you do it is you do it through speed. My colleague, Roy Peter Clark, put it in three words: "Write like hell."

SCISSORS

Or its electronic equivalent: the delete key. Truman Capote said, "I believe more in the scissors than I do the pencil." And William Strunk said, "Vigorous writing is concise. A sentence should contain no unnecessary words, a paragraph no unnecessary sentences, for the same reason that a drawing should have no unnecessary lines and a machine no unnecessary parts. This requires not that the writer make all his sentences short, or that he avoid all detail and treat his subject only in outline, but that every word tell."

A TRASH CAN

Isaac Singer says, "The main rule of the writer is never to pity your manuscript. If you see something is no good, throw it away and begin again. A lot of writers have failed because they have too much pity."

Journalists will have little pity for sources, but we will pity the weakest prose because it flows from our keyboard. "Hey, I spent two hours on that lead." We can't throw it away. But remember Singer: "I say that a wastepaper basket is a writer's best friend. My wastepaper basket is on a steady diet."

So there you have it, one writer's list of indispensable tools. Scrounge around, dust off one of your unused tools. Try a new one. Writing is a craft you can never perfect. That's the bad news. The good news, in newsrooms, is that that you always get another crack at it tomorrow.

Annual bibliography

BY DAVID SHEDDEN

WRITING AND REPORTING BOOKS 1996

Applegate, Edd. *Literary Journalism: A Biographical Dictionary of Writers and Editors.* Westport, CT: Greenwood Press, 1996.

Baskette, Floyd K., Jack Z. Sissors, and Brian S. Brooks. *The Art of Editing.* 6th edition. Boston: Allyn and Bacon, 1996.

Frazell, Daryl F., and George Tuck. *Principles of Editing: A Comprehensive Guide for Students and Journalists.* New York: McGraw Hill Text, 1996.

Friedlander, Edward Jay, and John Lee. *Feature Writing for Newspapers and Magazines: The Pursuit of Excellence.* New York: HarperCollins, 1996.

Hutchison, Earl R. *Writing for Mass Communication.* 2nd edition. White Plains, NY: Longman, 1996.

Lieb, Thom. *Editing for Clear Communication.* Madison, WI: Brown & Benchmark, 1996.

Lorenz, Alfred Lawrence, and John Vivian. *News: Reporting and Writing.* Needham Heights, MA: Allyn and Bacon, 1996.

McAdams, Katherine C., and Jan Johnson Elliott. *Reaching Audiences: A Guide to Media Writing.* Boston: Allyn and Bacon, 1996.

Missouri Group. Brian S. Brooks, et al. *News Reporting and Writing.* 5th edition. New York: St. Martin's Press, 1996.

Mitchell, Catherine C., and Mark D. West. *The News Formula: A Concise Guide to News Writing and Reporting.* New York: St. Martin's Press, 1996.

Morrish, John. *Magazine Editing.* New York: Routledge, 1996.

Murray, Donald M. *Crafting a Life in Essay, Story, Poem.* Portsmouth, NH: Boynton/Cook, 1996.

Pitts, Beverley J., Tendayi S. Kumbula, and Mark N. Popovich, eds. *The Process of Media Writing.* Boston: Allyn and Bacon, 1996.

Providence Journal-Bulletin Staff Writers. *How I Wrote the Story.* 3rd edition. Providence, RI: Providence Journal Company, 1996.

Rich, Carole. *Writing and Reporting News: A Coaching Method.* 2nd edition. Belmont, CA: Wadsworth, 1996.

Scanlan, Christopher, ed. *Best Newspaper Writing 1996.* St. Petersburg, FL: The Poynter Institute.

Smith, Ron F., et al. *Editing Today.* Ames, IA: Iowa State University Press, 1996.

Steinbach, Alice. *The Miss Dennis School of Writing.* Baltimore: The Bancroft Press, 1996.

CLASSICS

Atchity, Kenneth. *A Writer's Time: A Guide to the Creative Process, from Vision through Revision.* New York: Norton, 1986.

Berg, A. Scott. *Max Perkins: Editor of Genius.* New York: Dutton, 1978.

Bernstein, Theodore M. *The Careful Writer: A Modern Guide to English Usage.* New York: Atheneum Press, 1965.

Biagi, Shirley. *Interviews That Work: A Practical Guide for Journalists.* 2nd edition. Belmont, CA: Wadsworth, 1992.

Blundell, William E. *The Art and Craft of Feature Writing: Based on The Wall Street Journal.* New York: New American Library, 1988.

Brady, John. *The Craft of Interviewing.* New York: Vintage Books, 1977.

Brande, Dorothea. *Becoming a Writer.* Los Angeles: J.P. Tarcher; Boston: distributed by Harcourt Brace, reprint of 1934 edition, 1981.

Brown, Karen, Roy Peter Clark, Don Fry, and Christopher Scanlan, eds. *Best Newspaper Writing.* St. Petersburg, FL: The Poynter Institute. Published annually since 1979.

Cappon, Rene J. *The Word: An Associated Press Guide to Good News Writing.* New York: The Associated Press, 1982.

Clark, Roy Peter. *Free to Write: A Journalist Teaches Young Writers.* Portsmouth, NH: Heinemann Educational Books, 1986.

Clark, Roy Peter, and Don Fry. *Coaching Writers: The Essential Guide for Editors and Reporters.* New York: St. Martin's Press, 1992.

Dillard, Annie. *The Writing Life.* New York: Harper and Row, 1989.

Downie, Leonard, Jr. *The New Muckrakers.* New York: NAL-Dutton, 1978.

Elbow, Peter. *Writing With Power: Techniques for Mastering the Writing Process.* New York: Oxford University Press, 1981.

Follett, Wilson. *Modern American Usage: A Guide.* London: Longmans, 1986.

Franklin, Jon. *Writing for Story: Craft Secrets of Dramatic Nonfiction.* New York: Atheneum, 1986.

Goldstein, Norm, ed. *The Associated Press Stylebook and Libel Manual.* 27th edition. Reading, MA: Addison-Wesley, 1992.

Gross, Gerald, ed. *Editors on Editing: An Inside View of What Editors Really Do.* New York: Harper & Row, 1985.

Howarth, William L., ed. *The John McPhee Reader.* New York: Farrar, Straus and Giroux, 1990.

Hugo, Richard. *The Triggering Town: Lectures & Essays on Poetry & Writing.* New York: Norton, 1992.

Mencher, Melvin. *News Reporting and Writing.* 5th edition. Dubuque, Iowa: William C. Brown, 1991.

Metzler, Ken. *Creative Interviewing: The Writer's Guide to Gathering Information by Asking Questions.* 2nd edition. Englewood Cliffs, NJ: Prentice Hall, 1989.

Mitford, Jessica. *Poison Penmanship: The Gentle Art of Muckraking.* New York: Knopf, 1979.

Murray, Donald. *Shoptalk: Learning to Write With Writers.* Portsmouth, NH: Boynton/Cook, 1990.

— . *Writing for Your Readers.* Old Saybrook, CT: Globe Pequot Press, 1992.

Plimpton, George. *Writers at Work: The Paris Review Interviews.* Series. New York: Viking, 1992.

Ross, Lillian. *Reporting.* New York: Dodd, 1981.

Scanlan, Christopher, ed. *How I Wrote the Story.* Providence Journal Company, 1986.

Sims, Norman, ed. *Literary Journalism in the Twentieth Century.* New York: Oxford University Press, 1990.

Snyder, Louis L., and Richard B. Morris, eds. *A Treasury of Great Reporting.* New York: Simon & Schuster, 1962.

Stafford, William, and Donald Hall, eds. *Writing the Australian Crawl: View on the Writer's Vocation.* Ann Arbor, MI: University of Michigan Press, 1978.

Strunk, William, Jr., and E.B. White. *The Elements of Style.* 3rd edition. New York: Macmillan, 1979.

Talese, Gay. *Fame & Obscurity.* New York: Ivy Books, 1971.

Wardlow, Elwood M., ed. *Effective Writing and Editing: A Guidebook for Newspapers.* Reston, VA: American Press Institute, 1985.

White, E.B. *Essays of E.B. White.* New York: Harper & Row, 1977.

Witt, Leonard. *The Complete Book of Feature Writing.* Cincinnati, OH: Writer's Digest Books, 1991.

Wolfe, Tom. *The New Journalism.* New York: Harper & Row, 1973.

Zinsser, William. *On Writing Well.* 4th edition. New York: Harper & Row, 1990.

— . *Writing to Learn.* New York: Harper & Row, 1988.

ARTICLES 1996

Auman, Ann, and Betsy B. Alderman. "How Editors and Educators See Skills Needed for Editing." *Newspaper Research Journal,* Winter/Spring 1996, pp. 2–13.

Brown, Karen F. "Reporting with Kick, Writing with Punch." *Workbench: The Bulletin of the National Writers' Workshop.* Vol. 3, 1996, pp. 2–3.

Clark, Roy Peter. "A New Shape for the News." *Workbench: The Bulletin of the National Writers' Workshop.* Vol. 3, 1996, pp. 6–7.

Davis, Carolyn Joyce. "Editorial Writing and Investigative Journalism: Reporting on the Way to Judgment." *The IRE Journal,* July/August 1996, pp. 6–9.

Fry, Don. "Coaching Planners and Plungers." *Workbench: The Bulletin of the National Writers' Workshop.* Vol. 3, 1996, p. 8.

— . "Unprickling Your Newsroom's Attitude." *The American Editor,* July/August 1996, p. 24.

Giles, Robert H. "Writing Awards Push Us to Do Better Each Day." *The American Editor,* November 1996, p. 2.

Giobbe, Dorothy, Tony Case, and Jodi B. Cohen. "80th Annual Pulitzer Prizes." *Editor and Publisher,* April 13, 1996, pp. 9–13, 56.

Hammond, Ruth. "Reflections of a Lapsed Freelancer." *The IRE Journal,* March/April 1996, pp. 16–17.

Hart, Jack. "Five Steps to High-Impact Writing." *Editor and Publisher,* Oct. 19, 1996, p. 25.

Higginson, Charles. "Solutions Brought to Copy Desk Problems." *The American Editor,* November 1996, pp. 8–11.

Hynds, Ernest, and Erika Archibald. "Improved Editorial Pages Can Help Papers, Communities." *Newspaper Research Journal,* Winter/Spring 1996, pp. 14–24.

Larocque, Paula. "No Writer Can Be Too Rich or Too Thin in Use of Allusions." *Quill,* December 1996, p. 23.

McGrath, Kevin. "Just a Feature? Not If It Has News Value." *The American Editor,* January-February-March 1996, pp. 20–21.

Scanlan, Christopher. "Top Ten Tools for Today's Journalists." *Workbench: The Bulletin of the National Writers' Workshop.* Vol. 3, 1996, p. 4.

— . "What the Best Writers Learn, What They Can Teach Us." *The American Editor,* July/August 1996, pp. 22–23.

Sumner, David E. "A Few Tips on How to Do Well in Writing Contests." *Editor and Publisher,* July 6, 1996, p. 48.

Tankard, James, and Laura Hendrickson. "Specificity, Imagery in Writing." *Newspaper Research Journal,* Winter/Spring 1996, pp. 35–48.

Weaver, Janet S. "Wichita is Doing Fine Without a Copydesk." *The American Editor,* January-February-March 1996, pp. 14–16.

Weinberg, Steve. "Writing Investigative Books." *The IRE Journal,* March/April 1996, p. 17.